For Women and the Nation

For Women and the Nation

Funmilayo Ransome-Kuti of Nigeria

Cheryl Johnson–Odim
and Nina Emma Mba

University of Illinois Press

Urbana and Chicago

Publication of this book was supported by a grant from
Loyola University of Chicago

1 2 3 4 5 C P 6 5 4 3 2

This book is printed on acid-free paper.

Library of Congress Cataloging-in-Publication Data
Johnson-Odim, Cheryl, 1948–
For women and the nation : Funmilayo Ransome-Kuti of
Nigeria / Cheryl Johnson-Odim and Nina Emma Mba.
p.   cm.
Includes bibliographical references and index.
ISBN 0-252-02313-7 (alk. paper). —
ISBN 0-252-06613-8 (pbk. : alk, paper)
ISBN 978-0-252-02313-2 (alk. paper). —
ISBN 978-0-252-06613-9 (pbk. : alk, paper)
1. Ransome-Kuti, Funmilayo, 1900–1978. 2. Ransome-Kuti,
Israel Oludotun, 1891–1955. 3. Women political activists—
Nigeria—Biography. 4. Political activists—Nigeria—Biogra-
phy. I. Mba, Nina Emma. II. Title.
HQ1815.5Z75R355   1997
305.42'092—dc20   96-25390
[B]
CIP

Printed and bound in Great Britain by
Marston Book Services Limited, Oxford

For all our children,

    Adi, Benjamin, Chaka, David, Maya, Nnenna, Rashid

    and for our mothers,

    Elayne Isom and Dorothy Gantman

Contents

Preface

Funmilayo Ransome-Kuti (née Thomas) was a first-born daughter and the first female student at the Abeokuta Grammar School. Hence she acquired the affectionate nickname Béère, which means "first-born daughter" in the Yoruba language. Béère also became the *nom de guerre* of this first Nigerian woman to head a movement to attempt to depose a king, to travel with a nationalist delegation to London, and to hold office in an international women's organization.

▲▲▲

We came to the study of African women as graduate students in the early 1970s, Cheryl at Northwestern University in Evanston, Illinois, and Nina at the University of Ibadan in Ibadan, Nigeria. Our interests and research preceded the explosion of scholarly literature on women in Africa. By that time, however, a burgeoning interest had developed in expanding the contours of African historiography to include women's experiences and contributions and the analysis of the role of gender in African history.

We met at the University of Ibadan in 1975 while in the midst of research and fieldwork for our doctoral dissertations. Both dissertations were studies of women, Nina's on the political history of women in Southern Nigeria, 1900–1965 and Cheryl's on Nigerian women and British colonialism. Though Funmilayo Ransome-Kuti's "story" formed only a portion of our focuses at the time, we remained intensely interested in her remarkable life. Because of the limitations of time and subject imposed by the structure of our dissertations, neither of us could do full justice to the complexity and diversity of Funmilayo Ransome-Kuti's life and significance.

At various times between 1974 and 1976 we were each privileged to conduct many personal interviews with her at her home in Abeokuta where she was always a gracious hostess and a witty and inspiring informant. We each undertook extensive research in her voluminous personal papers, which were then simply stored, rather haphazardly, in her basement. They are now housed in much more hospitable surroundings at the University of Ibadan Library, Manuscripts Section.

Our dissertations were completed in 1978, unhappily the same year Funmilayo Ransome-Kuti died. We mourned her death but were grateful we had been able, in some small way, to share her life with others. In our search for a fitting memorial, we conceived the idea to write a "proper" biography. Competing priorities intervened as we each had two more children, changed jobs, and finished other research projects. Still, we remained friends as well as colleagues through letters, visits, and conferences, often discussing the proposed biography of Funmilayo Ransome-Kuti. Finally, in 1987, we formulated concrete plans to co-author it. The rest, as they say, pun intended, is history.

Among the most valuable of the written primary sources for this biography were the private papers of Funmilayo Ransome-Kuti and those of her husband, Rev. Israel Oludotun Ransome-Kuti, which provided us with a wealth of material on her personal, professional, and public life. Also useful were the private papers of their close friend, Ladipo Ṣolanke, who was based in London and corresponded with them both from 1930–54. These letters illuminate the relationship between Funmilayo and Oludotun Ransome-Kuti as well as other aspects of their family life in Abeokuta and that of their children studying in England. The Egba Council Archives, Abeokuta, contain some of the records of the Abeokuta Women's Union and data on events and personalities in Abeokuta. The National Archives, Ibadan, provided material on the interactions among the colonial administration, Funmilayo Ransome-Kuti, and the Abeokuta women. The Lagos and Abeokuta newspapers published between 1930 and 1978 supplied information about Ransome-Kuti's activities, her contemporaries, the lives of her children and other family members, and the circumstances of her death. Among the most valuable of the oral primary sources were interviews with Funmilayo Ransome-Kuti herself, members of her family, her associates in women's organizations, her former students, and her contemporaries.

As for secondary sources on Funmilayo Ransome-Kuti specifically, it is interesting to note that we found only one published account (that was not authored by either of us) since our dissertations of 1978.[1] However, two biographies of Fela, the second son of the Ransome-Kutis, have appeared.[2] Both books have information on Fela's family background. In addition, the Nobel laureate Wole Soyinka, grandnephew of Oludotun Ransome-Kuti (Funmilayo's husband), has published an autobiography of his childhood in Abeokuta, *Ake: The Years of Childhood,* which recalls his experiences of staying in the Ransome-Kuti home and of observing the women's agitation led by Funmilayo Ransome-Kuti in 1948. Two other Soyinka books, *Isara* and *Ibadan,* were also very useful for contextualizing the Yoruba area of Western Nigeria during much of Funmilayo Ransome-Kuti's lifetime.

The research for this biography spanned, off and on, twenty years (1974–94). During that time, the location, management, and classification of much of the archival material used has changed. For instance, from at least 1974 until the mid-1980s, the records of the Egba/Abeokuta Councils were kept in the Afin (Alake's palace) in Abeokuta. In the mid-1980s, these records were transferred to the new National Archives Abeokuta. Some of the colonial records pertaining to Abeokuta that were at the National Archives Ibadan in the 1970s were also subsequently transferred to the National Archives Abeokuta. It is especially the documents in the Funmilayo Ransome-Kuti Papers, however, that have been disturbed. In 1974–76, when the authors first used these papers, they were stored quite haphazardly in cupboards and boxes (mostly in the basement) in the Ransome-Kuti home in Abeokuta. Some of them were in quite fragile and/or deteriorating condition—particularly the handwritten letters. After Funmilayo Ransome-Kuti's death in 1978, her family donated her papers to the University of Ibadan Library in Ibadan, Nigeria. Though we used the FRK Papers in 1989 when they were (mostly) indexed and catalogued by the library staff, our greatest usage of them was in the mid-1970s when they were in her home. Thus, the citations for those documents from the FRK Papers vary.

One problem we faced almost immediately was how to refer to Funmilayo Ransome-Kuti throughout the text. Before her marriage she was Frances Abigail Olufunmilayo Thomas and then just Funmilayo Thomas, but after that she is referred to in letters, documents, newspapers, and other written sources (and interviews) as Funmilayo Ransome-Kuti, Funmilayo Anikulapo-Kuti (from the early 1970s), Mrs. Kuti, *Iya Egbe, Iyalode, Béére,* and Funmi—among other names. We have used several of these names and made an attempt to be clear (when it was not obvious) that the reference was to her. We have used her initials (FRK) frequently.

A brief explanation of the chapter titles we have chosen may be of interest to our readers. Chapter 2, " 'We Two Form a Multitude,' " is a quote from the pictorial essay *The Family of Man* (Edward Steichen, ed. [New York: Museum of Modern Art, 1955]). Chapter 3, " 'When Love Whispers' " is the title of a novel by the Nigerian author Cyprian Ekwensi. In 1948 Ekwensi asked FRK to write a foreword to his novel. The *West African Pilot* (Nov. 29, 1947) referred to Ransome-Kuti as the "Lioness of Lisabi" during the campaign against the *Alake*. Lisabi was a great hero of the Egba, who are sometimes referred to as the "children of Lisabi." The subtitle comes from a pamphlet, *The Fall of a Ruler,* by A. Aloba, commemorating the campaign against the Alake, which chapter 4 chronicles. The title of chapter 5, " 'A True Citizen,' " is from a speech on citizenship that FRK made at a convention of the National Council of Nigeria and the Cameroons in Kaduna, April 5, 1948, in which she said: "When you contribute your own quota to the welfare and progress of a place, you are a true citizen." The speech is among her personal papers. The title of chapter 6, " 'For Their Freedoms,' " comes from an August 1976 interview with Ransome-Kuti, when she remarked about her struggles for the freedom to travel to communist countries: "All our big men and women now travel to China and Russia. I suffered for their freedoms." " 'Virtue Is Better than Wealth,' " the title of chapter 7, is a Kenyan proverb.

▲▲▲

Coauthoring a biography, especially given our residences on different continents, was not easy. Though Cheryl spent time in Nigeria and Nina in the United States during both the research and writing, it was mostly mail, phone, and fax that enabled, and sometimes frustrated, our work. Undoubtedly, it took twice as long to produce given these constraints. While we take responsibility for errors and interpretations, we wish to share any credit with those who, in a variety of ways, provided resources, inspiration, and support.

There are many people who were extremely helpful in granting interviews, locating sources, and providing intellectual, emotional, and financial support. We cannot name them all and beg the forgiveness of those whom we do not mention. We wish first to thank our families, who put up with our intercontinental travel and absences from home and provided all of the above-named support plus love and faith in our effort. Our husbands, Carlton Odim and Ben Mba, were especially helpful in both practical and intangible ways. We give our heartfelt gratitude to the Ransome-Kuti extended family (including the Thomas and Jibolu-Taiwo-Coker relatives) for their time, trust, patience, and reflection in interviews as well as for priceless photographs and access to special items only they could have given, such as the family Bible. We hope this book is recompense. To them we say: "*Eshe. A dupe pupo*" (Yoruba for "Thank you. We are very grateful").

We also express our gratitude to the staffs of the Egba Council Archives in Abeokuta, the Africana and Manuscripts Sections of the University of Ibadan Library, the National Archives in Ibadan, the Gandhi Memorial Library at the University of Lagos, the Melville J. Herskovits Africana Collection at Northwestern University, the Library of Rhodes House, Oxford, and the Records Office of the House of Lords, London. Both Judy Ugonna of the University of Lagos Library and Hans E. Panofsky, formerly curator of the Africana Collection of Northwestern University Library, were especially helpful in guiding us to elusive sources. In addition, the secretariat of the Women's International Democratic Federation in East Berlin responded kindly to our several inquiries. We also acknowledge Loyola University Chicago, which provided funds for international travel at a critical stage in our collaboration on the work. Last but not least, our editors at the University of Illinois Press—first Carole Appel and then especially Elizabeth Dulany—were patient and very supportive.

▲▲▲

A biography is a complex enterprise involving several different historical approaches: the life history, contextual background, and sociopsychological interpretations. There is more than a little risk involved in the attempt to "get inside" someone's mind and analyze such subtle issues as intent, motivation, reasoning, and emotions. Despite the risks, we trust we have not dodged the need to do so where we deemed it appropriate.

In a foreword to *Leadership in Nineteenth-Century Africa* by Obaro Ikime, the eminent Nigerian historian J. F. A. Ajayi wrote, "Biography . . . highlights the subtle ways in which the circumstances of history shape personalities, and how strong personalities and leaders help to make history." Funmilayo Ransome-Kuti was a strong personality who helped make history—we hope we have conveyed both the personal and political aspects of her life and of her role in history.

Notes

1. Byfield, "Women in Nigerian Politics."
2. Moore, *fela, fela: this bitch of a life;* Idowu, *Fela.*

Abbreviations

AG	Action Group
AGS	Abeokuta Grammar School
ALC	Abeokuta Ladies' Club
ASUP	Abeokuta Society of Union and Progress
AUDC	Abeokuta Urban District Council
AWU	Abeokuta Women's Union
CMS	Church Missionary Society
CPP	Commoner People's Party
DO	District Officer
ECC	Egba Central Council
ENA	Egba Native Administration
EUBM	Egba United Board of Management
EUG	Egba United Government
FNWS	Federation of Nigerian Women's Societies
FRK	Funmilayo Ransome-Kuti
NCNC	National Council of Nigeria and the Cameroons (after 1960, National Council of Nigerian Citizens)
NCWS	National Council of Women's Societies
NEPU	Northern Elements Progressive Union
NNDP	Nigerian National Democratic Party

NPC	Northern People's Congress
NUS	Nigerian Union of Students
NUT	Nigerian Union of Teachers
NYM	Nigerian Youth Movement
NWP	Nigerian Women's Party
NWU	Nigerian Women's Union
SNA	Sole Native Authority
UPP	United People's Party
WASU	West African Students Union
WIDF	Women's International Democratic Federation
WILPF	Women's International League for Peace and Freedom

For Women and the Nation

Historical Background

Funmilayo Ransome-Kuti (née Thomas) was born in 1900 in Abeokuta, a formerly autonomous kingdom that, by the time of her birth, lay within the British-ruled colonial protectorate of Southern Nigeria. She died in 1978 in the same city, then the capital of Ogun State in the independent Federal Republic of Nigeria.

Her life encapsulates much of the twentieth-century history of Nigeria while the record of her ancestry depicts the evolution of Abeokuta in the nineteenth century. Funmilayo Ransome-Kuti was deeply attached to her hometown, where she spent the major part of her life, and concern for its progress, as she visualized it, was the initial motivation for her entry into public life. Even later when she was a participant in national and international politics and the acknowledged leader of women throughout Nigeria, Abeokuta remained her springboard and her inspiration. It is appropriate therefore to begin this chapter with a brief history of Abeokuta.[1]

Funmilayo Ransome-Kuti was Yoruba. By 1900 the Yoruba people had inhabited southwestern Nigeria for over a millennium. Though they shared common cultural and political institutions, over time the Yoruba divided into a number of groups that, though speaking mutually intelligible dialects of the same language, were politically autonomous.[2] One such group is the Egba, to which FRK belonged. Sometime between the eighth and thirteenth centuries C.E. the Egba migrated from the Yoruba homeland at Ile-Ife to a forest area whose boundaries were the Ogun River to the west, the Ijebu area to the east, and the Eko (Lagos) lagoon to the south. Within the Egba forest the people divided into many homesteads (orile) that eventually clustered into three provinces: Egba Alake, Egba Gbagura, Egba Oke-Ona.

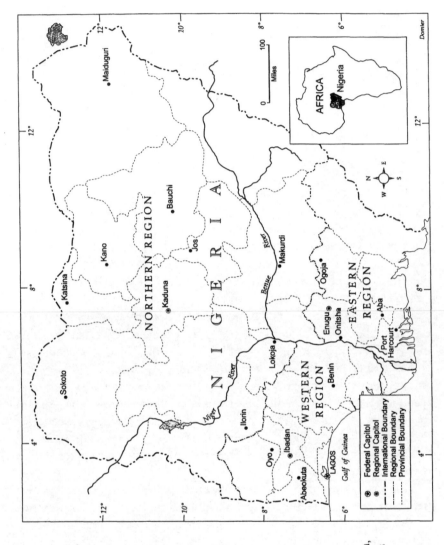

Map I. Nigeria,
ca. 1940s–1950s

Among the provinces a confederal political relationship operated. Each province had a paramount ruler or *Oba,* who were equal to one another: the *Agura* of Gbagura, the *Osile* of Oke-Ona, and the *Alake* of Alake. The Oba was "much more the symbol of authority than the instrument of its exercise."[3] Active legislative, executive, and judicial functions were performed by the civil chiefs, the *Ogboni,* who were distinguished by wearing the *saaki* (a woven towel) on their shoulders and the *ege* (a kind of sombrero) on their heads. Women were eligible to be members of the Ogboni as holders of the *Erelu* title and were selected, as were the men, on the basis of merit in terms of leadership ability, wealth, and contributions to the well-being of the town. Within the Ogboni was the *Oro,* a secret ancestral organization. Women were not allowed into the Oro nor were they admitted into the society of trade chiefs, the *Parakoyi,* even though women were the majority of traders; they were also not allowed in the society of hunters, the *Ode,* nor into the society of military chiefs, the *Olorogun* (or later, *Ologun*). This comprehensive exclusion of women from three of the four orders of government was countered to a degree by the exclusively female *Iyalode* society (literally, "mother of the town"), which may be seen as the female equivalent of the Ologun; the Iyalode enabled women to be represented in decision making and administration.

Toward the end of the eighteenth century, the Egba were threatened by incursions from the imperialistic Oyo Empire. Their successful resistance was spearheaded by the warrior leader Lisabi, who has been regarded ever since as a kind of savior and hero of the Egba, such that "Lisabi land" is synonymous with Abeokuta. (During her public life, FRK was hailed as the "Lioness of Lisabi" [chap. 4] and the "daughter of Lisabi.") From the beginning of the nineteenth century, the military and political situation in Yorubaland was transformed by internecine wars that brought the full impact of the trans-Atlantic slave trade down upon the Yoruba.

The Owu War (1821–25) signaled the general disruption of Yoruba country.[4] The Owu were defeated by the slave-raiding Ife allied to the slave-purchasing Ijebu. The victorious allies pursued the Owu into Egba territory and the divided Egba towns could not resist the invasion. Thousands were killed and thousands more were captured and later sold to European slave traders in Lagos and Porto Novo. The dispersed Egba regrouped and, under the leadership of Sodeke, eventually decided to resettle under a massive outcrop of granite rock (highest point on that outcropping: 137 meters) that the Egba hunters had discovered by the Ogun River. They named the rock "Olumo" [last ditch] and the new home "Abeokuta" [under the rocks].

The main body of the Egba entered Abeokuta during a lull in the rainy season of 1830 and settled on the western side of the Olumo rock, which is situated on Itako land between Ikija and Ikereku townships. The three divisions of the Egbas in the forest were preserved — the Alake, Gbagura, and Oke-Ona. Remnants of the old towns formed townships or wards, and the three provinces were maintained. Sodeke allowed all Egba refugees to enter and extended that policy also to the Owu refugees who formed a fourth province. The new settlement was besieged by the Ijebu and their Ibadan allies in 1832 and then was defeated by the Ijebu with the help of Lagos under the leadership of Adele I. Though defeated, the settlement remained.

Some of the Egba and other Yoruba captives during the wars who had been sold to the European slave traders had been resettled in the 1820s in Freetown, Sierra Leone, by the anti-slave-trade British naval patrols. Granted their freedom, they became known as Saros and in Freetown many converted to Christianity and received Western education and vocational training. One such liberated Egba Saro was Funmilayo Ransome-Kuti's paternal great-grandmother, Sarah Taiwo (chap. 2).

Once news of the new Egba settlement in Abeokuta spread to Freetown in the late 1830s, the Egba Saros decided to return to their homeland. The first batch migrated around 1838, and then another group in 1842, when 500 to 600 were estimated to have resettled. The Saros were followed shortly by European Christian missionaries, the earliest of whom, Thomas Birch Freeman and Rev. Henry Townsend, arrived in December 1842 and January 1843, respectively. Permanent mission stations were established in Abeokuta from 1846. The first missionary schools were established around St. John's Church, Igbein, and St. Peter's Church, Ake, in 1847. The missionaries were welcomed because they could help get weaponry from Lagos through the Ijebu blockade. The parents of Funmilayo Ransome-Kuti were among the many converted Egba who were educated in mission schools.

The new settlement at Abeokuta was vulnerable to attack from the same forces that had forced the Egba to flee from the forest. To deal with the problem of security, Sodeke devised a central administration for Abeokuta that had not existed in the traditional Egba confederation. He created a federal military government that then embarked on a series of wars of "aggressive defense," especially in the Egbado and Awori areas such as Ota and Ilaro. The conquered lands were made subordinate to Abeokuta through the introduction of the *Ajele* (consul) system, an imperial administration in which each of the territories was placed under the control of certain powerful war chiefs in Abeokuta. Some of the acquired lands were scarcely populated and the Egba, whose population had increased enormously since 1830, moved there to farm. Up to that time, the Egba had farmed fertile areas of the Abeokuta Egbaland within the boundaries of Abeokuta. Farmers established settlements on both their old and new farmlands but continued to regard Abeokuta as their home.

Once Abeokuta was secured, the Egba revived their traditional economic practices. As among the Yoruba generally, there was a gendered division of labor in which men specialized in agriculture, hunting, and warfare and women specialized in cloth production, marketing, and trading, both local and long distance. One reason often given for men's specialization in agriculture (unlike most of sub-Saharan Africa where women take primary responsibility for cultivation) is the many Yoruba wars of the nineteenth century, which posed security problems. The expansion of the British commercial and political presence in Lagos (the city was colonized by the British in 1861) provided a ready and profitable market for Abeokuta's agricultural products, such as palm oil, palm kernels, kola nuts, and later, cocoa. Cotton, which had been produced and consumed domestically, was expanded into a major export, and three hundred cotton gins were set up in Abeokuta to augment local processing. During the U.S. Civil War (1861–65), which interrupted the U.S. cotton trade to Europe, the Abeokuta cotton trade to England was substantial. Lagos in turn supplied Egba traders with tobacco pipes, alcoholic beverages, finished cloth, processed food, salt, umbrellas, mirrors, beads, and weapons.

The profitability and diversity of the new local and international trade attracted many men and women in Lagos and Abeokuta. Many Saros who had no farmlands had gone into trade immediately when they returned to Lagos or Abeokuta. Until the 1880s when large expatriate firms began to dominate trade and commerce, indigenous Lagos and Abeokuta merchants, male and female, had flourished. Examples include Funmilayo Ransome-Kuti's paternal uncle and great-uncle: Olufashabe and Moses (Aderupoko) Coker (chap. 2).

One of the most famous figures in the trade was the Egba woman,

Madam Tinubu. She traded in cotton, palm oil, salt, tobacco, arms, and slaves and was a leading trader in the hinterlands of Lagos. Tinubu's wealth gave her access to political power that she used to safeguard her economic empire against the British, the Saros, and the Brazilian returnees who threatened the slave and arms trade. Tinubu's success in the arms trade enabled her to provide Egba warriors with guns and ammunition during the 1864 Abeokuta-Dahomey War, for which she was rewarded with the first ever title of Iyalode of all the Egba.[5]

Tinubu's significant role in Lagos and Abeokuta politics between the 1850s and 1880s has been discussed elsewhere.[6] What is important here is to appreciate Tinubu's symbolic value to Funmilayo Ransome-Kuti. Tinubu was an Egba woman who possessed economic and political power. She had opposed both the British and the Lagos and Abeokuta rulers. She was a proud Egba nationalist who rejected Christianity and the missionaries and upheld indigenous values and culture. Thus, for FRK, Tinubu was both a feminist and a nationalist heroine, an inspiring role model and an emotive rallying cry that FRK used to good effect in mobilizing Egba women in the 1940s. FRK was seen by many Egbas as a second Tinubu, an analogy heightened by the ironic coincidence that Tinubu had supported the succession of Oyekan as Alake against Ademola (later Ademola I and father of Ademola II [chap. 4]) to the throne in 1869. When Ademola I won, Iyalode Tinubu withheld support from the acknowledged Alake. As will be seen in chapter 4, Funmilayo Ransome-Kuti opposed Alake Ademola II, was largely responsible for his leaving office, and after he was reinstated withheld *her* recognition and support.

In the 1860s, the Egba repulsed the last of a series of invasions from Dahomey (1864) and fought several other wars aimed at strengthening the military power as well as the political influence of the Abeokuta state. But a new danger emerged from the British, who annexed Lagos in 1861 and threatened Abeokuta's control over the Egbado and Awori areas. To counter this intrusion, the Egba leadership, influenced by the Saros and Christian missionaries, created a new, strong, central administration combining traditional Yoruba and European governmental structures. This institution became known as the Egba United Board of Management (EUBM).

When Lagos imposed duties on Egba traders, stationed constabulary on the border posts who harassed Egba women traders, and refused to allow Abeokuta to collect tolls in areas Lagos regarded as under its sphere of influence, the EUBM retaliated in 1867 by closing all churches in Abeokuta. This was meant to intimidate Lagos. The patriotic Egba people spontaneously expressed their hostility to the actions of the British in Lagos by attacking the churches and property of Europeans in Abeokuta in the *Ifole* (literally, "housebreaking") incident of October 13, 1867.

Since the Europeans in Abeokuta were mainly missionaries, the uprising was wrongly seen by the British as a persecution of Christians. The missionaries and many of their Egba converts fled, including members of the Coker/Thomas family—FRK's paternal relatives. Some Egba refugees settled in Ebute-Metta, outside Lagos, others on Egba farmlands. One group of Christian warriors led by John Owolotan Okenla, first Balogun of the Egba Christians who had won fame through his defense of Abeokuta against the Dahomey invasion of 1864, moved into the recently conquered/acquired Egbado area of Ifo near Ota, southwest of Abeokuta. Ifo was seen by the Egba as a strategic post on the overland route to Lagos and as a buffer area against the Awori. Okenla and his supporters, who included Ebenezer Ṣobowale Thomas (FRK's grandfather), colonized several villages near Ifo. One was named after Okenla, another was Igbogun where Thomas decided to settle (chap. 2).

The land was fertile and already sustained a flourishing kola nut crop. The Egba farmers initially concentrated on food crops, then on cash crops such as palm oil and kernels, kola nuts, and cocoa. The agricultural production stimulated the development of Ifo as a large market town.[7] In 1898, Ifo's importance was greatly augmented by the construction of a railway line between Lagos and Abeokuta with a junction at Ifo. The government in Abeokuta established a customs and tolls post at Ifo in 1900. The overland route from Lagos to Abeokuta, which had taken three days, took less than half a day by train. Trade in cash crops was greatly expanded and the population of the European merchant community in Abeokuta increased. The Ifo junction proved so profitable that an extension was constructed to Ifo town in 1913. Also, a road was built from Ifo to Igbogun. This meant that it was relatively easy for the Thomas family in Igbogun to move regularly between their home and Abeokuta. The Egba in the farmlands and settlements outside Abeokuta continued to regard themselves as citizens of their respective townships in Abeokuta and journeyed there for the celebration of important occasions in the life of the township or the family. Politically and judicially, Ifo and its Egba villages were controlled from Abeokuta.

In 1892 the British, intent on controlling the entire country—in the era of officially mandated imperial expansion—invaded Ijebu and, threatening to repeat the event with Abeokuta, persuaded the Egba authorities to enter into a treaty of "trade and friendship." In this treaty, the Egba promised to keep open the trade routes between Abeokuta and Lagos and in return managed to elicit a guarantee of territorial integrity that allowed Abeokuta to remain autonomous until 1914.[8] In 1898, after a leadership tussle in Abeokuta, leading members of the Egba mercantile community in Lagos won British colonial government support for a new "modernized" system of government, the Egba United Government (EUG). Part of the aim in establishing the EUG (just as for the EUBM before it) was to try to maintain autonomy from the British. The EUG ruling council consisted of the new Alake, Gbadebo I, as president, a membership of the other three Obas, representatives of the Ogboni, Ologun, Muslim, and Christian interests, and one or two members of the educated Egba elite. The EUG set about centralizing power in its hands and carrying out political, judicial, and economic "modernization." It also attempted to maintain its autonomy from Lagos and secure control over the territories between it and Lagos.

When Funmilayo Ransome-Kuti was born in 1900, the progressive EUG had been in existence for two years. Around this time it was estimated that the area of Egbaland was six to seven thousand square miles and its population between 350,000 and 400,000.[9] Having created an administrative superstructure to implement its modernization program, the EUG appointed Prince Oladapo Ademola as its ambassador to Lagos. He accompanied Alake Gbadebo on his official visit to Great Britain where they were received by the king.[10] The EUG did not have the funds to establish its own schools but encouraged people to contribute and raise money for education. In 1908, an Egba businessman in Lagos, R. B. Blaize, set up a technical institute (named after himself), one of the earliest institutions for technical/vocational education in Nigeria. Many Egba people agreed with the EUG that it was wrong that secondary grammar education should be available only in Lagos and contributed to funds for the Abeokuta Grammar School (AGS, see chap. 2).

Apart from promoting education, the EUG administration gradually extended its area of control by establishing courts in Abeokuta and in rural areas, by introducing sanitation and health facilities and regulations and by mobilizing labor for road construction. However, pressures from Lagos aimed at undermining the EUG's autonomy increased as the British government tightened and reorganized its administration.[11]

In 1906, the Yoruba protectorate was merged into the Protectorate of Southern Nigeria. Relations between the EUG and Lagos were increasingly strained as the EUG was dependent on the import duties levied on traders bringing goods from Lagos. In 1914 the government in Lagos threatened to withdraw its support of the duties, and the EUG was forced to propose direct taxation as an alternative source of revenue. This proposal excited great opposition and, coupled with a local dispute over labor, precipitated an uprising by the Ijemo (in the Egba Alake Province) on August 8, 1914. The EUG asked the Lagos government to assist in quelling the uprising but, when the Hausa constabulary stationed at Abeokuta fired on the demonstrators, the result was the "Ijemo massacre." Faced with this apparent evidence of the EUG's loss of control, the Lagos government decided finally to end Abeokuta's autonomy.

On October 1, 1914, Abeokuta was formally absorbed into the Protectorate of Southern Nigeria, which was then amalgamated with Northern Nigeria and the Colony of Lagos. The amalgamation marked the end of the first phase of the consolidation of British rule in the Yoruba hinterland, a rule described by the historian A. I. Asiwaju as being paramilitary in character.[12] The EUG was renamed the Egba Native Administration (ENA). The ENA pushed its role much further than the EUG in the areas of enforcing labor recruitment and sanitation regulations. Under the ENA, courts imposed heavier fines for infractions of regulations, and thus increasingly courts became revenue-producing agencies.

In 1917, the British Colonial Governor Frederick Lugard finally received his long demanded permission to introduce a system of direct taxation to the Yoruba areas of the protectorate, slated to begin in January 1918. Before then, the ENA had promised to abolish customs, labor recruitment, and sanitation fines in an attempt to appease the people's anger over ENA interference and direct taxation. After the taxes were collected, there were no other reductions and the Egba people rose in protest against all the incursions of the British-controlled ENA rather than just against taxation. The Adubi War of June 1918 was a massive uprising in which hundreds were killed, and railway and telegraph lines destroyed. Again the British army was called in to restore order. The commission of inquiry into the "disturbances" concluded that one of the main causes was the "illegal and oppressive sanitary fines." Many of the witnesses complained of the way women were exploited by the authorities in order to raise revenue from fines. One of the witnesses was Funmilayo Ransome-Kuti's father-in-law, the Reverend J. J. Ransome-

Kuti, who confirmed that the excessive enforcement of sanitary regulations was one of the main grievances that led to the uprising. Several women had been arrested and fined for not observing sanitary regulations. Men were particularly angry because the searches and arrests occurred while they were absent performing forced labor.

During the Adubi War, Funmilayo Ransome-Kuti was a student at the Abeokuta Grammar School and, though we have no evidence of her reactions, there is no doubt that she would have witnessed, if not the uprising itself, then the "cleanup" operation that involved troops searching homes in Abeokuta for "rebels" and destroying "fetish" places (i.e., Ogboni meeting houses). She would have heard discussions about it at home and at school—the proud Egba were horrified at the way their sovereignty had been violated by the British government in Lagos. Moreover, her uncle J. K. Coker was the leader behind the formation of the Lagos Egba Society just after the Adubi War. The society aimed to protect Egba interests by lobbying the government in Lagos. Coker used his own money and raised funds to restore the Ogboni houses.

Coker and the Lagos Egba Society of which he was president supported the candidacy of Prince Ademola II for succession to the throne of Alake when Gbadebo died in 1920. They thought that a well-educated and experienced businessman and administrator would be better able to protect Egba interests and preserve Egba culture against the British than had Gbadebo. They expected Ademola to modernize and democratize the ENA.

The British administration originally opposed and then approved the appointment of Ademola as Alake—for the opposite reason: that he would be able to fulfill the new role of Sole Native Authority (SNA) that had been devised as a means of indirect rule in the southwestern provinces. Under this system, the government conferred much greater administrative and judicial responsibility upon recognized Obas or Bales who replaced the British commissioners as presidents of the native courts and councils. Excessive authority was thus concentrated in the hands of the recognized "native" authorities, while the Western-educated elite were excluded from the "native" administration, as were institutions such as the legislative council and courts that moderated the conduct of British rule in the colony. Thus was initiated the second stage of British administration, described by Asiwaju as "authoritarian."[13] The traditional powers of the kingmakers and chiefs who had acted as checks on the Obas were removed. Though the chiefs were

members of the native authority councils, the SNAs were responsible
for the chiefs' appointments to the councils and, at any rate, the councils
were only advisory. The loss of the traditional powers of chiefs, kingmakers, Ogboni, and priests also meant the loss of the powers of the
female chiefs (Iyalode and Erelu) and priestesses. But where the male
chiefs were able, if they chose, to enter the new centers of power, such
as native authority councils and courts, the women were never granted
such access. The female titles rapidly became vacant and meaningless.

Tinubu's successor as Iyalode of all the Egba, Miniya Jojolola, was
Muslim and a wealthy trader. Among her businesses was a large *adire*
cloth dyeing establishment. She played a negligible role in Egba politics and government, however. No woman was ever a signatory to the
various treaties between Lagos and Abeokuta, no woman was ever a
member of the Egba United Board of Management, the Egba United
Government, or the Egba Native Authority. After Jojolola died (c. 1928),
the Iyalode title was allowed to lapse, though township Iyalode Societies remained and the Christian title of Iyalode of all Christians was
introduced by Alake Ademola II.

The erosion of women's access to political power was intensified
under the Abeokuta SNA system. No woman was ever a member of the
advisory ENA council or native courts nor employed in the bureaucracy.
The Alake personally advocated the education of girls, and several of his
daughters were educated in Britain. He also provided scholarships for
Egba boys and girls. But as head of the SNA he rarely consulted women,
even on matters that affected them. For instance, the Abeokuta Province Annual Report of 1937 notes that "during discussion of the 'rules
for Marriage and Divorce' His Honor elicited the information that the
women of Egbaland had not even been consulted on a matter which
concerned them so very closely." When he did consult the women, as
during the preparations for the celebration of the centenary of Abeokuta's founding, he berated them for not doing exactly as he wished:
"Anybody who disobeys my call must not be allowed to go away un-
challenged. . . . She will incur my displeasure."[14]

This diminution of women's status and power was reinforced by the
prejudices and assumptions of the British colonial administration officers who worked for a government in which there were scarcely any
women and who therefore did not expect—or wish—to find women
involved in Southern Nigeria's government. In Britain, the franchise for
women was first introduced in 1918, but only for women over thirty.

When elections to the Lagos and Calabar Legislative Councils were introduced in 1923, it was hardly surprising that Nigerian women did not get to vote.

Several chiefs soon protested about their loss of authority and revenue. The ENA paid the Alake an annual salary of £3,000 while the other three Obas received £500 as annual salaries. Ademola II aggressively maintained the elevation of the status of Alake above the three sectional Obas. This policy provoked tension and resistance in Abeokuta to what was seen as the Alake's autocracy (chap. 4).

In 1939 the Colony and Protectorate of Southern Nigeria was reorganized into the Eastern and Western Provinces with Lagos and Abeokuta as two of the seven constituent Western Provinces. From the mid-1930s, the British initiated an ad hoc gradual democratization of the SNA system in the Western Provinces and the warrant chief system in the Eastern Provinces, which had been so threatened by the 1929 Women's War. World War II put that process on hold, but the British postwar Labour government committed itself to the decolonization of the empire. The pace and nature of the process was determined by events within each colony.

In Nigeria there had been several anticolonial and nationalist movements and organizations since 1922, when the first political party, the Nigerian National Democratic Party (NNDP), had been founded by the Lagosian Herbert Macaulay. The Lagos Market Women's Association, led by Alimotu Pelewura, had actively supported the NNDP and initiated a successful campaign against the payment of taxes by women in Lagos in 1940 and the wartime policies of the control of food and supplies distribution.[15] Thus, there was a precedent in Yorubaland for political action against the colonial authorities by market women before Funmilayo Ransome-Kuti's political career began.

Moreover, both FRK and her husband, the Reverend I. O. Ransome-Kuti, sympathized with the nationalist Nigerian Youth Movement (NYM) led by E. Ikoli, S. Akinsanya, H. O. Davies, N. Azikiwe, and O. Awolowo in the 1930s and 1940s. The NYM included a women's wing led by Oyinkan Abayomi, who later formed the elitist, conservative, exclusively women's political party, the Nigerian Women's Party (NWP), in the 1940s.[16]

Rev. I. O. Ransome-Kuti was one of the founders of the Nigerian Union of Teachers (NUT) in the 1930s (chap. 3) and of the Nigerian Union of Students (NUS). This student union, particularly its King's

College branch, initiated a mass meeting to protest against the colonial government's educational policies in August 1944, a demonstration that led to the formation of a new political organization (later party): the National Council of Nigeria and the Cameroons (NCNC). Indeed, both Ransome-Kutis were founding members of the NCNC (chap. 5).

The colonial government responded to the nationalists' demands for the democratization of the government and full representation of Nigerians in it with a proposal for a new constitution named after the then colonial governor, Sir Arthur Richards. Despite the previous governor's assurances that Nigerians would be consulted beforehand, in fact they were not and the Nigerians found that unacceptable. Nigerians viewed the Richards Constitution proposal for Nigerian representation in an enlarged central legislative council and three regional councils as inadequate, especially as there were still colonial government–appointed members on all the councils. Moreover, the constitution provided for an extremely narrow franchise limited to Lagos and Calabar. It also established three administrative regions (North, East, and West), with provision for the creation of further regions if administrative needs warranted it.

The nationalists and NCNC argued that the Richards Constitution was an example of Britain's divide-and-rule policy, effected by establishing regional councils that roughly approximated the areas where different ethnic groups lived.

Though proposed in 1945, the new constitution would not be operational until 1947, and this gave the nationalists the time to organize a national campaign to protest against it. The NCNC sent a delegation to Britain to present a petition of protest to the secretary of state for the colonies. Funmilayo Ransome-Kuti was one of the seven members of the delegation (chap. 5). Although the delegation failed to stop the constitution's implementation, the colonial government recognized the defects of the constitution, which operated effectively only from early 1948.

In 1949 the new governor, Sir John Macpherson, called for regional and all-Nigeria constitutional conferences to discuss a new constitution. Funmilayo Ransome-Kuti was the only woman representative at the Western Regional Conference in Ibadan. All the regional conferences and the national one agreed on a federal rather than unitary system of government. Regional legislatures were established as well as a central House of Representatives in which the Northern Region was allotted half of the seats. There was an indirect system (electoral college) of election to the federal legislature, and the franchise was restricted to male taxpayers. A number of powers were allocated to the regions, such as control over local government, health care, education, agriculture, public works, and regional finance. The powers of the House of Representatives were limited. In other words, the constitution did not provide full powers of self-government. Indeed, it was a compromise between the sharply divided views of the various political leaders and as such did not win their commitment to its successful operation. Because it provided for regional and federal elections and governments, it prompted the formation of two further political parties early in 1951: the Action Group (AG), which was based in the Western Region and headed by Obafemi Awolowo, and the Northern People's Congress (NPC), headed by Ahmadu Bello. Only the NCNC led by Nnamdi Azikiwe was national in both concerns and membership, and it was the only party to contest in two regions—the Eastern and Western. Funmilayo Ransome-Kuti contested for the NCNC in Abeokuta for the Western House of Assembly—the only woman candidate in the country to get beyond the first stage (chap. 5). The election results of December 1951 revealed the regional divisions and the ethnically based support of the parties: the NPC won in the North, the AG in the West, the NCNC in the East. When it came to the July 1952 elections to the House of Representatives, members were elected by the regional legislatures. In the Western Region, Lagos was allotted five seats in the Western Regional Legislature and was entitled to two elected members in the federal House of Representatives. Azikiwe was one of the five members elected to the Western House. Suspecting that the majority might not elect him to the House of Representatives, Azikiwe and the other four members (all NCNC) agreed that three of them would step down so that Azikiwe would be automatically elected. At the last moment, two of them reneged and Azikiwe was defeated in his bid to enter the federal House.

The outcome of this imbroglio was that Azikiwe left the national stage and withdrew eventually to the Eastern House of Assembly and, after regional self-government was implemented in 1957, to the premiership of the Eastern Region. Likewise, Awolowo became premier of the Western Region, and Ahmadu Bello of the Northern Region. Thus, all three party leaders operated from a regional base and left federal politics to their "lieutenants" whom they tried to control. This intensified the regionalization and ethnic character of politics in Nigeria. Only a minority of the political activists remained national in outlook and practice, and Funmilayo Ransome-Kuti belonged to that group. She was very critical of the political divisions in the country and courageously criticized publicly her own party's leader.

The rift between the North and the South, first evident in the 1950 constitutional conferences, deepened in 1953 when the southern parties demanded self-government by 1956. But the NPC said that the North was not ready for such a move. This reflected colonial policies in the North, an area that had been insulated from the encroachment of Western education and training and felt itself at a disadvantage compared to the South. The resultant political crisis convinced the British that it was, in the words of the historian G. O. Olusanya, "impossible for the three regions to work effectively in a federation as closely-knit as the [Macpherson] one." [17] The British convened a constitutional conference from which emerged the 1954 Lyttleton Constitution (named after the then secretary of state for the colonies), which provided the basis for the constitution of Nigeria at independence.

Under the new constitution, the first direct federal elections were held in December 1954. Though unsuccessful, Funmilayo Ransome-Kuti was the only woman candidate (chap. 5). The overall majority party was the NPC, so its deputy leader Abubakar Tafawa Balewa became the Leader of Government Business. The NPC, however, had to govern in coalition with the NCNC. This continued until 1957 when, after further constitutional changes, the position of prime minister was created and held by Balewa. He decided that progress toward independence was so important that a national government was required, so he invited the AG to join the government. In 1957, the Eastern and Western Regions became self-governing, followed by the Northern Region in 1959.

Within each region there were large minorities: the Efiks, Ibibios, Kalabari, and Ijaw in the East; the Binis, Itsekiris, Urhobos, and Igbo in the West; and the Tiv, Igala, Idoma, and Nupe of the Middle Belt in the North. These minorities feared domination and oppression by the larger group in each region and demanded the creation of more states based on ethnic groups. In response to their pressure, the British set up a Minorities Commission that decided against the creation of more states but provisions for their creation in the future were inserted into the independence constitution. Nigeria remained a country unbalanced among three competing regions governed by three political parties that were each identified with the major ethnic group in their region.

At the federal level, as a result of the bitterly fought elections in

December 1959, in which Funmilayo Ransome-Kuti stood as an independent because the NCNC did not nominate her (chap. 5), the NPC again won the highest number of seats. Unable to form a government on its own, the NPC formed a coalition with the NCNC. The AG constituted the opposition, a status that seemed to many within the party to be indefinite unless one of two options was followed: (1) join the governing coalition and create a national government so that the Western Region and the Yoruba would not remain "outside," or (2) since the AG seemed unable to win power through the electoral system, aim to win control through extra-constitutional means. The debate within the party over the two options, coupled with ideological and personal disagreements, led to a split in 1962 and precipitated a state of emergency in the Western Region. FRK's response to this crisis was one of deep concern at the way she felt politicians were damaging the region and the country, and she supported the appointment of a nonpartisan administrator of the Western Region, Dr. Moses Adekoye Majekodunmi (with whose family she had associations).

This regional crisis led to a national political realignment after 1963 and a series of severe blows to the federal system. The federal elections of 1964 and Western Region elections of 1965 almost tore Nigeria apart.

The national political crisis and the state of incipient civil war in the region were resolved by the intervention of the army in a coup d'état on January 15, 1966. Under the military, secession, which each region had threatened at various stages in the colonial and independence periods, became a reality when the Eastern Region seceded in 1967 as Biafra. This led to a three-year civil war in which hundreds of thousands (some estimate millions) lost their lives. From then until 1978 when Funmilayo Ransome-Kuti died, there were a series of coups and successive military administrations. FRK and her children were brave and articulate critics of the actions of various military governments. For this they were victimized and in the aftermath of one such fiasco she lost her life (chap. 7).

In 1979, the military withdrew and an elected government, the Second Republic, took power under President Shehu Shagari. In December 1983, the Second Republic surrendered in ignominy to a military coup. From 1983–93, Nigeria was under military rule. June 1993 saw the first elections held since 1979. Chief Moshood Abiola was widely believed to have won the election, but before the results were released, the military government of General Ibrahim Babangida annulled the 1993 elections. Interestingly, a few months earlier in March 1993, Abiola had given an address at the launching of a published biography of the Reverend Ransome-Kuti, *The Reverend Israel Oludotun Ransome-Kuti: Teacher and Nation-Builder,* by Chief Tunde Adeyanju. In the March 15, 1993, edition of the newspaper *Concord* (owned by Chief Abiola), Abiola is credited with lauding the Ransome-Kutis' attention to the needs of Muslim students at the Abeokuta Grammar School in the 1940s and 1950s. He specifically mentions the predawn and late night meals they provided during Ramadan and the provisions they made for Friday prayer services. In August 1993, some top military officers coerced General Babangida into handing over power to the Interim National Government, headed by Chief Ernest Shonekan who is also an Egba. Three months later, this civil administration was usurped by the Minister of Defense, General Sani Abacha, who installed another military government which remains in power in Nigeria at this writing. As will be seen, the Ransome-Kuti children, particularly the youngest son, Dr. Bekolari Ransome-Kuti, have been active in protests against human rights violations in Nigeria (chap. 7).

Notes

1. This chapter draws on a rich body of literature on Abeokuta, notably works by Ajisafe, Biobaku, Folarin, Harunah, and Pallinder-Law.

2. Akinjogbin and Ayandele, "Yorubaland before 1800," 281.

3. Biobaku, *Egba and Their Neighbours,* 50.

4. For details on the Owu War, see Mabogunje and Omer-Cooper, *Owu in Yoruba History.*

5. It does not seem as though the title Iyalode existed in the Egba forest but was adapted from the Oyo pattern in 1829 along with the titles of *Balogun* and *Seriki.* For studies on the institution of the Iyalode, see Awe, "Notes on the Institution of the Iyalode" and "Iyalode Efunsetan Aniwura."

6. Biobaku, *Eminent Nigerians.*

7. Iṣola, "History of Ifo."

8. Pallinder-Law, "Government in Abeokuta."

9. These figures were in Governor MacGregor's 1904 estimates, quoted in Tamuno, *Evolution of the Nigerian State,* 67n.

10. Ademola had been educated at St. Peter's, Ake, and St. Paul's school, Lagos, and trained as a printer. Gbadebo was illiterate. The secretary to the EUG was Adegboyega Edun who was well educated.

11. A series of acts gradually increased British influence over the EUG: in 1900, the British commissioner in Abeokuta became ex officio chairman of the

Financial Advisory Board; in 1903, the British secretary of state was given control over EUG toll tariffs; and a judicial treaty of 1904 gave the Supreme Court of Lagos (already a British colony) jurisdiction over all capital cases as well as over all non-Egba people in the Egba territories. See Pallinder-Law, "Government in Abeokuta."

12. Asiwaju, "Western Provinces," 436.

13. Ibid.

14. Minutes and correspondence of Abeokuta women's centenary celebration committee, 1930, FRK Papers.

15. See Johnson-Odim, "Madam Alimotu Pelewura," 1–10.

16. See Johnson-Odim, "Lady Oyinkan Abayomi"; Mba, *Nigerian Women Mobilized*.

17. Olusanya, "Constitutional Developments," 536.

"We Two Form a Multitude": The Ancestors

The family is an important institution everywhere and is of primary importance in Africa. While it is difficult to speak generally of so huge and diverse a continent, particularly for the sub-Saharan region, "family" can mean a wide and extended network of kin, all of whom somewhere along the line claim descent from a single ancestor. This wide network of kin is connected by more than emotion, as a deep and complex web of mutual dependency and obligations also cements the bond of "belonging" and determines one's place in society. Therefore, lineage, the telling of the tale of "who begot whom" and how they passed through the world, is important in establishing that connectedness, sense of duty, and legacy. While the late twentieth century has seen some disruptions in this process among impoverished, urbanized populations, these disruptions are still the exception rather than the rule. Thus, to begin the story of Funmilayo Ransome-Kuti's life with attention to her lineage is to situate her not only historically but culturally and socially as well (see figures 1–3).

Appropriately perhaps, Funmilayo Ransome-Kuti's oldest remembered ancestor was a strong woman — Sarah Taiwo, her paternal great-grandmother.[1] Sarah Taiwo was born in the early nineteenth century in Erunwon, an orile (homestead) in the Egba forest. Probably as a result of widespread warfare among the Yoruba during this period, she was captured and sold into slavery. Though the wars were related more to internal power struggles than to the slave trade, the fact that the wars produced captives who could then be sold to obtain guns meant that many Yoruba were sold into slavery in the first half of the nineteenth century. Before 1820 the Yoruba had mainly taken captives from wars

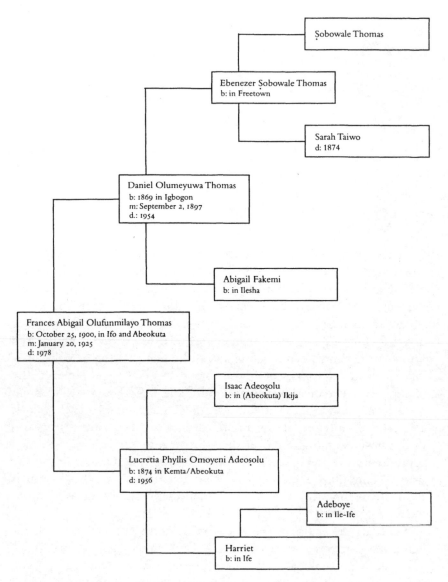

Figure 1. Ancestors of Frances Abigail Olufunmilayo Thomas.

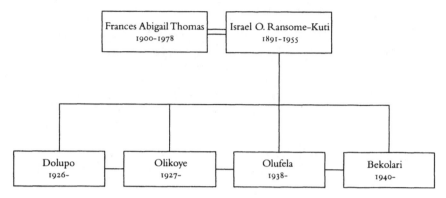

Figure 2. Descendants of Frances Abigail Olufunmilayo Thomas Ransome-Kuti.

with people to their north, but after that date captives mainly came from among the various Yoruba groups themselves.[2]

Sarah Taiwo was only a child at the time, yet old enough to remember her native land and to be remembered by the family she left behind. She was called simply Taiwo then, a Yoruba name signifying that she had been born a twin. The slave ship on which she was eventually boarded was surely headed across the Atlantic Ocean, but fate intervened. In 1807, England had outlawed the slave trade. Shortly thereafter the British government created a special branch of its powerful navy to deter the continuing but illegal slave trade: the British West Africa Patrol. This patrol's task was to cruise off the coast of West Africa in an attempt to intercept ships carrying captives who were bound for the Americas in an illegal slave trade that continued until the 1870s in some places. Taiwo's ship was seized, and with many others before and after her, she was resettled in Freetown, Sierra Leone (a territory west of Nigeria and also on the coast), where the British had recently founded a small colony partially for the purpose of repatriating such captives. There was a fairly large Christian missionary presence in Freetown and, although the details are sketchy, it is most likely this community that christened the newly arrived Taiwo as Sarah. She kept her Yoruba name as well and became known as Sarah Taiwo.

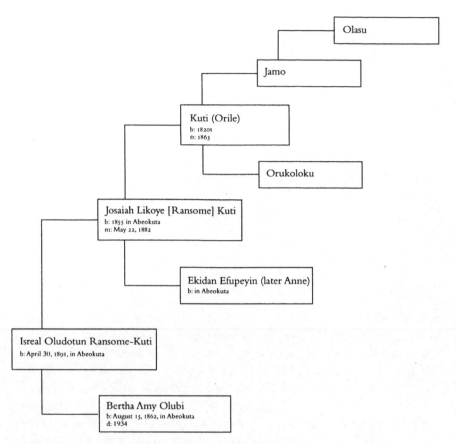

Figure 3. Ancestors of Israel Oludotun Ransome-Kuti.

Sarah Taiwo grew up in Freetown and eventually married a man named Ṣobowale Thomas, a Yoruba man whose background is obscure but who adopted, as did many converts of the time, the surname of a missionary or other British patron. The two had a son, Ebenezer Ṣobowale Thomas, who would be Funmilayo Thomas's grandfather. Shortly after Ebenezer's birth, his father died. After her first husband's death, Sarah Taiwo married again to a man named Jibolu Coker. This marriage produced three children, two of whom, their sons Ṣowemimo and Olufashabe, were born in Freetown.

Many of those who were resettled in Sierra Leone sought to return to their homes in other parts of Africa. The historian J. F. A. Ajayi observes: "The vision of home had a great power of attraction for the liberated Africans in Sierra Leone. . . . To the missionaries [in Freetown, Sierra Leone,] they were just liberated 'Africans,' but among themselves they were Ibo or Nupe or Hausa. . . . The Yoruba, who as a result of the wars of the [nineteenth century] quickly became the most numerous group, were . . . Oyo, Egba, Ijebu or Ife."[3] Those Yoruba who made their way back to Nigeria from Sierra Leone were called Saros. Between the 1830s and 1880s many first settled on the coast at Badagary before moving inland. It was not unusual for families of captives to send messages to Badagary to ascertain if they had relations among the returnees or if anyone knew if their kin were still in Sierra Leone.[4]

Eventually, in this tradition, Sarah Taiwo returned to Nigeria with her second husband but was shipwrecked on the coast at Badagary on her journey. She discovered at Badagary that she was pregnant; she gave birth to a son, Arungbamolu, whose name means "sickness means pregnancy." It is said she named him this because during her voyage back to Nigeria she had thought she was only seasick, not pregnant. In Nigeria, Jibolu Coker died, and Sarah took a third husband whose surname was Wickliffe. He was a Yoruba but had taken the name of a British patron.

Sarah became a trader for a while at Badagary and gave birth to a child by Wickliffe, this time a daughter, Efunjokogun. Shortly after this birth, messages from her family reached her at Badagary and with her children she made her way back to her family home in Abeokuta. Sarah died in Abeokuta on April 18, 1874. There is a large cenotaph erected to her memory and located on family land in Abeokuta. It is inscribed with the names of her five children and her date of death.[5]

All of Sarah's children settled permanently in and around Abeokuta. Her second son Ṣowemimo became a farmer in Ogbe and eventually took the traditional title of *Asalu*. Her third son Olufashabe became a trader in Itesi; his son, Moses Coker, also a trader, later arranged for Funmilayo Thomas (later Ransome-Kuti) to go to England to further her education. The fourth son, Arungbamolu, became a pioneer missionary of the Anglican Church in Ijebu and was known as Rev. Robert A. Coker. He studied music in England and was both a musician and songwriter. He composed several original hymns in the Yoruba language, at least two of which are still popular in the Anglican Church in Nigeria today.[6] His compositions are also sung at many family affairs.

Sarah Taiwo's son by her first husband, Ebenezer Ṣobowale Thomas (born in Freetown, Sierra Leone), was Funmilayo Thomas's grandfather. The Thomas family members were the first Christians at Igbogun, the nearest village to their family farmland at Ifo.[7] Ebenezer Ṣobowale Thomas was an Anglican and a talented carpenter who built St. Thomas's Church on the family farmland at Ifo. His first wife died childless. He and his second wife, Abigail Fakemi, a woman from Ilesha, had a son born in 1869, Daniel Olumeyuwa Thomas, who would be Funmilayo Thomas's father. Ebenezer died while Daniel was still young. As a result, Daniel's uncles took responsibility for raising him. His uncle Arungba-molu (Rev. R. A. Coker) took him to Lagos to the Aroromi Mission where he was educated and trained as a tailor. He returned to Kemta township, Abeokuta, and apprenticed as a carpenter to his uncle Olu-fashabe. With his new skills, Daniel built houses for two of his uncles, Olufashabe and Ṣowemimo, and later he built his own house on the family farmland at Ifo.

On her maternal side, Funmilayo's oldest remembered relative was a man from Ile-Ife named Adeboye. His wife's name is now lost to history, but they had a daughter named Harriet (born in Ife) who married an Egba man named Isaac Adeoṣolu. In 1874 in Abeokuta, Harriet and Isaac had a daughter, Lucretia Phyllis Omoyeni Adeoṣolu, who would be Funmilayo Thomas's mother. Funmilayo's mother was also Western educated, attending the Church Missionary Society (CMS) school at Ikija, where she trained as a seamstress. For a while, Lucretia boarded with the Reverend and Mrs. Wood (English missionaries to Abeokuta) and was baptized at St. Jude's Anglican Church in Abeokuta.[8]

The details of Daniel and Lucretia's meeting and courtship are not much remembered, though the circles of devout Anglicans in Abeokuta would still be relatively small, so they must have met fairly easily. On September 2, 1897, they were married at St. Jude's Church, Ikija, Abeo-kuta, where the young Lucretia had been baptized. The Thomas's first two children, a boy and then a girl, died in infancy. Their next two children, Frances Olufunmilayo Olufela Abigail Folorunsho (known as Funmilayo and born October 25, 1900) and Comfort Harriet Oluremi (known as Oluremi and born March 3, 1903), however, would have long, productive lives.

The Thomas family owned property in three locations: a two-story house at Igbogun that they usually rented out, a home in Kemta town-ship, Abeokuta, and family farmland at Ifo, where Daniel had con-structed a two-story home with eleven rooms. Though both Funmilayo and Oluremi were born in Abeokuta, the family farmland at Igbogun village outside Ifo figured prominently in their lives.

As noted in chapter 1, Ifo village had been founded in 1870 by Egba Christians fleeing from Abeokuta. The village became an Egba outpost for farming and marketing. The land at Ifo was very fertile and it appears that the Thomas family owned land there from near the beginning of the settlement. By 1898 the railroad from Lagos went to Ifo, making it an important crossroads for other villages and towns in the region. Though Islam had a large number of converts in the area by 1870, Christian denominations, particularly the Anglican Church, had a strong core of converts.[9]

Both Daniel and Lucretia Thomas were pious Anglicans. Shortly after their marriage, Daniel rebuilt the church at Ifo (St. Thomas's), which his father had originally constructed, only this time using stone.[10] Still, with the death of his infant son and daughter, and after the birth of his two surviving daughters, his desire for a son remained strong.[11] Despite his Christian piety, Daniel Thomas took a second wife. The practice of polygyny, even among Christian converts, was in fact widespread around this time.

There was a major cultural nationalist movement in Western Nigeria beginning in the 1890s and cresting at the turn of the century. In large measure the rise in cultural nationalism was a reaction to many missionaries' denigration of African culture as "primitive" and inferior to European culture. This was exacerbated by the growing racism of the colonial administration that, as more European bureaucrats arrived, increasingly marginalized even highly qualified Africans from certain positions.

Central to the denigration of African culture was the question of polygyny, which the overwhelming majority of missionaries believed was incompatible with a pious life and with Christianity itself. Though many Africans of the period believed that monogamy went hand in hand with "progress" and elite status, there were many others who disagreed, saying monogamy and polygyny were cultural practices independent of religious affiliation and that polygyny did not violate any law of God.[12] As early as 1884, it was illegal in Lagos for a man married in a Christian ceremony to take another wife even in a "customary" or "traditional" ceremony.[13] By the 1890s, many missionaries in fact viewed monogamy as a precondition for adult conversion and considered polygyny as grounds for excommunication, even to the extent of asking a convert to "give up" all but one of the wives he had married before conversion.

In reaction to such requirements, as well as to protest and circumvent their inability to rise to leadership positions in the Christian denominations, many Africans began to form separatist African Christian churches. These churches took issue with the marginalization of Africans from the hierarchy of European-run churches and with those churches' negative attitude toward polygyny. Daniel Thomas's uncle, Samuel Coker, was active in the separatist church movement in Lagos.[14] The movement that spawned the formation of separatist churches also spurred an increasing interest in promoting the Yoruba language, the use of Yoruba names, and the wearing of African dress as opposed to European apparel. Daniel and Lucretia Thomas could not have been unaffected by this groundswell, a fact attested to by their actions.

Daniel's second wife, Rebecca Olushade Thomas, was the sister of one of the workers on the Ifo farm. She was not wed in a Christian ceremony but in a Yoruba one. Under traditional Yoruba law, she and her children enjoyed the same rights as Lucretia and hers. Under colonial law, a woman who married a man who already had a Christian wife had few, if any, legal rights to his property. For the Yoruba, however, children's legitimate rights to property lay in their recognition by their father, whatever the status of their mother. Polygynists shared their resources roughly equally among the children of all wives. As will be seen in chapter 7, Daniel Thomas held to this tradition. Daniel and Rebecca had five children who lived to adulthood and two who died in infancy. Rebecca remained a full-time resident of Igbogun while Lucretia lived full-time in the house in Abeokuta. That each wife had her own home would have been consistent with traditional Yoruba practice. Children of both marriages reported that the relationships among the two wives and the two sets of children were not only cordial but close. Lucretia often brought Funmilayo and Oluremi to visit on the farm at Ifo and one of the younger sons of the second marriage, Ebenezer Taiwo Thomas, went to Abeokuta to study and stayed with a then grown and married Funmilayo. He fondly remembered that the children referred to his mother as "Mama Igbogun" (after the village farmlands outside Ifo where she resided) and to Funmilayo's mother as "Mama Kemta" (after the township in Abeokuta that was the site of the Thomas family home).[15] In addition, both sets of children were active members of the Jibolu-Taiwo-Coker clan, an extended family organization founded in 1930 (chap. 3). The children referred to one another as brothers and sisters. Despite the second marriage, Daniel and Lucretia continued to practice Christianity and to raise their daughters as Christians. Daniel's children with Rebecca were also raised as Christians. Of course, part of the lure of Christianity was that nearly all available Western education occurred in mission-centered schools.

Rebecca Thomas continued to work on the farm, while Lucretia Thomas was a dressmaker. Lucretia also helped Daniel in his trading activities. They were both trading agents for the British merchants John Holt, John Horsfield, and the United Africa Company. Lucretia primarily managed their trade in palm oil, palm kernels, and cocoa. Though elite Christian women were discouraged from engaging in trade, it was consummate Yoruba practice for women to be so engaged. Daniel managed the trade in rice, cloth, nails, and gunpowder. They had a trading stall in Kemta township in Abeokuta.[16]

Despite their grounding in both Western education and Christianity, the Thomas family was still very much rooted in their own cultural heritage. Though they both wore Western clothing, were churchgoing Anglicans, and spoke fluent English, they also spoke and taught their children their own Yoruba language, ate many traditional foods, and were in a polygynous marriage. They were of a generation on the cutting edge of the interplay and overlap of African and European cultures. From all indications, they were as proud of their Africanness as of the privileged status that Western education accorded them in a colonial setting.

Funmilayo was born to Lucretia at 2:55 A.M. on October 25, 1900. FRK reported being told that the day before FRK's birth her mother helped carry iron sheets to carpenters who were constructing a new roof on their home. Her mother reportedly had a short labor that lore attributes to the traditional practice of keeping busy in a healthy pregnancy right up to the onset of labor pains.

Funmilayo seems to have had a pleasant and secure childhood. She was born and reared in the same town, Abeokuta. Her parents were not wealthy but were comfortable and respected in both the African and European communities. Whatever disapproval may have existed among the European Anglican community over her father's polygynous marriage never seems to have surfaced in any way that hurt the family's influence or opportunities in business and education. According to her sister, Oluremi, and her half-brother, Taiwo, the young Funmilayo and her sister spent holidays on the farm at Ifo—at young ages they enjoyed riding the train to a station near the family lands and then trekking by foot several miles to the farm. The Ifo land would, in fact, always remain close to Funmilayo's heart; even after marriage and the birth of her own children, she often went there and continued to dabble in marketing farm produce.

Family members describe a young Funmilayo as often exhibiting behavior that in the words of one informant "was usually associated with boys," such as "assertiveness, daring, and cunning." As a child, it was often claimed that she "took after her mother's uncle" in personality.[17] Funmilayo's favorite food was "bush meat," which she often begged her mother to cook for her and which was usually provided at least once a week.[18] Yet Funmilayo did not escape or shirk, at least as a young girl, the domestic chores usually assigned to women. Oluremi hated the chore of ironing and fondly remembers that Funmilayo would often offer to do it for her. Oluremi recalls their mother as being loving but very strict, with a tremendous sense of duty and service. If the girls slept too late in the morning, their mother would douse them with cold water to wake them up.[19]

Funmilayo was regarded as a very good student and, luckily for her, both of her parents believed in the power of education; they felt girls were as entitled to its benefits as boys. This was an uncommon attitude in both Nigeria and Britain at the time, though it would have been less uncommon in the socioeconomic class from which Funmilayo and Oluremi hailed. Nonetheless, her father had to defend to relatives his decision to invest in the education of a daughter.

The social community in which the girls were raised rated education so highly that it was prepared to sacrifice and pay for schools. Abeokuta was in fact one of the first areas in Nigeria (other than Lagos) to levy itself to build schools which it then invited the Anglican Church to staff. One historian remarked, "These schools could not have been opened or maintained but for the financial help of the community channeled through the church."[20] Though the Anglican church staffed the schools, pupils of all religious denominations, including Islam, attended.

Both girls were sent to the infant mission school at Kemta and then to primary school at St. John's, Igbein. After her primary education, Funmilayo's parents discussed the possibility of sending her to Lagos or to the Annie Walsh Girls' Grammar School in Sierra Leone to continue her education, as the local secondary school, the Abeokuta Grammar School (AGS) was all-male.[21] The AGS had been founded in December 1908 with forty-four boys as the first class of students. The school did not receive any financial assistance from the government until after

1918, when an inspection concluded it could be put on the "Assisted List" of schools that qualified for government aid. In the initial class of boys at the AGS, the name of Israel Oludotun Ransome-Kuti (later FRK's husband) appeared first on the roll, hence his nickname, Daodu, or "first-born son" (of the AGS).

During his years at the AGS, Daodu first noticed Funmilayo. She later reported that one day in 1912 she was on her way home from shopping in the market and was approached by a young man whom she knew. Daodu was at that time instructing choirs at the AGS. The young man said to Funmilayo, "Tutor [Daodu] asked me to salute you. Perhaps you know him? He has accepted coming to teach the school songs for the forthcoming Christmas entertainment, which will give you an opportunity of getting to know him." Funmilayo remembered getting to be great friends with her husband and having at first what she described as a "warm brother-sister relationship." They spent many hours talking and coming to know one another well. Eventually, they had a heavily chaperoned courtship and fell deeply in love.[22]

In 1914, the year Funmilayo completed her primary education, there were several girls whose families were interested in their further education. Funmilayo's father discussed this development with his friend, the Reverend (later Bishop) S. L. Phillips, who then discussed it with the principal of the AGS, Rev. M. S. Cole, who supported the idea of admitting girls. In 1914, the first class of girls, six in all, was admitted to the Abeokuta Grammar School.[23] Coincidentally, as with her future husband, Funmilayo Thomas's name appeared first on the list of girls, earning her the nickname Bèèrè, or "first-born daughter" (of the AGS).

By the third year of coeducation, the number of female students had risen to forty and a new classroom was constructed for the girls in Igbein; in 1917, the girls' school was relocated to Ake (both districts in Abeokuta). In that same year, because she was such a good student and had taken her junior preceptor's examination, Funmilayo was chosen to teach the younger girls. From 1917–19 she taught, receiving her own instruction after school from Cole. Funmilayo was not fond of Cole, whom she considered too strict a disciplinarian, but she enjoyed teaching and seemed resigned to the arrangement. In a sketchy sixteen-page memoir begun in the 1970s, she remarked succinctly: "Principal arranged with my father that I would be teaching the girls and he would teach me after school to continue my studies."[24]

Oluremi later attended the AGS as well but left in 1919 to become a trader in her own shop in Kemta, Abeokuta. In July 1928 she married George A. A. Adebayo, a government official in the Egba Native Authority. Oluremi bore three sets of twins and one single child but only four of the children survived to adulthood.[25]

According to Oluremi, Funmilayo showed great intellectual promise; her parents therefore determined to send her to England to further her education. They were not really able to afford such an expense now that, counting Rebecca's children, there were six children (and another would be born in 1922). Nonetheless, in 1919, with the help of family and friends, Funmilayo went to England to continue her education. In a letter to her future husband, she quoted something that her father had said to her at the time:

> My daughter, I want you to be a competent lady, a helper to any man you may be married to, and to know everything about school, therefore, I am sending you to England for three years. You will go to school for two years and you will be a boarder. . . . You will stay a third year [to learn] dressmaking, you will be spending your holidays in London with Miss Parkes, the Principal of the school where you are going . . . [and] for one year after your arrival [home to Nigeria] you will teach in the Abeokuta Girls' School, not for Reverend Cole's sake, but for your country's sake.[26]

Funmilayo did not wish to leave Dotun—a name by which her future husband was known to those close to him (a shortened version of his middle name Oludotun). Yet her father was insistent that she continue her education, remarking that if Dotun could wait for her they would surely have a solid relationship. In the same letter, addressed to the "only suitor of my future life," Funmilayo told Dotun, "My heart has been so much filled of you that I could scarcely part with your portrait for a good two days. . . . I cannot and I must not change Papa's plans; I must do whatever he tells me, so that I may have his blessings. My Darling, I cannot force you to wait for me, for you are now old enough to have a partner; but how sad it will be at this age of our match to break. . . . *Never shall I forget you;* the man to whom I first gave my heart."

In 1919, Funmilayo left to attend the Wincham Hall School for Girls, Lostock Graham, Cheshire, England. As with many girls' schools of the time, it had as much a "finishing school" as an academic curriculum. Among other subjects, she studied domestic science, dressmaking, education, elocution, French, millinery arts, and music. She boarded with a British family named Horsfield, a contact made through her father's cousin, Moses Coker, who was a commercial agent for several British merchant firms. She later reported being well treated by the Horsfield family but that she did have some negative experiences connected to her race and national origin. While in England she chose to drop the use of Frances (her first given name) and use only Funmilayo.[27] Though it is not clear if there is any connection, interestingly, given their parents' backgrounds, not one of Rev. I. O. and Funmilayo Ransome-Kuti's children have biblical or European names, only Yoruba names. Yet, though their children's names may have been a culturally affirming statement by the Ransome-Kutis, neither of them professed political philosophies that were racially or ethnically exclusive. Nonetheless, as will be seen in later chapters, FRK remained sensitive to issues of race and national origin.

Except for a few anecdotes, little information remains of her stay in England. Her sister Oluremi reported that Funmilayo sent hats, shoes, and underwear for Oluremi to trade in Abeokuta. Also during this first period in England, Funmilayo picked up the skill of bike riding.

In September 1922, Funmilayo returned to Abeokuta to teach; in 1923, she was named head teacher of the girls' branch of the AGS. She taught algebra, drawing, English, geometry, and Latin. The courtship between her and the Reverend I. O. Ransome-Kuti resumed immediately upon her return. They had corresponded while she was in England, and he had stayed in close contact with her family. In addition to their deeply felt love for one another, she and the reverend shared education, religion, and social status in common.

▲▲▲

The Reverend I. O. Ransome-Kuti's great-grandfather was a man from Igbein (one of the Egba forest townships) named Jamo, who married a woman named Orukoloku. Together they had a son, born sometime in the late 1820s, named Kuti. Shortly after the settlement's founding, the family moved to Abeokuta, where Kuti was raised. Kuti is described as "a cloth weaver, a musician, and a warrior."[28] Christian missionaries were present in Abeokuta by the time of Kuti's adulthood, but he rejected conversion and, in fact, all things European. Kuti married a woman from Abeokuta, Ekidan Efupeyin. She belonged to the royal line of Igbein and Imo townships. After her conversion to Christianity in about 1848, she took the name Anne. Her husband found her conversion totally unacceptable and they often fought over her practice of Christianity. Kuti and Ekidan Efupeyin (or Anne) had a son, born in 1855, whom Anne called Josiah Jesse (his Christian name) but who was always called Likoye (his Yoruba name) by his father. The son was a focus of religious arguments between his parents. In 1863 Kuti died, leaving a young Likoye to the care of his mother, who was now unhampered in her efforts to raise him as a pious Christian. Mother and son joined the Church Missionary Society (CMS) in Abeokuta and later Josiah attended the CMS Training Institute in Lagos where he was called to the ministry. By 1877 he was a music teacher at the CMS School, Ake, Abeokuta. In July of that year his mother died and he left Abeokuta to teach at the CMS Girls' School in Lagos.

Josiah was a talented musician especially known for setting Christian hymns to indigenous music, which he often sang in marketplaces. He was extremely concerned with melding Christianity to his Yoruba cultural heritage. At some point around this time, Josiah Jesse added the name Ransome to his own name of Kuti and came to be known as the Reverend (later Canon) J. J. Ransome-Kuti. It is believed that he took the name Ransome from a British missionary who had some profound influence on him, a common and even fashionable practice among nineteenth-century converts. One biographer attributed the founding of at least sixteen churches in and around Abeokuta to Rev. J. J. Ransome-Kuti.[29] In 1895 he was ordained a deacon in the Anglican Church.

While teaching at the CMS Girls' School in Lagos where he taught both traditional Yoruba and European musics, Josiah met Bertha Amy Erinade Olubi, a student whose family was originally from Abeokuta but who now resided in Ibadan. After several proposals that her family initially rejected, Bertha and Rev. J. J. Ransome-Kuti were married on May 22, 1882. In 1887 they relocated to Gbagura, one of the four sections of Abeokuta, where Rev. J. J. Ransome-Kuti pastored a church. They had six children together, two daughters and four sons.[30]

Israel Oludotun Ransome-Kuti, their third child and second son, was born at Ija-Ofa parsonage in Gbagura on April 30, 1891. Oludotun attended the Gbagura Primary School and St. John's Primary School, Sunren Village, Ifo. In 1904, a visitor and friend of Oludotun's father, the Reverend (later Archdeacon) S. A. Delumo took a liking to Oludotun (as he was called) and asked Rev. J. J. Ransome-Kuti's permission to take the child back to Lagos with him and enroll him in the CMS Grammar School there. Permission was granted. When the senior tutor of the CMS Grammar School, the Reverend M. S. Cole, was invited to establish a grammar school in Abeokuta, Oludotun accompanied him and thus became the first pupil of the AGS. There he quickly completed his secondary education begun in Lagos.

From 1909–12, Oludotun was a junior assistant teacher at the AGS which he then left to enroll at Fourah Bay College in Sierra Leone. From that college, he received his bachelor of arts degree in 1914. In 1915 he received his licentiate in theology from the University of Durham (England) through a program with Fourah Bay College, and in 1916 earned his first-class teacher's certificate (in 1940 he earned his master's degree from Durham through Fourah Bay). In 1916 he became an assistant master at the CMS Grammar School in Lagos, and in 1919 at just twenty-seven, he was appointed principal of the Ijebu-Ode (a town quite near Abeokuta) Grammar School.

Funmilayo came to love Oludotun deeply. Two years after her return from England, he proposed marriage and this time her father joyfully agreed, saying that after such a patient wait: "Now I know you really want my daughter."[31] In December 1924, Funmilayo resigned her position at the AGS to marry and relocate with her husband.

Funmilayo and Oludotun were married at St. Peter's Church, Ake, Abeokuta, on January 20, 1925. Their relationship, begun blithely in 1912 with a salutation through a mutual friend and lasting through thirteen years and many separations, was now consummated. In 1960 Funmilayo Ransome-Kuti recounted this time, "The first contact, which developed into a big relationship later, was in 1912. . . . We didn't get married until thirteen years later. How both of us kept our heads during that interval of thirteen years was due in part to his unending desire for higher education and also to the influence my parents exerted on me. . . . Perhaps the younger generation would find this long waiting unendurable. We endured it."[32]

Notes

1. The information on Taiwo and her children has been provided by several sources: FRK, interview, Lagos, Mar. 14 and 15, 1975, and Apr. 6 and 13, 1976; Chief Oluwole Coker (FRK's cousin), interview, Lagos, Aug. 2, 1981; Ebenezer Taiwo Thomas (FRK's half-brother), interview, Lagos, June 16, 1989; Oluremi Adebayo (FRK's sister), interview, Ibadan, June 7 and 10, 1989. Unless otherwise noted, all interviews were conducted by the authors. Information also came from FRK, handwritten memoir, begun in the 1970s and now in FRK Papers. The family Bible, made available by Sonia Ransome-Kuti (wife of FRK's son)

in June 1989, was also very helpful. In addition, in June 1989 the authors also visited Sarah Taiwo's cenotaph, located in the Olufashabe compound on Aderunpoko Lane in Itesi, Abeokuta; it is inscribed with her date of death and the names of her children.

2. For further information on this period of Yoruba history, see Ajayi and Smith, *Yoruba Warfare;* Afigbo, Ayandele, Gavin, Omer-Cooper, and Palmer, *Making of Modern Africa.*

3. Afigbo et al., *Making of Modern Africa,* 25.

4. Ibid., 27.

5. Inscribed on the cenotaph is the following: Sarah Taiwo, 4/18/1874, Iya (mother of), Ebenezer Ṣobowale Thomas, Ṣowemimo, Olufashabe, Arungbamolu, [and] Efunjokogun.

6. These are "Ose Ose Rere" [Respected (good) Sunday] and "Lehin Aiye Buburiyi" [After this very wicked world]. On papers in family bible in possession of Sonia Ransome-Kuti. Seen in Lagos, June 8, 1989.

7. Ebenezer Taiwo Thomas, interview, Lagos, June 16, 1989, and Chief Oluwole Coker, interview, Lagos, June 15 and 16, 1989.

8. The information on FRK's mother is from FRK, interview, Abeokuta, Mar. 14 and 15, 1975, and Apr. 6 and 13, 1976; Oluremi Adebayo, interview, Ibadan, June 7 and 10, 1989. In 1846, shortly after the founding of Abeokuta, the CMS established a mission there.

9. Information on Ifo is from Iṣola, "History of Ifo."

10. Oluremi Adebayo, interview, Ibadan, June 7, 1989.

11. Oluremi reported that her father's great desire to have a son inspired his second marriage (interview, Ibadan, June 7 and 10, 1989). This was confirmed by Ebenezer Taiwo Thomas (known as Uncle Taiwo), himself a son from that second marriage (interview, Lagos, June 16, 1989).

12. For further discussion of this debate, see Mann, *Marrying Well,* 71–74.

13. Ibid., 44.

14. Ibid., 73.

15. Ebenezer Taiwo Thomas, interview, Lagos, June 15, 1989.

16. Oluremi Adebayo, interview, Ibadan, June 7 and 10, 1989, and Ebenezer Taiwo Thomas, interview, Lagos, June 7, 10, and 16, 1989.

17. Ibid.

18. Bush meat is an indigenous game meat from an animal in the rodent family that grows to the size of a large rabbit or possum. Oluremi Adebayo, interview, Ibadan, June 10, 1989.

19. Ibid.

20. Fajana, *Education in Nigeria,* 176.

21. FRK, interview, Abeokuta, Mar. 14 and 15, 1975, and Apr. 6 and 13, 1976.

22. Ibid., Apr. 13, 1976; radio program honoring Rev. I. O. Ransome-Kuti, Abeokuta, Aug. 1960, produced by Ṣegun Oluṣola and edited by Rev. (later

Canon) Adeniyi, transcript, Rev. I. O. Ransome-Kuti Papers (hereinafter cited as IORK Papers).

23. In addition to FRK were Misses Kuye, Lipede, Olumide, Jibowu, and Adeyinka, the last of whom would be one of FRK's few lifelong close friends. See the brochure on the seventy-fifth anniversary celebration of the AGS, IORK Papers.

24. FRK, handwritten memoir, Funmilayo Ransome-Kuti Papers (hereinafter cited as FRK Papers).

25. Oluremi Adebayo, interview, Ibadan, June 7, 1989.

26. FRK to I. O. Ransome-Kuti, Mar. 25, 1919, FRK Papers.

27. FRK, interview, Abeokuta, Apr. 13, 1976; Oluremi Adebayo, interview, Ibadan, June 7, 1989; FRK, handwritten memoir, FRK Papers. See also *Nigerian Tribune*, Apr. 14, 1978.

28. These early details of the Ransome-Kuti ancestry are from Delano, *Josiah Ransome-Kuti;* and from recollections of Oludotun's brother Azariah Olusegun (Segun), in the transcript of radio program on Ransome-Kuti, IORK Papers. Some information also came from Holy Trinity Church, *History,* and from "The Ransome-Kutis of Abeokuta," *West Africa,* May 12, 1951, 413–14.

29. Adebesin, *Egba History,* 133.

30. The children's names and dates of birth are listed in the family Bible: Josiah Oluyinka (Feb. 27, 1883), Anne Lape Iyabode (Oct. 20, 1885), Israel Olu-dotun (Apr. 30, 1891), Joshua Oluremi (Jan. 6, 1894), Victoria Susannah Tinuade (June 20, 1899), and Azariah Olusegun Orisale (June 29, 1902). Two children were born dead: Olufela Daniel Kuti (1887) and Susannah Olubade (1898). Bertha's mother, Susanna (née Daley), was born in 1821 and was a pupil of the Anglican missionary teacher Anna Hinderer. She died in 1924 at the age of 103. Bertha's father, Olubi, was ordained a deacon in 1891.

31. Radio program on Ransome-Kuti, transcript, IORK Papers.

32. Ibid.

"When Love Whispers":
Early Marriage and Family Life

On the day of their marriage, the Ransome-Kutis moved to Ijebu-Ode, an Ijebu Yoruba town just southeast of Abeokuta and nearer to the Atlantic coast on the land side of the Lagos lagoon. Ijebu-Ode was a Yoruba town much older than Abeokuta: as early as 1507 its first European visitors described it as "a very large city."[1] In the nineteenth century, the Ijebu Yoruba of Ijebu-Ode and the Egba Yoruba of Abeokuta had in fact often been at odds over the slave trade and the position of the Ijebu as brokers in the trade between Lagos and Abeokuta, though they were also allied for a while against the power of the city of Ibadan. In 1892, as seen in chapter 1, the British defeat of the Ijebu was a prelude to a treaty with Abeokuta that eventually brought Abeokuta under British rule.

Rev. I. O. Ransome-Kuti became principal of the Ijebu-Ode Grammar school in 1919 while his future wife was studying in England. He was twenty-seven when he assumed the principalship, the youngest Nigerian to be principal of a secondary school. He arrived in Ijebu-Ode at a time when there were few schools in Nigeria but a great deal of interest in Western education. Still, there was some lingering distrust between Egba and Ijebu Yoruba, and one of his missions, consonant with his increasingly nationalist orientation, was to eliminate rivalry between the two groups of Yoruba and to increase their awareness of being one people in common circumstances. One of his pupils at Ijebu-Ode later commented that the reverend expended a great deal of energy toward this goal and that his candor and broad-minded attitude gained the trust and admiration of the people of Ijebu-Ode.

In 1931, when the Reverend I. O. and Funmilayo Ransome-Kuti left Ijebu-Ode to return to Abeokuta they were escorted from the town by an honor guard of hundreds of parents of the grammar school pupils. When the new principal arrived at Ijebu-Ode, many remarked, "This new Kuti is not as good as the old one," so identified had the reverend become with the office of principal.[2] By the time of his marriage, he had already become involved in civic activity in Ijebu-Ode, organizing its first boy scout troop.[3]

When Funmilayo Ransome-Kuti accompanied her husband to Ijebu-Ode, she was much impressed with his popularity among the towns-people and his dedication to his pupils. Later, she remarked that the first years of their marriage there were "unforgettably happy."[4] Her marriage and relocation required her to resign her teaching position at the Abeokuta Grammar School (AGS) but immediately on her arrival at Ijebu-Ode she set about assisting as unpaid "help" at the school where her husband was principal. She did this until 1928 when she founded a kindergarten class, known simply as "Mrs. Kuti's class," for four- and five-year-old children. The class began with nine pupils and was certainly one of the pioneering preschool classes in Nigeria. The class became well known and widely respected in the town and grew at a constant rate. In 1931, when the Ransome-Kutis returned to Abeokuta, FRK began a kindergarten class there.

In the late 1920s, FRK also organized a "young ladies' club" in Ijebu-Ode. The club started out as a small organization to teach singing, handicrafts, and cooking to the young daughters of the elite. It primarily offered "self-improvement" instruction with a goal of creating fairly traditional, Christian, Western-educated wives. The club began to see itself as having a slightly broader constituency and branched out to do "civic" work with nonelite women, though its mission was little changed save for the addition of literacy classes. Still, this early involvement with education and civic organization laid the seeds for what would become, from the 1940s on, FRK's radicalized perspective on gender relations in the indigenous as well as colonial context, appreciation for class analysis as a tool for demystifying the impact of colonialism, and deep concern with exposing the racism inherent in imperialist ideology.

In the early days in Ijebu-Ode, though, she was engaged in the type of activities that many "new elite" (those who were both Christian and had some Western education) women prized. Like many of her near contemporaries in other places, such as Charlotte Obasa and Oyinkan Abayomi in Lagos, she pursued activities suitable to her "station." There are several things, however, that led her on a different, more radical, trajectory.

She was always described as "aggressive," a common appellation for women whose forceful personalities lay outside the bounds of acceptable "female" behavior. Many of those who knew her well described her "cynicism" as an overriding character trait, but this was a later observation, predicated on hindsight. No one considered her sentimental; she was frequently described as stoic. But this too seems to be hindsight, for in her courtship correspondence with her fiancé and her optimism in the early years of her marriage emerges a portrait of a woman of deep sentiment and feeling.

In 1948, FRK was asked by the Nigerian writer Cyprian Ekwensi to write a foreword to his novel *When Love Whispers*. She liked the novel, calling it a "typically African love story" and saying, "This little book of Mr. Ekwensi is just the kind which is most needed at this very stage of our development as progressive units of the human race ready to take our place among the other nations of the world." She wrote this at the same time that she was leading massive demonstrations of women in Abeokuta; the foreword is evidence that there was room for romantic love in her vision of the new world. In an entry in her diary in June 1946, she wrote, "White cat has two kittens," a small but seemingly sentimental observation.[5]

Even her confrontational activist tactics seem inspired by a concern for people. Her stubbornness was well known, though her allies were more often apt to label it tenacity. In an October 1, 1985, article in the newspaper *Vanguard*, entitled "Life and Times of Nigeria's First Woman Nationalist," one aging contemporary reflected, "She never gave up. She didn't allow those who worked with her to give up. And the fight was to the end."[6] Among those FRK most admired were Madam Tinubu (chap. 1), Kwame Nkrumah, Mohandas Gandhi, and A. B. I. Olorun-Nimbe (the first mayor of Lagos)—activists and "take charge" personalities all, each a leader of the "people."[7] She abhorred the flaunting of material wealth and, in that regard, she and her husband were well suited to one another.

Yet, there was another side to FRK. There is evidence that her concern with her appearance included the use of imported hair dyes and other toiletries, such as perfume and cosmetics—and even stockings—many of which were sent to her (often at her request) by the Ransome-Kuti family friend Ladipo Ṣolanke, who lived in London.[8] Though at the height of the women's demonstrations in the 1940s (chap. 4) she would all but abandon Western clothing for the wrapped cloths worn by market women, in previous years there are pictures of her adorned in Victorian clothing—in one she even sports a pith helmet.

During the first half of her life, FRK was squarely of those generations of early Yoruba women nationalists who sometimes straddled the cultural discourse between Africa and Europe, women like Charlotte Obasa, Oyinkan Abayomi, Tinuola Dedeke, Elsie Femi-Pearse, and others. Though Christian, Western-educated, and often married to activist men, they sought to define an identity for themselves that was neither traditionally African nor traditionally European. They insisted on the use of Yoruba names and Yoruba language and took up the causes of their poorer, often uneducated sisters. They also insisted on the right to be employed in the civil service, the right to an academic education, and the right to participate equally with men in the nationalist political parties. FRK, however, was to be among those very few women of her generation who, while perhaps never totally resolving all of her contradictions, began to propose systemic solutions that went beyond the mere reform of colonial institutions or even independence, to propose a new social order that more evenly distributed wealth and power.

Her vision was that of both a nationalist and a democratic socialist. Her nationalism was informed by a number of circumstances and experiences. She spent nearly two-thirds of her life as a colonial subject in a colonized country. Her experience of colonialism was exacerbated by the fact that the colonizers were European and the colonized were African: white supremacist ideology was a fundamental tenet of the colonial enterprise in Africa. Nationalism (whether it was Pan-African or country-centered) was a fundamental tenet of the anticolonial struggle, even if it was sometimes obscured or fractured by ethnic allegiances— one false premise to which FRK never fell prey. Though she also successfully defended against a purely racial analysis of colonialism, she saw race as a critical factor, for instance, when she dropped her one European name while in England.

Her views are also elucidated by an example described by her grand-nephew Wole Soyinka in his book *Ake: The Years of Childhood*. According to Soyinka, who often spent time in the Ransome-Kuti home in Abeokuta and for a short time was a student at the AGS, FRK was appalled by the dropping of the atomic bomb on the heavily populated Japanese cities of Hiroshima and Nagasaki in 1945. In a heated conversation with a British district officer of Abeokuta after the bombing, she insisted that it was a racist act. She raised her voice to point out that they would never have dropped it on Germany, "because Germany is a white race, the Germans are your kinsmen. While the Japanese are just a dirty yellow people. I know you, the white mentality: Japanese, Chinese, Africans, we are all subhuman. You would drop an atom bomb on Abeokuta or any of your colonies if it suited you!"[9] FRK thought the bomb should have been dropped—if at all—where there were no people, as a warning.

In the early 1970s when she began using Anikulapo-Kuti as a last name (dropping Ransome), many identified her Pan-Africanist son Fela (see esp. chap. 7) as the cause. Though he may indeed have suggested it, she always made up her own mind, and much in her past suggests that such nationalist feeling was not new to her. Yet, she counted a number of Europeans among her closest comrades. She recognized racism as a factor, yet she never identified it as other than one enemy among many, including gender and class oppression, both of which she saw as "raceless," and it was that recognition that informed her politics as a democratic socialist.

Nationalism sometimes, albeit temporarily, obscured her vision. In a 1961 article in the *Journal of Human Relations,* written about a year after Nigerian independence, FRK, in the midst of demanding women's equality, simultaneously counseled women to be more tolerant and even to forgo temporarily their own personal interests for those of their husbands.[10] These were the heady days of early independence when nationalist voices everywhere proscribed women as "helpmates" to their husbands in constructing the nation. FRK was not much of a champion of such proscription, contradicting herself even in the very same article.

She had a reputation for both industriousness and parsimoniousness. The number of small-scale trading ventures and business schemes in which she became personally involved (in addition to her teaching and the collective business of the Abeokuta Women's Union [chap. 4]) were legion. She did everything from selling eggs to marketing farm produce from the Thomas family farmlands at Ifo to acting as a retail agent for the Olubadan of Ibadan when he was manufacturing mineral waters in the 1930s. Yet she kept tight purse strings. When she was treasurer of the Jibolu-Taiwo-Coker family union, it was said, "Anything that gets in her purse doesn't get out."[11] She often kept records of the smallest financial losses, noting in her diary in June 1946, for instance, that an egg was broken by a student and that half a bag of grain was missing. It seems, however, that much of her careful financial accounting was motivated by need rather than greed. Both she and the Reverend Ransome-Kuti eschewed showy materialism, though they were concerned about some degree of financial security. They existed on the economic margins, never amassing any real wealth and constantly struggling to educate their children. Their major material possessions were their home, small plots of land (inherited as well as purchased), and an old car. The school building Funmilayo Ransome-Kuti owned was bought after her husband's death. Her careful financial accounting was also likely motivated by a background that disparaged waste of any kind.

The Ransome-Kuti marriage looms large as a factor in FRK's increasing political awareness. It lasted for thirty years, until the death of the reverend in 1955 (chap. 7). Her husband was nine years older than she was, and both his involvement in nationalist politics and his international connections proved very useful for her. By all accounts, theirs was an atypical marriage for its time in that the partners operated from a sense of equality and were highly supportive of each other's public activities. In a 1951 article in *West Africa* magazine, a reporter described Funmilayo Ransome-Kuti as having an "air of authority and the look of one whose decision was final." The reporter further observed, "I felt confronted by a woman who has to be assessed on her own merits and not as a shadowy reflection of her husband. . . . Emancipation of women has indeed come to the Ransome-Kuti household."[12]

Thus, the Ransome-Kutis did not have the typical male-dominated marriage of their time. One former student of the AGS, among whose duties was cleaning the Ransome-Kuti bedroom, remembered the reverend as "the most democratic man I have ever known."[13] The reverend enjoyed such a reputation with many of his students, who reported that when he was principal students always felt they got a fair hearing and were never afraid to report to him their mistreatment at the hands of older students or even teachers.

Both Ransome-Kutis objected on principle to the Yoruba custom of kneeling or prostrating to an elder or titled person. They refused to do so themselves and taught their children not to do so, nor would they allow anyone to curtsy or kneel to them. This was equally true, however, of a number of Christian, Western-educated, elite families. It was another example of attempting to reject those African customs perceived as conflicting with an egalitarian worldview while preserving those that were not.

Many people described the even temper, fairness, and joviality of the Reverend Ransome-Kuti and attested to the egalitarian relationship that characterized the marriage. In fact, some felt that FRK, who was much more likely to show anger or intransigence in public than was her husband, wielded the most power in the relationship. Yet those who knew them well disagree, insisting that the difference in their public personas — she the firebrand, he the rock — was the foundation of a complementary union built on honest communication, mutual support, and deep respect. In several interviews in the 1970s, FRK herself spoke gently and with conviction of the role her husband's support and love played in her activism. In an interview given long after her husband's death she remarked: "He was a fine man, hardworking, understanding, and cooperative. He was a woman's man. He hated women being exploited. Many times he was sent for and told 'Come and see what your wife is doing, O!' He merely smiled and told them to leave me alone as I had my own mind. He never went against anything I did."[14] As will be seen in chapter 7, after his untimely death, she strove to preserve his memory. Indeed, there is some indication that she deeply regretted having traveled so much during his last few years of life, when he was quite ill. In one posthumous tribute to the reverend, a writer observed: "The incomparable partnership, cooperation and understanding between Mrs. Kuti and her husband, a trend which runs through their lives, accounts in particular for the success of her contribution to, and achievements in that past of Nigeria [sic] public life with which they were involved."[15] While no one remembers seeing the Ransome-Kutis quarrel publicly, there is evidence that they sometimes disagreed. One former student remembered times when they ate separately and there seemed to be a coolness between them and concluded it only happened when there was a disagreement.[16]

The Reverend Ransome-Kuti was very concerned about women's treatment and their opportunities. He was very much in favor of co-education. Though a minister, he never had his own parish, and there is conflicting evidence about whether or not he desired one. As a member of the Abeokuta District Church Council and the Lagos Diocese Synod, he supported women's admission to the synod. Yet, as will be seen below, he invested far more of his energy in educational rather than religious work.

Described as a patriot by many contemporaries, one friend also called him "a fearless man of great ability and discipline."[17] He had a great zest for life, an animated conversational style, and a tremendous sense of humor.[18] Both he and FRK were very organized. One student reported that when he cleaned the couple's bedroom, if everything was not replaced exactly as he found it, Funmilayo Ransome-Kuti would find him on the school premises and watch as he rearranged things to their original order. Rev. Ransome-Kuti was supposedly fanatical about punctuality, the neatness of his study, and the cleanliness and attractiveness of the school grounds.[19] The students in both Ransome-Kuti-run schools (Ijebu-Ode and Abeokuta) were required to participate in cleaning, cooking, and landscaping, as were the Ransome-Kuti children. Both the reverend and Funmilayo also participated in the manual labor of the schools. When the reverend first became principal of the AGS, for instance, the building was only partially completed and without landscaping. He personally worked with the pupils to complete and landscape the school buildings.

Both Ransome-Kutis were considered strict but fair disciplinarians. Several former students commented that they were disciplined for erratic academic performance but never for consistently poor performance per se, in which case they would be offered academic help.[20] Infractions of school rules could result in a variety of punishments, including added housework duties or corporal punishment administered by caning the buttocks, a common punishment in British schools of the period. The reverend, in fact, had a reputation for "taming" incorrigible youth. He also, however, often took students who were not succeeding academically elsewhere and brought them to AGS. He made a number of trips to Britain in the 1930s and 1940s to observe educational institutions and curricular changes, several at the couple's own expense, so interested was he in ensuring that his students were being competitively educated.

FRK sometimes intervened on behalf of female students in an attempt to convince their families to educate them beyond the secondary level. One such student recalled Funmilayo's repeated efforts to convince the girl's father to send her for further education; eventually, the girl attended Queen's College (a secondary school) in Lagos.[21] This former student had very warm feelings toward Funmilayo Ransome-Kuti even though later her former teacher was unsuccessful in convincing her father to send her for a university education, a privilege that, given his limited resources, he reserved for his sons.

Like FRK, the Reverend Ransome-Kuti was a Pan-Africanist and nationalist. Indeed, he wrote an anthem for Abeokuta.[22] He and Funmilayo Ransome-Kuti coauthored a song exhorting the African people to prepare themselves for the work that lay ahead.[23] The reverend was very interested in researching traditional African music, much like his father. When corresponding with his close friend and fellow activist, Ladipo Ṣolanke, the reverend often signed his letters, "Long live mother Africa!"[24] According to his eldest son, he was once offered a high honor by the British but refused because it was a foreign honor.[25]

While in Ijebu-Ode the Ransome-Kutis became involved in several organizations beyond those they founded locally. One in which the reverend was particularly active was the Association of Principals of Independent Schools. This group included principals from all nongovernment schools, some of which were started by particular communities and others by missions, from the cities of Abeokuta, Ijebu-Ode, Ondo, and Ibadan. The group used the acronym AIONIAN. The principals were called the Aionian chiefs (none was actually a chief) and as a special distinction Rev. Ransome-Kuti was called Chief Aionian.[26]

Also while in Ijebu-Ode in the 1920s, the Ransome-Kutis joined the West African Students Union (WASU) of which they were among the founding members in Nigeria. WASU had been formed in London in 1925 by the close friend of the Ransome-Kutis, Ladipo Ṣolanke. The organization was nationalist and anticolonialist in orientation and sought support from West Africans in Africa as well as in London (chap. 5). The Ransome-Kutis were very active in raising funds for WASU both in Ijebu-Ode and later in Abeokuta.

The Ransome-Kutis were also very involved in other organizations, particularly those concerned with education. In 1926, a year after their marriage, the reverend inspired the formation of the Association of Headmasters of Ijebu Schools (AHIS), one of the earliest associations of teachers in Nigeria. Significantly, the association included both primary and secondary school headmasters, who were usually divided on the basis of the greater prestige and salaries for the latter. One member later said of the Reverend Ransome-Kuti: "He did not think himself too eminent to associate with headmasters of primary schools."[27]

The first AHIS meeting was held at the Ijebu-Ode Grammar School where the reverend was principal; he became the association's first president. The AHIS aimed to unify the teachers to effect their greater empowerment in setting the conditions of their work and to carve out a greater decision-making role for them in setting educational standards. The Reverend Ransome-Kuti later remarked, "It was in the year 1926 that a few lovers of their country in the teaching profession— headmasters all—came together."[28] Clearly, patriotism was part of the inspiration for the AHIS. One historian pointedly remarked that the reverend's vision was a nationalist one.[29] The AHIS not only sought to participate directly in educational decisions but also offered social and political recommendations. Soon after its founding, for instance, it proposed that government hospitals treat schoolchildren free of charge.[30] In 1929, the association also cooperated with WASU's organizing efforts in Ijebu-Ode.

In November 1930, AHIS affiliated with the Lagos Union of Teachers, an affiliation that spawned the formation of the Nigerian Union of Teachers (NUT) in July 1931. The reverend played a prominent role in the founding conference of the union. A colleague who attended the inaugural conference, E. E. Esua, reported that the reverend said, "Today, we come from Lagos and four neighboring towns, but the union we are inaugurating now will soon grow into a mighty organization with branches in all the important towns of Nigeria."[31] The Reverend Ransome-Kuti served as president of the NUT from its founding in 1931 until his retirement in 1955. The position of president was without any financial remuneration until 1942, when a small salary was instituted.[32]

Funmilayo Ransome-Kuti was also among the charter members of the NUT and attended its inaugural meeting. Later, she served as NUT's representative on the Western Provinces Regional Board of Education and in 1949 she was among three NUT representatives on the Central Board of Education of Nigeria, inaugurated in that year. For the latter, she was a member of a board subcommittee charged with developing a plan for technical education for girls. An active member of the board, she supposedly always checked the minutes carefully to be sure her views had been noted accurately. She was particularly concerned that women receive the same educational monetary allowances as men, pointedly remarking that women, too, had dependents. Moreover, she was quick to respond when she felt the abilities of Nigerian teachers were being disparaged.[33] In describing the twenty-first annual conference of the union in 1952, one historian wrote, "Mrs. Funmilayo Ransome-Kuti, a long-time crusader for the rights of Nigerian women, urged the NUT to see to it that more women attended its annual conferences in the future, with the hope that the new legislators would do something to improve Nigerian womanhood."[34]

Though nationalist in orientation, the NUT often strove for cordial relations with the colonial government even while it sought to change British policy. In addition, the union maintained several international links. In 1939, it affiliated with the National Union of Teachers in England, which helped provide access to governmental bodies when Nigerian union's members, particularly Rev. Ransome-Kuti, traveled there seeking to raise Nigerian educational issues with British government officials. Also of great help in providing contacts in England was WASU. In fact, the NUT and WASU often cooperated in their projects. In August 1941, WASU held a conference in London; on a long list of reforms the union advocated that the British undertake in Nigeria appeared several educationally centered proposals of the NUT.[35] In 1942 in an address to the NUT annual conference, Rev. Ransome-Kuti specifically thanked WASU, calling it a body of patriotic Africans, for its efforts in helping make his 1939 tour of British educational systems a success.[36] Throughout the 1930s, the NUT corresponded also with the Gold Coast Assisted Schools Teachers' Union in an effort to compare British educational policies in various African colonies, particularly attempting to use evidence of negative disparities to argue for greater consistency. The NUT's policy was to keep membership open to all teachers regardless of their religion, academic qualifications, race, or ethnicity.

By 1948, the NUT claimed twenty thousand members in 155 branches throughout Nigeria. Among its particular concerns in the late 1930s and throughout the 1940s was the increasingly regional and ethnically based nature of the nationalist political organizations. Sometime in July 1939, Rev. Ransome-Kuti founded an organization known as the Nigerian Union of Students (NUS), an organization composed mostly of his students from the AGS, whose major purpose was to counteract separatism based on regional and ethnic origin among the students.[37] At the seventeenth annual conference of the NUT in January 1948, the reverend expressed his fears that ethnic politics might negatively affect the NUT's progress in organizing teachers on a national basis.[38]

In the midst of their political activities, family life continued apace for the Ransome-Kutis. In March 1926, approximately fourteen months after their marriage, Funmilayo Ransome-Kuti gave birth to their first child, a daughter, Dolupo. Dolu, as she was affectionately called, was born in the home of her mother's paternal relatives, the Cokers, on Princess Street in Lagos. Apparently, FRK had traveled to Lagos to have her first baby in the absence of any family in Ijebu-Ode.

A second child, a son, Olikoye, was born in December 1927 in a hospital in Ijebu-Ode. Several years passed before FRK again became pregnant. In addition to her teaching duties and civic activities, two such young children must have kept her extremely busy.

In 1931, the Anglican District Church Council invited the Reverend Ransome-Kuti to become principal of the Abeokuta Grammar School. Thus, he, FRK, and their two children returned to Abeokuta in 1932. Almost immediately, Funmilayo Ransome-Kuti earmarked two rooms in the new school building into which she transferred "Mrs. Kuti's kindergarten class." Shortly thereafter, she petitioned the Nigerian Department of Education to turn the endeavor into a primary school; her petition was approved. In running her own school, she operated within an ongoing tradition of educated elite women who opened educational institutions in towns like Lagos, Ibadan, and Abeokuta. Particularly frustrated by the lack of facilities for girls' education and the absence of career prospects for married women, these women often founded and ran their own schools.

In Ibadan, Wuraola Esan founded the Ibadan People's Girls' Grammar School in 1944. Esan was also one of the founders of the Private Schools Proprietors' Association, Western Provinces, in 1949, an association in which FRK was active. In 1948 in Ibadan, T. Ogunlesi set up her Molete Girls' Home School. Much later the first school for Muslim girls was founded by Alhaja Humani Alaga in Ibadan in 1964. All of these women used their status as school proprietors as a launchpad for their involvement in civic activities and politics. Opening her school in 1932 placed FRK at the forefront of such efforts.

On March 13, 1934, the Reverend Ransome-Kuti's mother died, which had a profound effect on him. He wrote to his friend Ṣolanke that it "nigh well paralyzed me" and subsequently spent a short while in a small "vacation" bungalow the couple had bought not far from Abeokuta.[39] Just eight months before, the reverend's younger brother, Joshua Oluremi (J. O.), had committed suicide.[40]

Between March 1935 and July 1936, the Ransome-Kutis carried on a running correspondence with Ṣolanke about two cars; they had sent him money to purchase the vehicles in England and to have them delivered to Nigeria. The reverend had been riding a motorized bike and FRK had sometimes ridden a bicycle, a practice she had begun in England.[41] The reverend had a moderately serious accident on his motorbike, and apparently after that the couple decided to buy a car.[42] In fact, FRK became the first woman to drive a car in Abeokuta.[43]

The cars were shipped separately; the second arrived as a replacement of the first, which never ran properly. Given the couple's limited means, they were forced to purchase used cars. Both the Ransome-Kutis, however, were scandalized by the condition of the cars Ṣolanke sent them and felt that he had been careless, not choosing the cars well. Probably he bought the best he could for what they could afford.

FRK apparently read a lot about cars, at one point cautioning Ṣolanke about the second, replacement car: "Before the car is sent please see that the following are good: the brakes, the plugs, the clutch, the gear . . . and that the battery is practically new. I had never had anything to do with cars in my life and you can see that this car has taught me a lot about cars."[44] She was also concerned about the availability of spare parts, even if they had to be shipped from England. At another point, she excoriated Ṣolanke, saying a mechanic in Nigeria had labeled the car "fifth hand" and adding, "Cursed was the day on which we cabled you money for a car!"[45] In separate letters, both Ransome-Kutis demanded their money back for the car. It is not clear whether Ṣolanke refunded the money but the friendship certainly survived the crisis and the couple maintained their close relations with him.

In 1935, FRK had another child, a son, born in Sacred Heart Hospital in Abeokuta, who died two weeks after his birth.[46] In October 1936, she had a miscarriage in her sixth month of pregnancy. The child, a daughter, lived for two days. The Reverend Ransome-Kuti was very concerned for Funmilayo's health after the miscarriage and was much relieved when she seemed completely recovered. He maintained a vigil by her bedside and afterward wrote his friend Ṣolanke about the experience.[47] Two more children, both sons, were born to the Ransome-Kutis in the General Hospital in Abeokuta: Olufela in 1938 and Bekolari in 1940.

The Abeokuta Grammar School served as the family's home until the reverend's death in 1955. One former pupil described the AGS as "a toughening school, a training ground for later survival in life."[48] Expectations for the students were high and discipline, while fair, was strict. In every classroom was displayed a sign that read, "My good name is greater than my books." On average, there were a hundred boarding students and three hundred commuters. Learning academic skills was not all that was required of students. Both commuters and boarders were required to learn vocational skills (e.g., woodworking, technical drawing, and agricultural skills) and boarders were also given chores that included cleaning the school and the Ransome-Kuti living quarters and caring for the school grounds. The Reverend Ransome-Kuti was regarded as a perfectionist by a number of ex-students, a man whom one described as searching the ceiling for cobwebs and checking to see that only the "bad" and not the "good" grass was trimmed (by scythe or sometimes weeded by hand).[49] The school was coeducational, and students of various Christian denominations as well as Muslims and practitioners of traditional African religions attended. Students were from diverse ethnic backgrounds as well, and one former student pointedly recalled that Funmilayo Ransome-Kuti was especially adamant in enforcing a ban on the use of derogatory names or epithets based on ethnic origin.[50] When Rev. Ransome-Kuti traveled, FRK was in charge of the boarding students—and he traveled quite a lot in 1939–45, spending nearly all of 1943–45 abroad.

The boarding and teaching sections of the school were housed in the same building as the family's residence. Though their living quarters were in a separate area, much of the domestic life of the family was integrated into that of the school. As Funmilayo Ransome-Kuti became increasingly involved in political activity in the 1940s, this integration of domestic and institutional life provided support for her political activity. All of the Ransome-Kuti children attended Mrs. Kuti's kindergarten class and then the AGS. In general, the Ransome-Kuti children took their meals with the school boarders, the exception being if the family was entertaining company. Even FRK and the reverend, while they often ate separately from the boarders, usually ate the same food. All of the Ransome-Kuti children, notably the three sons, were taught to cook and bake. The eldest son's culinary skills were well honed, according to his wife.[51] Because all of the students of the school (including the Ransome-Kuti children) were involved in the domestic chores, FRK's absences from home for political activity were much less problematic than might otherwise have been the case. The school and the family were also drawn into the Ransome-Kuti political orbit. Women's meetings were held in the school courtyard, and the inner circle of the Abeokuta Women's Union (AWU) convened in the Ransome-Kuti living quarters, which also served as a headquarters for the women's demonstrations (chap. 4).

In November 1936, Abeokuta celebrated WASU week, during which pansies were sold as a WASU fundraiser. Not only did the sale of the pansies provide money for the student union but wearing them was a sign of support for the organization. The Ransome-Kutis were very active in the sale; FRK even drafted her children to go around the town selling the flowers. The NUT was also a major sponsor of the pansy sale.[52]

All four Ransome-Kuti children recollect their parents as strict disciplinarians who believed in corporal punishment.[53] The two older children, Dolu and Koye, felt their parents were far more strict with them than with the younger Fela and Beko. This may have reflected "seasoning" as parents, less scrutiny of the younger children because of the couple's heavy political involvement by that time, or both.

In the early years of their marriage, the couple ran a pious Christian home where prayers were said first thing in the morning and last thing at night, though as time passed and both were drawn more intensely into the political arena, this seems to have waned. They were very concerned that their children be well educated, showing great disappointment when any one of them faltered in their studies. Truthfulness, fearlessness, and independence were preached in their home as cardinal virtues.

The integration of family and political life may have lightened the burden on Funmilayo Ransome-Kuti, but the children felt it created additional burdens for them. There was little "family space," such as dinner hour or quiet time when the children and their parents were together as a unit. The children therefore found it hard to know where school ended and home began. The two older children especially felt that their parents were harder on them, both because they had to serve as examples for the boarders and because their parents wished to ensure their impartiality toward their own children vis-à-vis the others at the school.

Dolu and Koye, as the oldest daughter and son, felt their mother had little time for herself and even less for them. To them, she seemed to conduct her life with a military discipline, "marching" off to teach by 7 A.M. and not sleeping before 3 A.M. Such a pace must have resulted in a seemingly distant and distracted mother. Though both Dolu and Koye were old enough to admire and respect their mother's choices, they felt keenly the lack of an intimate relationship with her. Dolu, however, fondly recalled family visits to the small bungalow with its many fruit trees that her parents owned just a few miles from Abeokuta. The family sometimes retired there just to "get away." Fela and Beko seem to have fared a little better because they were still at home in the 1950s when, just one year after their father's death, their mother took the new principal of the AGS (J. S. Adeniyi) to task because she disliked the way he treated the two boys.[54] Dolu, Koye, and Beko all agreed that Fela was their mother's favorite (chap. 7), Dolu even going so far as to say her mother would "rather die than see Fela suffer."[55] Fela seems also to have been the most rebellious (see below and chap. 7).

In 1944, Dolu went to England to further her education. Her mother expressed great concern because of World War II, writing to Ṣolanke, "I am really very nervous about her coming [sic] over during this terrible war."[56] In fact, Dolu's father was in England at the time with the Elliot Commission on Higher Education (chap. 6). Dolu first attended the Camden Town School for Girls. Wartime London could not have been a hospitable place for an eighteen-year-old Nigerian girl on her own for the first time. After completing her course at Camden, Dolu attended Southhampton University where she studied history, economics, and art. She lost interest in her studies at the university and instead entered a nurse training program at Halifax Hospital, Rochdale.

Dolu became involved with another Nigerian student in London, Dapo Ṣoetan, the son of an acquaintance of the Ransome-Kutis in Nigeria, Adegunle Ṣoetan. In the midst of her training program, Dolu gave birth to Dapo's daughter at Halifax Hospital on November 26, 1949. The child, a daughter named Frances Foloronsho Opeolu, took her mother's surname of Ransome-Kuti. When Dolu informed her parents of her pregnancy, they expressed extreme disappointment that she had not finished her studies first and that she had not married before having a child. Dolu described her father as "going wild" with anger when he heard. Since his disposition was usually so calm, he must have been terribly distraught. From the Ransome-Kutis' perspective, the worst was yet to come. Not only was Dolu not married to Dapo but, despite his deluge of letters describing his love for her, with the characteristic stubbornness of her mother, Dolu refused to marry him. She felt Dapo was irresponsible and had been unsupportive during her pregnancy. Not only had he continued to see other women, but he had three children by two women in the space of two years. In April 1951, more than a year after her daughter's birth, Dolu confided in a letter to her parents: "I have no intention of getting married to such a man. . . . Someone I love and who really loves me will come along someday."[57] In fact, Dapo was still married when Dolu became pregnant.

Though they were terribly disappointed and concerned, once it was clear that no amount of pressure could convince Dolu to marry, her parents remained supportive. They sent her money and visited her in England. They did not speak with Dapo's father (who lived in Abeokuta) about the grandchild they shared; when he discovered it, he was horrified because neither he nor his son had been contributing to the child's welfare. He was exceedingly worried that the Ransome-Kutis thought Dapo had told him and that he had merely ignored the plight of their daughter.[58]

Rather than send the child back to Nigeria and so far away from her, Dolu eventually placed her daughter in the foster care of a childless Anglican minister and his wife, the Ashmores, when the child was about two years old. Dolu did this so she could finish her education and still have the child near her.[59]

Indeed, FRK paid the Ashmores to care for Frances and visited the child as often as she could. When she was traveling internationally, she tried to route her trips through England in order to visit Frances. Rev. Ransome-Kuti also visited Frances in England, but he died when the child was only 5½ years old. Her uncle Koye visited her as well, once bringing her a doll for Christmas.

FRK also instructed the Ashmores that Frances's father was not to be allowed any access to her; consequently, Frances did not meet her father until she was a teenager. Frances later reported that the Ashmores found FRK intimidating, but apparently they were very kind to the child, who called them "Mom" and "Dad," though she often felt isolated as the only black person in her environment. The Ashmores were working-class people, often staying for short periods in rural parishes. Frances thought the Ashmores disliked FRK, not least because she did not fit their stereotype of Africans as being intellectually inferior to whites. At times Frances even felt that the Ashmores attempted to prejudice her against her strong-willed grandmother, though not on racial grounds. Nonetheless, they obeyed FRK's wishes as far as the child was concerned. From the time Frances was eleven years old, FRK sent regularly for her to visit Nigeria, especially during school vacations and other holidays. According to Frances, FRK "called the shots" with the Ashmores about her care even more so than her mother.[60] After attending Sheffield University where she became a dentist, Frances returned permanently to Nigeria in 1977.

After attending his mother's kindergarten class and the AGS, the eldest Ransome-Kuti son, Olikoye (Koye) received an intermediate degree in chemistry at Yaba Higher College in Lagos. He was offered a scholarship to study in Britain but his father preferred to pay his tuition and prevailed upon him to decline the scholarship. In 1948 Koye left Nigeria (with £800 supplied by his father) to attend the University of Dublin where he studied medicine. From 1960–62 he studied at the Institute of Child Health Hospital in London, and when he returned to Nigeria he taught at the College of Medicine, University of Lagos, and later became professor and head of the pediatrics department. Professor Ransome-Kuti has received several honors and is internationally known as a pediatrician (chap. 7). Perhaps his greatest contribution was his work, as Minister of Health for Nigeria, on shifting attention from elitist teaching hospitals to rural, community-based health clinics.

Koye felt that both the Ransome-Kutis were overly strict as parents and that their expectations for their children were so high as to be almost unachievable. He remembers being very tense about his academic performance as a student at the AGS. While he has expressed great respect for his parents' activist lives, he also bemoaned the extent to which that activism took them away from their children, especially the absence of his mother. Yet he credits his sense of obligation to others as having come from his parents. FRK's mother spent time at the Abeokuta home (until her death in 1956), and Koye remembers his grandmother as often being more available and attentive to the children than their own mother. Though he sometimes felt intimidated by and distant from his father, he holds one particularly poignant memory of him. In 1954 when his father was ill, Koye returned from Ireland by boat. The Reverend Ransome-Kuti, in a weakened condition, took a chair to sit on the wharf at Lagos, waiting hours for the boat to arrive and Koye to disembark.[61]

In June 1955, Koye married Sonia Doherty, whose father was a Lagosian doctor who had attended the AGS and been good friends with A. O. Ransome-Kuti (the reverend's brother). Sonia had attended the Methodist Girls' School in Lagos and met Koye at his Uncle A. O.'s home there. She and Koye had been sweethearts before they had both gone abroad to study, she to England, he to Ireland. Sonia was very fond of FRK, though initially overawed by her. Koye strove to shield his young wife from FRK's "bossiness," counseling Sonia to leave the room when he felt his mother was ordering her around.[62]

The second Ransome-Kuti son, Olufela (Fela) was extremely close to FRK and is perhaps the most overtly political and controversial of all the children (chap. 7). Born in 1938, Fela was still a relatively young child when his mother became heavily involved in women's protest activities in the 1940s. In an interview with his biographer, Carlos Moore, Fela recalled those heady days: "I liked to hear her talk, discuss. Something always made me sit with her, to listen. . . . As I got older she started taking me around with her in the car to her campaign meetings. . . . I admired her. . . . My mother was quite heavy politically."[63]

Though the other children often thought Fela was FRK's favorite and that her increasing political activity estranged them from her, Fela saw things a little differently. He reports that his mother flogged him frequently *until* she got into politics, when he felt that she had less time to flog him and he came to understand her better, getting closer to her rather than becoming more detached. He also, alone among informants (at least prior to the onset of Rev. Ransome-Kuti's serious illness in the early 1950s), felt that his mother's increasing political involvement created problems between her and his father (42–43; see also chap. 7). As a young child, Fela may have interpreted things this way, or he may be reflecting on the early 1950s when his father's increasing illness and his mother's increasing travel did in fact create a dilemma for the couple. All other evidence indicates that until that time there was no significant discord in the marriage and that, especially in political causes, the couple were mutually supportive.

From all indications, Fela was a creative and spirited child. In secondary school he formed a club known as the "Planless Society": "I was sixteen then. . . . The rule of the club was simple: we had no plans. You could be called upon to disobey orders at any time. Disobedience was our 'law.' We'd take my mother's car, for example. . . . We'd go to Lagos nightclubbing" (48). It's interesting to note that this was one year after the reverend's death and during a period of increased international travel by FRK.

One of Fela's most vibrant memories of sharing a political occasion with his mother was the day she introduced him to Kwame Nkrumah, then the first president of an independent Ghana: "She had met with Nkrumah many times in her life. But on that particular day she took me with her to see Nkrumah. . . . My mother thought a lot of him. . . . He was her friend, a very good friend. Nkrumah! Man, I'll never forget his face" (46–47).

Fela attended Trinity College of Music in England, where he married Remi, his first wife, also a Nigerian. But it was the next year (1969–70), which he spent in the United States, that he credits with changing his life. There he met and had an intense romantic relationship with an African American woman, Sandra Smith, who lived in Los Angeles and was active in the Black Panther Party. Of this relationship, Fela recollected: "Sandra gave me the education I wanted to know. She was the one who opened my eyes. . . . Sandra was my adviser. She talked to me about politics, history . . . she blew my mind really" (85).[64]

In 1970, Sandra visited Nigeria and spent some time in Abeokuta with FRK. Because Sandra didn't have a visa and had entered Nigeria illegally, Fela was constantly hiding her in various locations, one of which was his mother's home in Abeokuta. Sandra recalled: "While I was there Fela's mother turned me on to books. She turned me on to *Chariots of the Gods*. . . . She gave me this communist book to read, I believe it was called *Lenin*. . . . I talked to her about her going to China because that really fascinated me. . . . Everything she told me about communist China was good" (104–5). FRK had described to Sandra her meeting with Mao Tse-tung as well as her struggles undertaken with the women in Nigeria. FRK had been especially impressed with the success of the literacy campaigns in China and later recorded in a 1961 article in the *Journal of Human Relations:*

> If we could read and write in our own language, half of our battle is won. When we visited a Chinese women's adult education class we were greatly impressed by the women's zeal; they were so absorbed in their lesson that they hardly took their eyes from their books. Every one of them was keen because they wanted to equip themselves with the weapon of liberty. There was to be a total eradication of illiteracy in their country within five years after their liberation and no woman wanted to be left behind. We Nigerian women should be ready to emulate them and set to work vigorously. . . . Our women should be ready to learn and make good use of the knowledge imparted to them.[65]

During Sandra's first visit, FRK personally took her to immigration officials and succeeded in getting her a visa (106). Sandra later remarked of FRK's personality, "Fela's mama didn't take no sh-t!" (105). Sandra felt that FRK (and indeed the rest of Fela's family) was very disappointed by his lack of academic achievement, though in a second visit in 1976 she believed FRK to be very supportive of Fela's chosen vocation as a musician.

As controversial in his personal as in his public life, Fela simultaneously wed twenty-seven women in 1978. It is particularly his relationships with women that often seem opposed to the political perspective embraced by his mother. They shared, however, a fierce nationalism: both despised political corruption and gave little thought to material accumulation. FRK's support of Fela was not contingent on agreement with his political philosophy but more on his right to express his views.

After completing secondary school at the AGS, the youngest child, Bekolari (Beko), attended Coventry Technical College in England and then studied medicine at the University of Manchester, where he got his degree in 1963. In 1964 he returned to Nigeria where he opened a private medical practice and later became involved in human rights activism (chap. 7).

As the youngest (born in 1940), Beko's recollections of his mother's turbulent political activity in the 1940s are less vivid than those of his older siblings. Nonetheless, he recalls his feelings of not having enough of her time. He concedes that he might have been less strictly disciplined than the older children but as with his older brothers his mother taught him to cook, bake, and clean. As he grew older he came to appreciate his mother's political activity.[66]

While a student at the University of Manchester, Beko, at age twenty, fell in love with Brenda, an Irish woman who was four years his senior. He wrote to his mother, telling her of his intentions to marry. FRK immediately wrote to Brenda, saying in part: "I am not opposed to my sons marrying [women] from any nation but Beko is too young now to think either of engagement or marriage. He's only twenty years old and away from home and those who could give him good advice. You are older than him—use that to give him good advice."[67] Beko and Brenda married anyway but were separated in 1967; Brenda later died of cancer.

Though FRK received help in the form of the integration of her home life with that of the school, and some from her mother, it is clear that she could not entirely solve the dilemma of spreading her energy and attention between her children and her political activity. Though as adults all of the children take great pride in their mother's work and acknowledge the legacy of both their parents by their own acceptance of political and civic responsibility, they are all (to different degrees) haunted by the lack of intimacy they felt with their parents as children, especially their mother. In many ways, this is a systemic problem facing all women who engage in extra-familial activity to which they are committed or that is required of them to help their families survive, or both. Yet it is not simply a "women's issue" but an issue of how society constitutes itself—how obligations and expectations about child care and "housework" are assigned.

FRK's "tradition" as a Yoruba woman was to engage in such activity, whether economic or political. While such engagement may have plagued her foremothers with another set of problems (an impossibly long day and tiring labor intensive activity), FRK's circumstances were transformed by a certain degree of Westernization: monogamous Christian marriage and a more isolated nuclear family, both exacerbated by lengthy international travel. With a foot in each camp—one Yoruba, one Western—FRK was a trader, teacher, political activist, wife, and mother in a basically nuclear family constituted on a Western, industrialized model in a situation where most of her constituency was neither Western nor operating under conditions of industrialization. There were elements of both Yoruba and Western models that she rejected: anything that construed women as second-class citizens, marginalized the poor from the benefits of citizenship, or upheld ethnicity or race as legitimate criteria for assigning "rights." She must have been in a constant process of reconciliation and readjustment, just as she was in a constant process of growth and analysis. It is no wonder that several informants described her as always eating "on the go," having little patience with those around her, exhibiting a "military" discipline, being "bossy" in her desire to get things done yesterday. In addition to whatever her own personality added to such descriptions, perhaps such behavior was part of the compromise she made with the conditions of her life—the strategy she used to meet her own expectations, for by the 1940s, as will be seen in the next chapter, she was besieged and engaged on all sides.

Notes

1. The visitor was the Portuguese explorer Duarte Pacheco Pereira. See Connah, *African Civilizations*, 121.
2. Seth I. Kale, remarks, radio program on Rev. Ransome-Kuti, Aug. 1960, transcript, IORK Papers.
3. Ibid.
4. FRK, interview, Abeokuta, June 15, 1976.
5. FRK, diary, June 4, 1946, FRK Papers (hereinafter cited in text only).
6. The article was written by Dupe Alapafuya. Among those interviewed, all in their seventies or eighties, were Mrs. Ajibola, Chike Obi, and Iyabo Makinde, all former comrades of FRK.
7. Odugbesan, "Bééère," 2–3; FRK, interview, Abeokuta, June 15, 1976.
8. Letters, box 7, file 4, no. 41, Ṣolanke Papers; Olisa Chukura (who was a student at the AGS and who often had the task of cleaning the Ransome-Kuti bedroom, including FRK's dressing table), interview, Lagos, June 12, 1989.
9. Soyinka, *Ake,* 224.
10. Ibid., 69.
11. Ebenezer Taiwo Thomas (FRK's half-brother), interview, Lagos, June 16, 1989.
12. "Portrait: The Ransome-Kutis of Abeokuta," *West Africa,* May 12, 1951.

13. Olisa Chukura, interview.

14. FRK, interview, *Daily Times,* May 2, 1973.

15. Odugbesan, "Béère," 4.

16. Olisa Chukura, interview.

17. Babalola, *My Life Adventures,* 132–36.

18. "Portrait," *West Africa,* May 12, 1951.

19. Olisa Chukura, interview.

20. Ibid.; Winifred Olubunmi Thomas, interview, Lagos, June 15, 1989.

21. Winifred Olubunmi Thomas, interview. In 1941 Winifred Olubunmi married FRK's half-brother, Ebenezer (Uncle Taiwo) Thomas in Abeokuta. Apparently, FRK had served as matchmaker. In 1944, after living for three years with FRK's mother, Ebenezer and Winifred relocated to Lagos where he worked as a manager at G. B. Olivant (a general retail store).

22. The first stanza reads: "On the hill and down below there / I was born / There I was brought up in the / land of freedom / I will glorify Abeokuta / the land that stands on top of Olumo rock / I will rejoice on behalf of / the Egba / Rejoice Rejoice Rejoice on Olumo."

23. The song (translated here by Femi Taiwo of the philosophy department of Loyola University of Chicago) is in IORK Papers: "Ise ya / Ise ya / Omo Africa, e mura yin / Ise po fun wa lati se / Omo rere kii sojo / E bere gberu o / Oluwa mbe fun wa / Ifoya o si mo / Ise ya" [It is time to work / It is time to work / Children of Africa / Prepare yourselves / There is much to be done / A good person does not run away from work / A good person is not fearful / Get down and lift the load / God is with us / There is no more fear / Let's get to work].

24. For instance, see letters of R-K to Ṣolanke, box 3, Ṣolanke Papers.

25. Olikoye Ransome-Kuti, interview, Lagos, June 5, 1989. Koye couldn't remember if it was an officer or member of the Order of the British Empire.

26. Archdeacon E. O. Alayande (a close friend of Rev. Ransome-Kuti with whom the reverend always stayed when in Ibadan where Alayande was principal of Ibadan Grammar School), interview, Lagos, Feb. 12, 1991. All of the principals were Anglican. The man who had the first distinction of being called Chief Aionian was Bishop Alexander Babatunde Akinyele, the father-in-law of Alayande and the first principal of Ibadan Grammar School. The Reverend Ransome-Kuti began an annual sports competition for the Aionian Schools, the Aionian Sports Reunion Meeting.

27. A. E. Awolana (then NUT General Secretary), remarks at the Silver Jubilee Celebration of the Union at Ijebu-Ode in 1951. See *Silver Jubilee* (Ijebu-Ode: Okenla Printing Press, 1951), p. 1, University of Ibadan Library.

28. Ibid. He wrote this in a prepared statement to be read at the Silver Jubilee.

29. Smyke and Storer, *Nigerian Union of Teachers,* 20.

30. Ibid., p. 21.

31. Ibid., 25, reported by E. E. Esua. An important motivating factor for NUT organizing was that it was the depth of the depression and teacher salaries had been cut 10–15 percent.

32. For further information on NUT, see Smyke and Storer, *Nigerian Union of Teachers.* Among other important charter members were Rev. (later Canon) E. O. Alayande, E. E. Esua, Rev. (later Bishop) Seth I. Kale, T. K. Cameroon, and E. N. E. Nkume.

33. See correspondence, IORK Papers. The other three NUT representatives to the Central Board of Education were E. E. Esua, Hon. Alvan Ikoku, and Joseph F. Odungo.

34. Smyke and Storer, *Nigerian Union of Teachers,* 159.

35. Ibid., 65.

36. Ibid., 75.

37. Ibid., 60.

38. Ibid., 129.

39. R-K to Solanke, box 2, file 5, no. 16, Solanke Papers.

40. Editorial, *Daily Times,* Aug. 21, 1933. J. O. was a clerk for the Lagos Town Council for nineteen years. There had been an allegation that he had taken a very small amount of money as a bribe. In July 1933, he drowned himself in the Lagos lagoon. The editorial cited here expressed sympathy and hailed J. O. as a member of a "notable African Christian family," observing: "All we suggest is that young Kuti must have been a man of a highly strung nature with a queer conception of personal honor."

41. Oluremi Adebayo, interview, Ibadan, June 7, 1989.

42. For discussion of the accident, see Soyinka, *Ake.*

43. Ayo Rosiji, interview, Lagos, June 20, 1989.

44. FRK to Solanke, box 3, file 5, no. 156, Solanke Papers.

45. FRK to Solanke, box 3, file 5, no. 15, Solanke Papers.

46. The child was named Hildegart by a German missionary. Many years later another Ransome-Kuti son, Fela, claimed to have been that child, who died because he was given a foreign name and then came back a few years later. See Moore, *fela, fela: this bitch of a life,* pp. 29–30.

47. R-K to Solanke, Oct. 16, 1936, box 3, file 4, Solanke Papers.

48. Soyinka, *Ake,* 165.

49. Olisa Chukura, interview. See also Soyinka, *Ake,* 171–73.

50. Olisa Chukura, interview.

51. Sonia Ransome-Kuti (Olikoye's wife), interview, Lagos, June 3, 1989.

52. Olikoye Ransome-Kuti, interview, Lagos, June 5, 1989; box 3, file 5, Solanke Papers.

53. The information on the Ransome-Kutis as parents is largely drawn from separate interviews with three of the children, Dolupo, Olikoye, and Bekolari, all conducted in June 1989. Other sources include Moore, *fela, fela: this bitch of*

a life; Idowu, *Fela;* and various correspondence between the couple and their children in the FRK Papers, IORK Papers, and Ṣolanke Papers.

54. See correspondence with Adeniyi in the FRK Papers.

55. Dolupo Ransome-Kuti, interview, Abeokuta, June 18, 1989.

56. FRK to Ṣolanke, Mar. 22, 1944, box 7, file 4, no. 41, Ṣolanke Papers.

57. Dolu to parents, Apr. 24, 1951, box 8, file 4, no. 65, Ṣolanke Papers.

58. Rev. R-K to Ṣolanke, Oct. 6, 1950, box 8, file 4, no. 63, Ṣolanke Papers.

59. In 1953 Dolu graduated from Gracefield's nursing school at Rushgate; in 1965 she obtained a diploma in nursing administration from Halifax Hospital, Rochdale.

60. Frances (now) Kuboye, interview, Lagos, June 15, 1989.

61. Olikoye Ransome-Kuti, interview, Lagos, June 22, 1989.

62. Sonia Ransome-Kuti, interview, Lagos, June 12, 1989.

63. Moore, *fela, fela: this bitch of a life,* 41–42 (hereinafter cited in text by page number). This book is full of Fela's recollections (some of them divergent from others' opinions) and details of his life.

64. Shortly after meeting Sandra, Fela changed his last name from Ransome-Kuti to Anikulapo-Kuti.

65. FRK, "Status of Women in Nigeria," 69–70.

66. Bekolari Ransome-Kuti, interview, Lagos, June 15, 1989.

67. FRK to Brenda, Nov. 4, 1960, FRK Papers.

Lucretia Phyllis Omoyeni Adeoṣolu, mother of Funmilayo Ransome-Kuti (FRK). Unless otherwise indicated, the photographs gathered here appear courtesy of Olikoye Ransome-Kuti and Comfort Oluremi Adebayo.

Oluremi (FRK's younger sister), Lucretia (mother), FRK, c. 1917.

FRK in her late twenties.

Cenotaph of Sarah Taiwo located in the Olufashabe compound on Aderunpoko Lane in Itesi, Abeokuta. Photographed by the authors, June 1989.

The Reverend I. O. Ransome-Kuti (FRK's husband), 1940s.

The Ransome-Kuti family, c. 1941.

Abeokuta Women's Union (AWU) meeting, 1940s. FRK is behind the center of the table.

Members of the AWU.

FRK (in glasses) during 1947 demonstration. To her immediate left is Eniola
Soyinka, member of the AWU executive and mother of the Nobel laureate winner
Wole Soyinka.

NCNC delegation to London, 1947. FRK was the only woman delegate.

FRK (standing and speaking) is greeted by several supporters after one of her tax cases.

Amelia Osimosu (member of the AWU executive committee) maintaining order among the AWU members at a demonstration outside the Ajin palace, April 26, 1948.

The Reverend and Mrs. Ransome-Kuti surrounded by students from the Abeokuta
Grammar School, 1947.

"Lioness of Lisabi": The Fall of a Ruler

Funmilayo Ransome-Kuti and the organization she led, the Abeokuta Women's Union (AWU), are credited with being the primary force behind the abdication of the traditional ruler of the Egba, Alake (King) Ademola II, in January 1949. The women's role in the Alake's abdication has become not only a matter of history but of legend. Though other organized groups among the Abeokuta-based Egba, such as the Majeobaje and the Ogboni Societies, eventually rallied to the cause, in fact the women were the most visible in the struggle and the most venerated in the press and among the people.[1] After the Alake's abdication, FRK was compared to the historical heroine Madam Tinubu, who had defended the Egba against invasion, to Lisabi, a legendary hero of the Egba, and to Moses.[2] The process leading to the Alake's abdication catapulted FRK into the limelight and set her on the course of being recognized as a spokesperson for the women of Nigeria. Since she already possessed charisma and feminist convictions, the events gave her sufficient renown to embark on organizing women on a national basis, to be actively solicited by international women's organizations, and to articulate a vision of how an independent Nigeria should be organized—all issues explored in upcoming chapters.

FRK's childhood had prepared her to view women as equal to men. As noted in chapter 2, even as a child she was assertive and energetic. Undoubtedly, her experience of living thousands of miles away from her family while attending school in England also helped her to mature, develop confidence, and become self-sufficient. This sense of gender equality was also manifested in her marriage, encouraged by a communal lifestyle at the boarding school she and the Reverend Ransome-Kuti ran, and in his supportive attitude. It is not surprising therefore that her interest in women's education and treatment played a major role in her adult life. Her experiences as principal of the Abeokuta Girls' School and the literary classes she established for market women were building blocks toward her leadership of women in the 1940s, but her first attempts at organizing women began much earlier.

In 1923 while head teacher of the girls' branch of the Abeokuta Grammar School, FRK organized a group of young girls and women into a ladies' club. This group primarily concentrated on learning handicrafts and social etiquette. Its members were Western-educated Christians and mostly middle class. In 1925 when she married and moved to Ijebu-Ode with her husband, this first ladies' club broke up, indicating she was at the heart of it. In the late 1920s, she founded a similar ladies' club in Ijebu-Ode, but this club branched out to undertake civic and community-related projects. In 1932 after returning to Abeokuta, she again founded a ladies' club, which consisted of twelve women who, like her, were Western educated, Christian, and middle class. Similarly to the Ijebu-Ode-based ladies' club, these women undertook civic projects with community youth in Abeokuta. They organized teenagers of both sexes and held picnics, athletic games, and lectures for their entertainment and education.

In early 1944, FRK was approached by an old friend and former student who introduced her to a market woman who told FRK of her great desire to learn to read. The woman confided that she often purchased newspapers and saved them for the day when she could read. FRK had another friend who, whenever she went to church, held her hymnal upside down because she couldn't read. FRK undertook to teach these women to read.[3]

In March 1944, a revitalized Abeokuta Ladies' Club (ALC) expanded its ranks to include market women, who were most often neither Christian nor Western educated, and generally poor. The ALC continued with some of the catering, sewing circle, and charity work of its predecessor but was drawn more and more into explicitly political work on behalf of the market women. In its pamphlet on the "Rules and Regulations of the Abeokuta Ladies' Club," the group listed among its aims "to help in raising the standard of womanhood in Abeokuta . . . to help in encouraging learning among the adults and thereby wipe out illiteracy." FRK also drew her family into the literacy classes. Her two eldest children, Dolu and Koye, were recruited as tutors, as was their young cousin, Wole

Soyinka.[4] Other members of the ALC also tutored, including some of her relatives, such as Eniola Soyinka, a teacher and the mother of Wole.

Initially, the ALC established only literacy classes for the market women. In this context of increasing interaction with the mostly poor and illiterate market women, though, FRK confronted her own privileged status as a Western-educated elite. From her parents and likely from her religious education, she already had a strong sense of duty toward those less fortunate. Her life's experience thus far had conditioned her to believe women were equal beings entitled to fair treatment. Her husband's and her own involvement with the Nigerian Union of Teachers, the West African Students Union, and the National Council of Nigeria and the Cameroons provided a politicizing ferment. As the market women began to share their stories of woe, injustice, and ill-treatment at the hands of the Alake and other representatives of the colonial hierarchy, FRK's political consciousness matured and her ideology became more radical.

Unlike in Lagos, the Abeokuta market women were not organized into one overarching association but remained in smaller groups according to the commodities in which they traded. As FRK's reputation as a woman of integrity and strength grew among the market women, she became a focal point of the leadership in politicizing their struggles.

In 1945 the Abeokuta-based market women who sold rice complained to the ALC that their rice was being seized without compensation by the government. In fact, during the early 1940s the British government attempted to effect a series of price controls and confiscation of set quotas of food stuffs, ostensibly to offset certain shortages due to World War II and to provide for soldiers.[5] The confiscation of rice in Abeokuta was the tail end of this effort.

After hearing the rice sellers' stories, in September 1945 three members of the ALC and three members of the NUT went to the assistant district officer for Abeokuta to demand an end to the seizure of the women's rice. It is telling that the ALC and NUT worked together in this early effort, the former an organization headed by FRK and the latter one in which her husband was a founding member, for this was an important indication of his support for her political work.

The ALC sent several protest delegations to the district officer (DO), assistant district officer, and the Egba Native Administration Council, all to no avail—at first. Finally, they took their protests to the public realm, with a press conference. The *Daily Service* newspaper of November 12,

1945, published a summary of the women's protest efforts and quoted the ALC delegation: " 'We the members of the Abeokuta Ladies' Club, on behalf of all Egba women, appeal to the press of Nigeria to help to bring the seriousness of the position [of the market women] to the attention of the authorities before it is too late.' " Within a week of the article's appearance, the confiscation of rice ceased. Buoyed by this victory, the ALC expanded its role and attracted an even larger membership of market women to its ranks. Soyinka described the organization's transition: "The movement . . . begun over cups of tea and sandwiches to resolve the problem of the newlyweds who lacked the necessary social graces was becoming popular. . . . It became all tangled up in the move to put an end to the role of white men in the country."[6]

Later, FRK recalled her mounting anger as she became aware of the women's concerns. She listened to them speak of "conditional sales," a method used to force women to buy (in order to resell) certain unrelated goods in tandem. For instance, purchases of sugar were coupled with mandatory purchases of cutlasses. This was an attempt to force the burden of slower moving goods onto the women traders. Since the vast majority of the market women survived on small margins of profit and had traditionally exercised control of the commodities' prices, conditional sales placed most of them in an even more precarious economic position, as well as removed their autonomy as traders. The imposition of quotas of food to be sold to the government and attempted government control of what foodstuffs should be sold and where were also onerous to the women. The women charged that policemen, private subcontractors, and even representatives of the Alake, in an attempt to satisfy the quotas, confiscated the traders' wares or paid them less than market value and then resold to the government at higher than market value. Policemen were stationed at various roads leading out of Abeokuta to ensure that until the government quotas were filled no food could be sold in other major trading centers such as Lagos, Ibadan, or Ijebu-Ode.

FRK began to believe that, in her own words, "We educated women were living outside the daily life of the people."[7] She decided to abandon Western clothing, wearing instead the traditional Yoruba wrapped cloth in order to "make women feel and know I was one with them."[8] In fact, no photograph of her after the late 1940s, even those taken on her international trips, shows her in anything other than Yoruba dress. Given the more radical turn her philosophy and activities would take, this was likely as much a statement of class allegiance as of cultural pride and unity with the market women. In addition, she began using Yoruba rather than English in public speeches, which often meant British officials required translation.

Shortly after the protest of the rice sellers, the ALC became deeply involved in other protest actions. It composed a list of demands, including the establishment of health clinics and playgrounds at schools, sanitation improvements, financial aid to increase adult literacy, and provision of a safe water supply. Two key demands were a call to end government control of trading and for no increase in taxation on women. These demands were widely circulated among the colonial and traditional authorities, including the British resident, Egba Native Administration Council, prominent chiefs, and the Alake.

In fact, the issue of female taxation (and attendant to it, reform of the Sole Native Authority [SNA] system, including women's representation in it) would lead to the most dynamic and protracted of the women's struggles, culminating in both the temporary abdication of the Alake and reform of the SNA. Women's taxation had been a sore point for many years in Abeokuta, where women were among the first females in Nigeria on whom the British imposed a tax. As early as 1917, a poll (or "head") tax was imposed on the people. This reflected London's philosophy that the colonies should bear the cost of their own "development" and replaced the former systems of tribute payments and conscripted labor, which had included women. From the beginning, there were many complaints about women's taxation. Girls were taxed at age fifteen, boys not until age sixteen. Wives were taxed separately from their husbands whether or not it could be proven that they earned income. Moreover, the tax was a flat rate and over and above the fees women already paid, such as water rates and those to support the SNA. Women not only considered the taxation as foreign, unfair, and excessive, but they also objected to the methods used to enforce its collection. Homes were invaded and women were sometimes physically assaulted, including being stripped naked, ostensibly to assess their ages to determine their eligibility for taxation. And women were jailed for nonpayment of taxes.

Due to the British system of indirect rule, the collection of taxes, like that of food quotas, was subcontracted to local traditional authorities such as the Ogboni chiefs, who were paid for the privilege. Indeed, the introduction of indirect rule placed the Alake at the pinnacle of the hierarchy of traditional authority. Though, as shown in chapter 1, the office of Alake had previously been part of a complex system of checks and balances in which groups such as the Ogboni could effect the resignation (or even suicide) of the Alake, the new system invested the Alake with powers greatly exceeding those of the traditional title. The SNA, headed by the Alake, was now imbued with all-encompassing governmental powers, as well as some powers that had been traditionally reserved to the people themselves, such as control and marketing of foodstuffs and crafts. Women were particularly disenfranchised as the process of indirect rule rendered them invisible in the governing process and challenged their decision-making roles in the economy, particularly in the distributive or trading sector where they had previously been quite important in deciding such things as market locations, days, and prices of commodities and services.

Colonialism vastly changed the character of women's traditional offices and access to power. After the extremely powerful Iyalode Tinubu died in 1887, her successor Miniya Jojolola saw her own powers and influence continually eroded by the imposition of colonial rule; by the early twentieth century, the Iyalode was no longer a significant political force.[9] Though the Ogboni Society continued to wield political influence among the people, like all traditional authority, its governmental powers were severely curtailed with Abeokuta's absorption into the indirect rule system in 1914, placing the Egba Kingdom under the complete control of the British Protectorate of Nigeria.

In 1920, Alake Ademola II (Ladipo Ademola) acceded to the office at the death of his predecessor, Gbadebo I. Gbadebo had incurred the wrath of several groups of Abeokutans because the poll tax and sanitary regulations had both been instituted during his reign (chap. 1).

The succession of Ademola II was not without its initial problems. Apparently, the British opposed Ademola because he had once served jail time in Nigeria, probably for political reasons, though the exact charge is unclear. African members of the Egba Central Council (ECC), led by the prominent trader, J. K. Coker (a relative of FRK), were in favor of Ademola. The ECC argued that Ademola had been close to Gbadebo I, even groomed by him, that he was well-educated at both the Lagos CMS Grammar School and in England, and that he was a member of the Jibolu family from whom kings were chosen. The African faction prevailed and Ademola returned to Abeokuta from a kind of exile in Isara district to assume the title of Alake.[10]

While Alake Ademola often relied on "tradition" to criticize both FRK's and the women's protests, his own life had not been so "traditional." In an interview in 1954, he admitted that he had worn European clothing up until his coronation, after which he wore his robes of office. Several of his daughters were educated as nurses and teachers in England and returned to Nigeria to pursue their careers. He was raised by his sister and partially attributed his professed belief in education for both girls and boys to that circumstance.[11]

The relationship between Alake Ademola II and FRK's family was of long duration but not always smooth. As early as 1925, the same J. K. Coker who had supported Ademola had an argument with him. The disagreement revolved around the Alake's deposing of one of the sectional rulers of Abeokuta, the Osile of Oke-Ona. Coker felt the manner by which the Osile was deposed was high-handed, arbitrary, and untraditional, and he criticized the Alake for exceeding his traditional authority. In addition to other writers, the historian J. K. Ajisafe was also so publicly critical of the Alake's action that both he and Coker were sued for libel by Ademola, who won his case in 1929.[12]

Another FRK relative, Samuel Durojayi Ṣowemimo Coker, had been banished to Ibadan in 1898 (during the reign of Gbadebo I) for being a political nuisance to the British. He became so popular in Ibadan that the British brought him back to Abeokuta where he dropped the name Samuel (becoming D. S. Coker) and became Balogun (chief) of the Christians of Abeokuta. When Ademola II acceded to the throne, D. S. Coker was so much his political opponent and rival it was said of him during the reign of Ademola, "Ade wa l'ake oba wa l'ogbe" [The crown is at Ake, the king is at Ogbe]. Ake was the site of Alake Ademola's palace; D. S. Coker resided at Ogbe.[13]

In fact, a land boundary dispute between FRK's extended family and the Alake was in great measure responsible for the founding of the Jibolu-Taiwo-Coker family organization. In 1930 the clan was called together to arbitrate the dispute, and every year thereafter (to the present) a major family reunion has been held on the first Monday in August. During the colonial era, this date was a British holiday and was therefore a long weekend. The family organization grew quite strong, electing officers and setting up a monetary fund. The oldest living family member served as the head of the clan. FRK served in several positions (including treasurer and advisor on education). She was never the head of the family only because she was never the oldest living clan member, although a woman could serve as head. For example, in 1989 her sister, Oluremi Adebayo, was head.[14]

Still, some evidence indicates that direct and often cordial relations existed between the Ransome-Kutis and the Alake. During the 1930s, the Alake invited them both to tea at his palace. However, in a letter to his good friend Ladipo Ṣolanke in London, the Reverend Ransome-Kuti confided, "I have discovered that in order to help the Alake most one must not appear to go too frequently to the palace unless wanted there." And in discussing the Alake's proposal that the Ransome-Kutis accept a standing invitation to periodic teas at the palace, the reverend informed Ṣolanke, "That would be a splendid thing if half-fulfilled as we may then talk over informally affairs which would ordinarily be difficult to ask an audience for without running the risk of being suspected and distrusted by the young elements whom it is now our duty to convert to our view and use as a national asset."[15]

In September 1934, the Ransome-Kutis helped organize a welcome home reception for the Alake's eldest son, Adetokunbo, who had been studying abroad. In the same year, FRK wrote to Ṣolanke about their preparations for the Alake's coronation anniversary.[16] Interestingly, both Ṣolanke and the Reverend Ransome-Kuti referred to FRK by the title Iyalode in their correspondence, a clear reference to her public-spirited activity. The relationship the Ransome-Kutis were cultivating with the Alake had obvious political overtones. This may help explain why in 1945 the ALC, under Funmilayo Ransome-Kuti's direction, undertook to cater the twenty-fifth anniversary celebration of Ademola's accession to the throne, though the decision to do so was likely also related to the end of the food control laws.

In the 1930s, Alake Ademola experienced a great deal of unpopularity with the people of Abeokuta and surrounding townships. Again, a major issue of contention was the taxation of women. Despite being found guilty of libel two years previously, in 1931 the local historian Ajisafe charged the Alake with corruption and pointedly criticized the taxation of women.[17] In addition, the Abeokuta Society of Union and Progress (ASUP), composed mostly of Western-educated members (and led by the Reverend I. O. Ransome-Kuti), protested to the Alake that "the way in which our women are being treated, hunted down and dragged about on public streets . . . for non-payment of tax reflects unfavorably against the reputation of Abeokuta for progress."[18] The ASUP, under Rev. Ransome-Kuti's leadership, proposed the elimination of the tax on women with a concomitant increase in men's taxes. The tax collection process was often brutal, as previously noted, and women were often stripped naked by the tax collectors, ostensibly to assess their ages. The Alake defended the process on the grounds that it was more efficacious than fines. Nonetheless, this harassment had sexual overtones and was resented by the women on the twin grounds that it was an insult to their womanhood and a consequence of their class position. Of course, primarily poor and illiterate market women suffered such treatment.

In November 1939, several articles appeared in the *West African Pilot* also calling for an end to the flat-rate tax on women (Nov. 20 and 25, 1939). In addition, a number of complaints were lodged with British authorities, stating that the Alake was appropriating land that did not belong to him and then leasing it to European firms and commercial agents.[19] In a short memoir written in the 1970s, FRK detailed complaints against the Alake regarding the negotiation of leasing arrangements with Europeans without consulting African owners of the land. These arrangements were encouraged by a law inspired by the British and passed by the SNA that stipulated that no foreigner could rent a house or land without going through the Alake as a kind of central repository of indigenous citizens' rights. Though it is possible that the law was meant to protect both owners and lessors from taking advantage of one another, by ignoring Yoruba tradition and land law, it created a nightmare for everyone involved.

By the early 1940s, dissatisfaction with the Alake and the Sole Native Authority system had increased. In 1940 the Alake increased the tax on water, better known as the water rate. When news of the increase reached the populace, ten thousand people gathered outside the palace and the office of the British resident. When Alake Ademola appeared and gave a speech supporting the increase, the crowd chanted in Yoruba, "Awa ko gba!" [We do not agree!]. Subsequently, the *Daily Service* carried editorials questioning the increases (July 10, 21, and 22, 1940). In early 1942, several Egba chiefs were jailed for embezzling tax funds, which served to exacerbate the people's frustration with the taxation system (*Daily Service,* Feb. 28, 1942).

The Alake was quite popular with the British administration, however. The Abeokuta Province annual reports are full of praise for him. Complaints of his corruption and maladministration were dismissed as the disgruntled grumbling of an "undisciplined" populace. Thus, the women's grievances centered on the Alake as the most visible and accessible symbol of what they considered to be despotic rule. Undoubtedly, for many Egba, who had little direct contact with the British, the Alake *was* their only "real" symbol of authority. Still, some, including FRK, were aware that the Alake was a symbol of colonialism. In a May 1975 interview with *New Breed* magazine, she commented: "What people are saying is that I attacked Ademola. I didn't really attack Ademola, I attacked imperialism. Those Europeans were using him against his people. . . . I was attacking Europeans indirectly and they know it." Attacking a ruler who abused his power was not an imported ideal but very much a part of Egba tradition.

Alake Ademola II was between the proverbial rock and a hard place. On the one hand, the Egba held him responsible for their welfare and expected him to respond in traditional ways to local issues. On the other, the colonial authorities held him responsible for implementing their policies, which by the nature of colonialism evaluated the welfare of Abeokutans on the yardstick of the welfare of the colonial system rather than in terms of the local situation. Particularly when it came to women, the British imported their own views of women's proper arenas of activity and thus were often blinded to women's activities in precolonial Nigeria. Thus, the British failed to take due note of women's dissatisfaction with government interference in areas the women had previously controlled themselves, such as choosing market sites and setting prices. It did not help, of course, that there was ample evidence that the Alake did in fact engage in corrupt practices. Corruption at the top filtered through the ranks, and thus members of governmental bodies and committees, even policemen, also often demanded their "cut," negotiating bribes.

In March 1946, within months of the women's limited victory in getting the food control laws abolished, the ALC became the Abeokuta Women's Union (AWU). The name change signaled a new commitment to avowedly political purposes and an activist orientation. Thousands of market women began to swell the organization's ranks. In *Ake,* Soyinka refers to these women as "wrapper wearers," distinguishing their traditional Yoruba dress of wrapped cloths from the Western attire of the middle-class Christians. Soyinka described himself as having been as a child an "odd job man" for the women's movement—relaying messages and running errands. He vividly describes the "wrapper wearers" who descended upon the Ransome-Kuti residence at the Abeokuta Grammar School for the women's meetings:

> Women of every occupation—the cloth dyers, weavers, basket makers and
> the usual petty traders of the markets—they arrived in ones, twos, in groups,

they came from near and distant compounds, town sectors and far villages whose names I had never heard. They smelt of the sweat of the journey, of dyes, of dried fish, yam flour, of laterite and the coconut oil of their plaits. Some were tattooed on arms and legs, with cica-trices on their faces. In addition to the headtie, their shoulder shawls, neatly folded, were placed lightly on their heads for additional protection from the sun.[20]

FRK herself began to adopt an explicitly anticolonial position. She did not believe that an end to colonialism would resolve completely the problems of women or other disenfranchised groups, as she was equally critical of those elements of traditional culture that she felt oppressed women. Under her leadership and utilizing both indigenous and imported means of protest, the AWU began to articulate not only an anticolonial position but one that sought to democratize government and establish women's equality (especially giving women the franchise).

The AWU adopted the motto "Unity, Cooperation, Selfless Service, and Democracy." Included in its constitution under the title "Aims and Objectives" were "to unite women; to defend, protect, preserve and promote social, economic, and political rights and interests of women; and to cooperate with all organizations seeking and fighting genuinely and selflessly for the economic and political freedom and independence of the people."[21] The organization issued membership cards signed by FRK—under her name was the title *Iya Egbe*—"mother of the society."

The AWU focused first on the issue of taxation but early on developed a comprehensive list of demands that included complete abolition of the flat-rate taxation of women, the Alake's abdication because he was corrupt, elimination of the SNA system, and institution of a more representative system of government (including, of course, the representation of women).

Notably, the AWU did not simply call for the overthrow of existing arrangements but made concrete suggestions for what should replace them. For instance, the organization employed an accountant to audit the Sole Native Authority treasury books and, based on the audit, severely criticized SNA expenditures and submitted a detailed alternative budget. In analyzing the budget, the AWU particularly criticized the investment of Egba treasury funds in British stock, pointing out that to "loan to other countries at the time we are in great need of capital for local industries . . . is part of maladministration."[22] In place of the flat-rate tax on women, the organization proposed increasing taxes on expatriate companies, using royalties from the quarry located in Abeokuta, and the increase of government investments in other local industries. The crux of the AWU's argument against the flat-rate tax on women was that there should be "no taxation without representation." An AWU-sponsored publication of 1949 quoted both the U.S. Declaration of Independence and British statesman Charles James Fox, who was sympathetic to both the American and French revolutions. The quotes dealt with the right of the governed to overthrow unjust government.[23]

The women documented in detail what they felt were the Alake's abuses of power and his corruption—a list of charges for which they believed they provided sufficient proof to warrant his resignation. Among these were his negotiations of contracts to lease land that did not belong to him to expatriate firms, thereby cheating the proper landowners of the revenues, his support of food and price controls, the corrupt manner in which regulations were enforced, and allegations of profit-making from the *dipeomu* system. This system allowed wives who so wished to leave their husbands and take refuge at the Alake's palace. Ademola's predecessor as Alake, Gbadebo, had constructed separate quarters in the palace for housing dipeomu wives. The AWU charged that Alake Ademola had sexual relations with some of these women and charged fees for their maintenance so as to make a profit. Ademola eventually responded by creating a committee to oversee the dipeomu quarters.[24]

The women also complained that sanitation, medical, and educational facilities were woefully inadequate. In 1936, the Abeokuta SNA spent 0.52 percent of its income on education, and as late as 1947 there was only one SNA-supported school.[25] In a long document entitled "A.W.U.'s Grievances," the women charged that the SNA was "a great source of oppression and suppression to the Egba people. . . . We are not happy under it. It is foreign to the customs of [the] Egba."[26]

The AWU was well organized; its membership included both individuals and other organizations, such as the various commodity associations of market women. It included Western-educated and illiterate members, followers of Yoruba religions, Christians, and Muslims. Indeed, many market women were Muslim. There is an Egba saying: "Islam is as old as the hills but Christianity came in the noon of our life."[27] At the end of the mass demonstrations component of the womens' campaign, the AWU gathered at the Central Mosque, Igbein, Abeokuta, to "give thanks to Allah."[28] Even though a professed Christian, FRK had always been ecumenical in her outlook.

An executive committee, elected by all members, served as the

AWU's decision-making body. Included among its members were the president, vice president, secretary, treasurer, and representatives from the major market associations and from the four districts of Abeokuta. A number of those on the executive committee were members of FRK's extended family: Amelia Osimosu, FRK's cousin; Eniola Soyinka, a niece of the Reverend Ransome-Kuti; and F. W. Fagbemi, a goddaughter of the reverend.

FRK served as president from the AWU's inception until her death in 1978. One author observed that the women regarded FRK with "reverence."[29] Yet she had a strong personality, and there were others who felt she was not democratic enough in her leadership style, though none ever attempted to replace her. Some women outside AWU ranks labeled her a "rebel against nature." One such contemporary, Iyabo Makinde, was interviewed many years later for an article on FRK in *Vanguard* in which Makinde reflected: "I always considered her to be a rebel against nature, but when I look back now and remember the things she said and did . . . she was continually fighting one authority or another and it wasn't for her own sake but for someone else's. . . . We were not exactly close, you know. . . . I used to watch her from the sidelines and envy the way she pulled crowds and had people hang on to every word she uttered."[30]

The union had several strengths. Because it forged together several organizations and built upon FRK's reputation, the ALC's literacy classes, and the triumphant struggle on behalf of the rice sellers, there existed a network and infrastructure that could mobilize women quickly and count on their unswerving loyalty and discipline. For discipline was something about which the women were seriously concerned. For example, the AWU's charter rules stated: "All members must obey any order given by the leaders of the union as long as it is for the good of the member and for the union. Any complaint about an order shall be made at the general meeting and carefully examined for adjustment if necessary."[31] With a dues-paying membership of roughly twenty thousand women, organized demonstrations in which thousands of them participated, and the support of another hundred thousand women, it was important that everyone follow the rules to minimize chaos and the potential for conflict. FRK later recalled that her plans were that the women should not give the authorities any excuse to attack them. She was determined also that "no member of the union should think herself better than the others; all must move freely and happily together."[32] Though she possessed a body of able "lieutenants" in her executive committee, FRK's dedicated, charismatic, courageous, and politically savvy leadership was a mainstay of the AWU's protests. In addition to wearing Yoruba dress, she always spoke in the Yoruba language when addressing the women in rallies and meetings. Even when British officials were present, she spoke in Yoruba and translated the discussion in English into Yoruba so the vast majority of non-English speaking market women would understand. The fact that FRK spoke Yoruba and wore Yoruba dress made the women comfortable with her and increased their trust and belief that she was empathetic and one of them.

Funmilayo Ransome-Kuti stood about five feet four inches tall and had a slender frame. Her high cheek bones and piercing gaze could be quite intimidating. She had a hearty laugh and a strong, clear voice that many informants concurred could be heard well even by a large crowd. She spoke rapidly, often gesticulating with her hands when making a point, and displayed a great deal of passion in her speeches. Though many people commented that her manner could be brusque, they remember her as warm and concerned about people. In her role as a leader, she was able to capitalize on being simultaneously Western educated and grounded in tradition. The women looked up to her because of her education; the fact that she had been to England lent status and credibility to her role as their "representative" to the colonial government.

At the height of their demonstrations, the women composed a song of praise to her in which they called her their "king who made their life better." Several market women giving evidence to the SNA Council said, "It was their God who created Mrs. Kuti; that made a gift of her to them as their mother."[33] Many years later, one AWU member, Mrs. Ajibola, recollected: "She was like a goddess. We hung onto every word she said, even if we thought it was wrong, but hardly any of her words were wrong anyway. There was nothing hypocritical about Funmilayo. She just did not know how to pretend."[34]

FRK was passionate about the women's struggle, and that passion sometimes elicited charges of an autocratic leadership style, most especially from the other Western-educated members of the executive committee (though none resigned or provided any real opposition to her leadership). Diplomacy was not, in fact, her strong suit. In both public and private, her no-nonsense approach was not particularly tolerant of incompetence, dishonesty, pettiness, or disagreement, once she'd made up her mind. She listened to others, but she made up her own mind, and she took her role as leader seriously. The one thing of which she was never accused was wavering about what to do.

There was some brief and unsuccessful opposition from a tiny group of women who formed a women's section of a very small organization known as the *Egbe Atunluse,* founded in 1949 by disgruntled members of the Ogboni who opposed the Alake's abdication. Though the Ogboni later played a role in engineering the Alake's return, they were unable to decrease the effectiveness of FRK's leadership or her popularity.

The Reverend Ransome-Kuti was also well known and held in great esteem, which redounded to FRK's benefit, in addition to some of the practical aid that he rendered the women in their struggle against the Alake. Rev. Ransome-Kuti was among his wife's staunchest supporters. Undoubtedly, his political acumen and experience were a hidden force in the women's struggle. In an unpublished essay on FRK, Clara Odugbesan remarked on the mutual support the couple gave one another in their political activities. FRK reported that her husband helped author some of the women's petitions.[35] His presidency of the Majeobaje Society, one of the men's groups to lend early, strong support to the AWU, also proved of invaluable help. In the midst of the women's demonstrations against the Alake, the reverend wrote to Ṣolanke, "Iyalode [FRK] sends you all warmest love and please do not in the least believe all the nonsense you may read in the papers about her. . . . They are the doings of the hired agents of the Alake. . . . She continues to do her work for Egbaland and strengthens the children of Lisabi."[36]

Other men were initially less helpful, however. Besides the already noted opposition of the Egbe Atunluse, in 1947 several Egba chiefs held a meeting in support of women's taxation, claiming that half of their revenues came from that source (*Daily Service,* June 13, 1947). Though the *Daily Service* had earlier championed the women's cause, it too became critical, as did the *Daily Times* (on whose board of directors Alake Ademola sat). In an editorial on December 13, 1947, the *Daily Times* referred to Funmilayo Ransome-Kuti as a "dictatrix [*sic*]." The *West African Pilot* was generally more sympathetic, even referring to FRK as the "Lioness of Lisabi." Though her brother-in-law, George A. Adebayo (her sister Oluremi's husband), worked for the Egba Native Administration (ENA), he tried to stay neutral, supplying neither side with propaganda or support.[37]

As the struggle intensified, some male support was forthcoming. On

December 20, 1947, a mass meeting of Egba men was held at Sapon Market Square in Abeokuta where they resolved: "We wholeheartedly endorse and approve of all the lawful ways and means which Mr. and Mrs. Kuti employ in the cause of happiness, freedom from oppression, and the peace of Egbaland and the inhabitants thereof" (*Daily Service*, Jan. 17, 1948). The meeting was probably organized by the Majeobaje Society, led by Rev. Ransome-Kuti.

In June 1940, the AWU submitted a petition to the SNA Central Council in which they protested that women suffered "double" taxation, comparing Abeokuta women unfavorably to those in places like Ibadan where there was no direct taxation of women. In addition to paying income and water rate taxes, market women were required to pay the salaries of the traditional parakoyis or market supervisors. The women complained that any salary due the parakoyis should come from existing taxes and suggested that since both sellers and buyers used the market the general tax fund should support its physical upkeep. They ended with a call for no taxation without representation: "Inasmuch as Egba women pay taxes, we too desire to have a say in the management of the country, because a taxpayer should also have a voice in the spending of the taxes. We . . . request you please to give consideration to our being represented in this [SNA] council by our own representatives at the next general election" (*Daily Service*, July 8, 1946).

On July 5, 1946, the AWU held a "women's day" celebration. Shortly before, FRK had sent a letter to several Egba chiefs in which she outlined the Alake's abuses and corruption. On July 6, she recorded in her diary that there was a meeting in the Alake's palace about her letter to the chiefs but wrote, "I was too tired to be present," perhaps because of the celebration the day before. On July 11, there was a meeting of the chiefs, the Alake, and the Ransome-Kutis in an effort seemingly organized by the chiefs and/or the Alake to defuse the impact of FRK's letter. In her diary for that day, FRK recorded that she ended up shaking hands with the Alake, but the very next month there are several entries that chronicle continued protests led by her.

The women sent a number of petitions to various colonial authorities, asking that the tax on women be repealed and that the corruption of the Alake "and his agents" be investigated and stopped. On one occasion in August 1946, the women seemed to win the sympathy of the district officer (DO). The Alake had forced women traders from an area in Itoku market so that he could lease the land to a European firm, Bata Company. The DO directed the Alake to allow the women to return to the area to trade,[38] but this sympathy was short-lived. In 1947, FRK refused to pay her own flat-rate and special assessment income taxes in protest (see below), a strategy she employed several times. That same year she visited England with the National Council of Nigeria and the Cameroons (NCNC) delegation to protest the Richards Constitution, causing quite a controversy due to some of her actions there (chap. 6). By the time she returned from England, she had fallen totally out of favor with the colonial authorities in Nigeria who surmised in the 1947 Abeokuta Province Annual Report that she had "learnt a few tricks in England from those who do not like any form of constitutional authority."[39]

Though in 1949 she was appointed by the British resident to represent Abeokuta at the Western Provinces conference on a new constitution (to replace the Richards Constitution), women were not enfranchised at the time. Since this was at the height of the women's demonstrations against the Alake, her appointment may have been an attempt to rechannel her energies or, by involving her in the process, to take the steam out of her complaints. The only woman representative out of twenty-seven members, FRK argued vociferously for women's enfranchisement, arguing against the indirect electoral system and the requirement that a candidate post a monetary deposit before being allowed to contest an election.[40] She remained as central to the women's mass demonstrations as before.

Between August 1946 and May 1947, the AWU sent several petitions to the Alake, requesting an end to both the flat-rate tax on women and his other abuses of power. An AWU delegation even met with the Alake on October 5, 1946, but to no avail. Rather than having been initiated by FRK, this meeting seems to have been the result of the intercession of others, including Ladipo Ṣolanke, all the way from London, trying to bring the parties together, as FRK noted in her diary on October 1, 1946.

The Alake was upset that his decision regarding the women traders in Itoku market was reversed by the DO. Perhaps it was part of a rapprochement between the two that in late 1946 the Alake was inspired to actually *increase* the flat-rate tax on women, an action supported by the British resident.

The women had had enough. The increase of the flat-rate tax, adding insult to injury, spurred the beginning of the mass demonstration phase of their protests. In mid-October 1946, FRK led nearly a thousand women in a march to the *Afin* (Alake Ademola's palace) to protest the increase. Speaking in Yoruba, FRK told the Alake that the women had come to complain about the tax increase. The Alake replied that the Tax Assessment Committee had increased the taxes, which was warranted according to their findings. Interestingly, he added that any woman who felt she could not pay her tax should come to him to explain, alone, but that such a matter was "no group business" (*Daily Service,* Oct. 19, 1946). FRK then replied that before any increase in taxes, tax declaration forms should be printed and distributed to the populace to properly determine people's incomes. The Alake said such a suggestion was too late.

The women then decided to contest the tax levies in court. One trader, Janet Ashabi, had her tax assessed on an estimated yearly income of £150. She attempted to show in court that the figure was too high. The British resident who heard the case, E. N. Mylius, refused to accept Ashabi's figures, not only denying her appeal but directing the assessment officers to increase her tax![41] FRK recorded in her diary on November 7, 1946, "I dreamt I saw the late Gbadebo [the Alake previous to Ademola]—he said Abeokuta would soon be like his own time." On behalf of the AWU, she sent a letter regarding the Ashabi case to Mylius, in which she stated he was "not conversant with the conditions in which the women of Egbaland live" and requested that he reconsider his decision. He replied that he had nothing to add to his earlier remarks (*Daily Service,* Feb. 3, 1947).

In April 1947, as noted above, Funmilayo Ransome-Kuti refused to pay her income tax. At her arraignment she pleaded "not guilty," and eight thousand people, mostly women, came to the Ake grade "A" court to support her (*Daily Service,* Apr. 29, 1947). She petitioned for a transfer of venue to the magistrate court, and her lawyer subpoenaed the Alake to give evidence for the amount of the tax. The case was adjourned for a week. When the trial resumed, a crowd of over five thousand women demonstrated at the courthouse and paraded through the streets in her support (*Daily Service,* May 8, 1947). She was found guilty and fined £3 or one month's imprisonment. She was given one month in which to appeal (*Daily Service,* May 13, 1947). Though she filed an appeal just before she was scheduled to leave for England with the NCNC delegation, she eventually paid the fine in time to leave (chap. 6).

Almost exactly a year later, after several mass demonstrations by the women (see below), FRK again refused to pay her taxes. She led a demonstration of thousands of women to the Afin (palace), where she renewed her demands for the abolition of female taxation. The AWU had planned a mass demonstration for her day in court, but the day before an anonymous person paid the tax for her. The British resident even broadcast a radio message to inform the women that "some good soul" had paid FRK's tax and that the court date was canceled. He announced that a committee had been constituted to review the women's flat-rate tax and that women would be represented on the committee (*Daily Service,* Apr. 27, 1948).[42] This, however, followed a number of women's demonstrations.

By late November 1947, the women began organizing mass demonstrations in which up to ten thousand of them participated. The mass demonstration phase of the women's protests was impressive, disciplined, and well organized. The protests were always led by FRK, who held training sessions in her home to instruct the women on mass resistance. For instance, she showed them how to cover their eyes, noses, and mouths with cloth when tear gas was thrown. She also instructed them to pick up the tear gas canisters and throw them back at the policemen. Unable to get demonstration or parade permits, the women proclaimed that their demonstrations were "picnics" and used "picnic" as a kind of code euphemism during their planning sessions. Sometimes they referred to the demonstrations as "festivals." The women used their dues to have lawyers imported from Lagos for those who were arrested; these lawyers stayed in the Ransome-Kuti household, which was also the central planning headquarters.[43]

There is a story of FRK snatching "Oro," a fearless and forbidden thing for a woman to do. Oro is part of the power of the Ogboni society, the secret society of kingmakers (and deposers of kings) that operated as a kind of council to balance and monitor the power of rulers (chap. 1). Oro is both a "thing" and a ritual that "comes out" to compel people to obey Ogboni sanctions. Only men can parade during Oro (women must stay inside when they march); an instrument about fourteen to fifteen inches long and one and a half inches wide made of a light wood and with a hole at the end through which a piece of string is attached is whirled above the head. Depending on the size of the stick, a higher or lower pitched sound is emitted. Oro is said to have supernatural powers; those who do not obey its directives are punished. Several informants reported that Oro "came out" to stop women from demonstrating and that FRK approached, snatched the stick, and later displayed it in her home. The tenacity displayed in the story is testament to both FRK's fearlessness and the way in which she was perceived as nearly invincible by many of her followers.[44]

Wole Soyinka recorded an incident regarding FRK and Oro as well: "And then I heard the ultimate challenge of the women, for this was not just a rallying-song, even an ordinary war-song, but the appropriation of the man-exclusive cult—*Oro*—by women in a dare to all men, *Ogboni* or not. . . . I saw stocky, middle-aged men, the fearsome *Ogboni* abandoning their hats, shawls, staffs of office and [saw them] run on the wind." Then he heard the women's chant:

Oro o, a fe s'oro
Oro o, a fe s'oro
E ti'lekun mo'kunrin
A fe s'oro

[Oro—o, we are about to perform oro / Lock up all the men, we are bringing oro out] [45]

When one woman's husband refused to allow her to attend a pre-demonstration meeting, FRK reported that the woman ran to her doorway and sang to those outside, "Oh, women, my husband will not allow me to come to the meeting," whereupon the women ran to the house, grabbed the man, and rolled him outside in the dust. Following this, FRK pronounced, "Now we have no more opposition from men" (*Daily Worker*, May 14, 1952).

The first demonstration occurred on November 29–30, 1947, when ten thousand women held a twenty-four-hour vigil outside the Afin (*West African Pilot*, Nov. 29, 1947). FRK reported that as the women came near to the Afin in this first demonstration she commanded them to stop and close their eyes. Then, she closed *her* eyes and said that all who were afraid should desert the ranks now. None withdrew. Moreover, all the markets of Abeokuta were closed, so the women organized supplies of food and water in order to sleep and eat without leaving the vigil.

The use of songs is a Yoruba tradition of great longevity. People compose songs of praise or derision to raise morale and lighten workloads. Song is a way of circulating news and expressing political opinion. The AWU composed over two hundred songs in Yoruba to use in their protests. [46] Some songs, to boost morale, were ecumenical, reflecting the diverse religious allegiances of the members:

Because we are fighting on the right the Lord will make us victorious . . . for we are on the right.

The streets of Mecca are as bright as daylight, paradise is our home.

The women also praised the *Orisa,* the Yoruba pantheon of gods and goddesses. Others expressed the women's determination not to pay taxes, no matter what: "We are not paying tax, if you like, take us to prison. . . . If you like keep us in prison, no we are not paying tax." They expressed a sense of their power:

Idowu [Alake], for a long time you have used your penis as a mark of authority that you are our husband. Today we shall reverse the order and use our vagina to play the role of husband on [*sic*] you. . . .

O you men, vagina's head will seek vengeance.

They ridiculed the Alake and threatened the British:

Ademola
Big man with an ulcer
Your behavior is deplorable
Alake is a thief
Council members are thieves
Anyone who does not know Kuti will get in trouble

White man, you will not get to your country safely
You and Alake will not die an honorable death . . .

You pale-faced one keep off
That we may have a chance
To chat with father [Alake]

And they praised the Ransome-Kutis:

Béère [FRK], go on enjoying your life, All your plans have yielded
    successful results
Daodu [Rev. Ransome-Kuti] is deputizing for Kuti [FRK]
Just as the stars deputize for the moon
Daodu is deputizing for Kuti . . .
Let us all demonstrate our honesty
Let us all be kindhearted
Whosoever follows the crooked way
Shall incur Béère's displeasure
Let us all be kindhearted

The women performed mock traditional sacrifices and funeral rites for the Alake and were in concert with tradition by collectively and publicly demonstrating against policies inimical to their interests. However, it was unprecedented that they should attempt to depose a ruler, particularly without the concurrence of the Ogboni, whose support would not come for nearly another eight months (in July 1948, see below). The Egba Native Administration (ENA) Council held an emergency meeting on the first day of the demonstration, and the British resident, E. N. Mylius, lambasted FRK and the Reverend Ransome-Kuti by saying, "I am satisfied that Mrs. Kuti was the ringleader of the irresponsible women. I was with the Alake when Reverend Ransome-Kuti led a deputation of youths and adult men before the Alake. I condemn the spirit of irresponsibility shown by both husband and wife." FRK later sued him for libel.[47] The disposition of the case is unclear.

At one confrontation, a British DO reportedly yelled at FRK, "Shut up your women!" She allegedly retorted, "You may have been born but you were not bred! Would you speak to your mother like that?" Reportedly, women around her threatened to take the DO and "cut off his genitals and post them to his mother."[48]

After the November demonstration, the ENA Central Council informed the women that female taxation would be suspended pending further investigation. On December 3, several AWU members appeared before the council, were questioned, and then informed that the council would confer with them again. Instead, several women were charged with being in default on their taxes, convicted in court, and imprisoned. AWU-employed attorneys defended those arrested.

The second demonstration, December 8–10, was the result of the arrests, which the women considered both harassment and a breach of the council's promise of December 3. This demonstration lasted forty-eight hours, twice as long as that of November, and again reportedly involved over ten thousand women who ate and slept outside the Afin, threatening to remain there until all the women who had been arrested were released. On December 10, all those arrested were released and the vigil ended, although within a few weeks harassment and jailing began again. One woman with a nine-day-old baby tied to her back was arrested and jailed. FRK complained to the assistant DO who replied: "My dear Mrs. Kuti, what does it matter if a woman is jailed with a nine-day-old baby? What we want to know is that she pays her tax. We did not know she had paid before she was summoned and jailed" (Daily Service, Jan. 24, 1948).[49] Nonetheless, the women continued to protest by sending letters to the Daily Service, the Egba Central Council, the Alake, the chief secretary to the government, and the governor.

A few weeks after the December demonstrations, the Alake reacted by calling them unprecedented. He also announced that he wished to appoint two women councillors to the ENA Central Council and proposed to appoint an Iyalode and other women chiefs, though he said it would take time to find good candidates (*Daily Service,* Jan. 2, 1948).

On February 12, 1948, the Alake (with the concurrence of the ENA Central Council, the DO, and the British resident) banned FRK from the Afin. This represented a public censure as well as an attempt to render her leadership ineffective since she could now not attend meetings to represent women before the council, the Alake, or the British resident, all of whom met at and worked out of the palace. Perhaps the Alake also hoped it would curtail further demonstrations there.

Shortly thereafter, a letter addressed and delivered to FRK invited representatives of the AWU to a meeting convened by the DO at the Afin. Though addressed to FRK, the letter stated expressly that she was not to attend the meeting. Nonetheless, a delegation of the AWU, including FRK, approached the Afin to demand that she be allowed to attend the meeting; they were informed by the DO that due to the resolution barring her the women could either come without her or stay home. The women appealed to the Alake to allow FRK to enter, saying they were "all daughters of the soil." The Alake replied that the AWU women were like "vipers that could not be tamed" and "no woman who behaved as Mrs. Kuti did would come into his presence prior to making the customary apology" (*Daily Service,* Feb. 18, 1948).

Immediately after this ultimatum by the Alake, the DO attempted to leave the Afin but the women blocked his way, refusing to let him leave. He reentered the palace to inform the Alake and then summoned the British resident. When the DO and the British resident attempted to leave together, the women once again blocked the exit. In a third attempt to leave, the DO became involved in a fracas in which FRK held the steering wheel of his car until he pried her hand loose (*Daily Service,* Feb. 18, 1948).[50]

The tide had begun to turn. Even the *Daily Service,* previously extremely critical of the women, called for women's representation in all native administration systems, including the ENA Central Council. The Alake proposed that women be appointed to the ENA finance committee (*Daily Service,* Feb. 20, 1948). Egba men who were living in Lagos met and questioned the Alake's position on female taxation (*Daily Service,* Feb. 25, 1948). Even the Egba chiefs who had previously supported the tax began to waver. At a February 21 meeting with the chiefs at the Afin, the Alake informed them that unless they were willing to pay women's taxes in addition to their own—in other words, have their own taxes raised—nothing could be done (*Daily Service*, Feb. 24, 1948).

At a February 27 meeting of the ENA Central Council, the British resident read a pronouncement (referring to FRK and the AWU) in which he objected to their "insulting of the Alake" and "recent activities of certain persons who had disturbed the peace and tranquility of Abeokuta." He went on to support the banning of "certain persons" from the palace and stated that the administration's patience had run out and those "endangering the peace of Abeokuta" would henceforth be treated as criminals. He reiterated the government's position that female taxation was an unchangeable fact (*Daily Service*, Mar. 2, 1948).

The women continued their efforts to achieve successful negotiation of their demands. They held press conferences, sent letters to the editors of major newspapers, and submitted petitions to various colonial authorities, including the long, detailed "Abeokuta Women's Union Grievances." They documented complaints that the Alake used the power of his office to buy large quantities of salt at wholesale prices from European firms, such as the United Africa Company and G. B. Olivant, and then, with a monopoly of the available salt, demanded that the women salt traders purchase their supplies from him at inflated prices. They reported that in 1946–47 FRK and S. F. Adeyinka (a member of the AWU's executive committee and one of FRK's few close friends) visited several villages in Abeokuta Province and observed the poverty-stricken areas that were being required to pay taxes. The women again demanded female representation on the ENA Central Council "and all other committees that have to do with the management of Egba affairs."[51]

On April 28, the women held a five-hour demonstration, marching throughout the streets of Abeokuta and reiterating their demands for the abolition of the tax on women, for women's representation in the ENA, and for the abdication of the Alake. Shortly after this demonstration, FRK received a letter from a woman who signed her name Madam O.X.Y.A.Z.A., warning her to be wary of an assassination attempt.[52]

Within weeks of the April demonstrations the Alake was compelled to act. He appointed a special committee of both women and men to investigate the AWU's complaints, suspended the tax on women, and agreed that women should be represented on the ENA Central Council

(*Daily Service,* June 1, 1948). For a cooling-off period, the Alake left for the city of Jos—supposedly for a vacation.

In his absence, the Ogboni chiefs abandoned their earlier support of him and, with several members of the ENA Central Council, repudiated him as the king. On July 4, they passed a resolution rejecting the SNA system as "not in accordance with native law and custom" and charged the Alake with corruption and usurpation of powers not rightfully his. They also called for the abolition of the tax on women.

When the Alake returned from Jos, the Ogboni greeted him by sounding a bell and beating drums, the traditional method of rejecting a king. The Alake responded by accepting the terms of the July 4 resolution, except for their repudiation of him as king. The Ogboni then began a boycott of ENA Central Council meetings, preventing any administrative decisions from being made.

For their part, the AWU continued to protest, holding mass demonstrations on July 7 and 8. On July 26, the Alake resigned as SNA administrator to become chairman of the ENA Council, but retained his title as Alake. The AWU again responded with mass demonstrations on July 27 and 28, insisting that Ademola abdicate as the Alake. The British resident and the chief commissioner for the Western Provinces then advised him to leave Abeokuta to prevent further "disorder."[53] At the end of July, he left for the town of Oshogbo, proclaiming:

> That so fierce and unprecedented opposition should have been encouraged at this hour in my career on the stool of Egbaland is entirely beyond my capacity to understand, but as I have always placed the happiness of the people and progress of my dear country above everything, I cannot bear any longer the sight of turmoil, strife, and discontent. I have therefore decided . . . in order to avoid bloodshed, to leave the environ of my territory in the hope that after a time frayed tempers will subside and an atmosphere of calm prevail.[54]

Nora Majekodunmi, the wife of the Alake's physician, Dr. M. A. Majekodunmi, later reported that the Alake was in "shock" the night he left for Oshogbo and her husband was called in to see him.[55] From July 29 to August 2 the AWU held a celebration, which included dancing throughout the town and a "thanksgiving" service at St. John's Church, Igbein, at which Bishop S. L. Phillips (a friend of the Ransome-Kutis) gave a lecture on "The Emancipation of Women." The deputy director of education for the Western Provinces, S. Milburn, also gave an AWU-sponsored lecture on the education of women at Centenary Hall, Abeokuta.[56]

The AWU received publicity and support from London, where an article entitled "They Made the Ruler Run," chronicling the women's campaign against the Alake, appeared in the *Daily Worker* on August 18, 1948. FRK deliberately sought to publicize the women's cause in England. She wrote to at least one member of Parliament, Reginald Sorensen of the Labour Party (an anticolonialist who was also active with the West African Students Union), and to her old friend Arthur Creech-Jones, who was then secretary of state for the colonies. She complained to both not only about the Alake but also about the behavior of local British officials (chap. 6).[57]

During the second absence of the Alake, several of the women's demands were met. An Egba Interim Council was constituted to replace the old Native Administration Council, and four women, two of them AWU executive committee members (FRK and Mrs. Soleye) were appointed to the new council. Four members of the Majeobaje Society were also appointed to the council. Among the first official acts of the Interim Council were the abolition of the tax on women, including the water rate tax, and an increase in the flat-rate tax on men. The British agreed to this under the conditions that there be a cut in the salaries of council employees and increases in fees for certain licenses, as well as a decrease in capital expenditures.[58]

The AWU, supported by the Majeobaje Society, continued to demand the Alake's abdication. FRK maintained that the Alake had left town less in the interest of "peace and tranquility" and more to avoid facing the commission of inquiry into the women's charges.[59] Clearly, the women were "doubly" angry with the Alake. First, he abused his traditional authority and, rather than acting in the best interests of his people, enriched himself. Second, he was the visible mouthpiece of an onerous and undemocratic colonial system, which some of the women wanted to reform and others wanted to end. The battle between FRK and the Alake seems to have escalated to a personal level, a contest of will and power, for there is evidence that, despite others' numerous attempts to end their feud, it continued even after the Alake's abdication and reinstallation (see below).

Finally, on January 3, 1949, Ademola abdicated as Alake. Apparently the British also had to approve his abdication.[60] In his letter of abdication,

Ademola stated that since he had become Alake in 1920 there had been no "major" objections to his rule until the women began their protests (*Daily Service,* Jan. 5, 1949).[61] Though the women could not claim total credit for his resignation, since both the role of the Majeobaje Society and the Ogboni's rejection of the Alake were important factors, the women's actions (even in Ademola's own assessment) had clearly played a pivotal role in his downfall. The women initiated and spearheaded the movement against him and, perhaps even more importantly, for changes in the structure of the SNA system. The press also viewed the women, particularly FRK, as the initiators and mainstay of the movement, even many years later.[62] One observer wrote: "Inspired by Mrs. Ransome-Kuti, the Egba Women's Union [AWU] . . . was chiefly responsible for the agitation that . . . led to the abdication of the Alake of Abeokuta."[63]

After the Alake's abdication, the AWU published a pamphlet in both Yoruba and English, entitled *The Fall of a Ruler: The Freedom of Egba-land,* by A. Aloba, and celebrated amid dancing and drumming all over Abeokuta. Yet there were many battles still to be fought. In 1950, the ENA Council became the Abeokuta Urban District Council (AUDC). Although the number of representatives (both ex officio and elected) increased, the number of women representatives remained static at four. Objection to even this limited number of women resurfaced.[64]

The pro-Alake supporters, many of whom still sat on the reorganized council, began agitating for his return almost immediately. Though the British attempted to keep a public profile of neutrality in the whole affair, it is clear that Ademola neither abdicated nor returned without their approval.[65] An article entitled "Police versus Egba Market Women" in the September 15, 1950, issue of the *Nigerian Tribune* lambasted FRK, charging her with having given "the public cause to disregard the integrity of the E.N.A. as an effeminate [*sic*] authority" and labeling her followers "storm troopers." The article was also critical of the AWU's attempt to abolish the water rates, of the "coercive terrorism" of the Majeobaje Society, and of the British resident, J. H. Blair. The byline of the article was simply "Egba Youth." Some felt the article had been planted as an attempt to discredit FRK by Ademola's supporters while they struggled for his return as Alake.

Twenty-two months after his abdication, and after several votes, the Central Council by a narrow margin decided on November 30, 1950, to recall Ademola as the Alake. The AWU and the Majeobaje Society had both opposed his recall but were unable to prevent it. With the help of a relatively new party, the Action Group (AG), and its leader Obafemi Awolowo, Ademola returned to Abeokuta secretly, late at night on December 3, escorted by members of the Ogboni and the ENA police. His return was engineered in this manner to avoid a confrontation with FRK and the AWU. The AG supported Ademola's reinstatement as part of a general policy of supporting traditional rulers in return for their support of the party.[66]

Though the role of the Alake's reinstatement in it is unknown, on December 28 there was an attempt by the AUDC to ban the Majeobaje Society that was later rescinded. Ladipo Ṣolanke, who continued to be involved in Abeokuta politics, including corresponding with the Alake, was also against the Alake's return.[67] The AWU and the Majeobaje Society *were* able to participate in setting the conditions by which Ademola could resume his office; among these were recognition of the Majeobaje Society and a promise that any "political organization that works within the law and the spirit of the Constitution shall not be interfered with." The conditions, signed by Ademola on January 15, 1951, further stipulated:

> I, Ademola II, have decided to return to my homeland, and, with the approval of the Government, shall resume my position as Alake. . . . I hereby promise that I shall take no revenge of any nature against any person or persons who may have opposed my return in the past . . . and that I shall cause no interference either directly or indirectly, with the administration of the affairs of the Egba Native Authority, beyond executing the normal duties required as Chairman of the Egba Council.[68]

Despite everything, the Alake and FRK were once again on a collision course. On March 28, 1951, the Resident I. W. F. Schofield wrote to Rev. Ransome-Kuti, asking his intercession in persuading FRK "to make her peace with the Alake and to cooperate in amending the market rules where necessary as well as getting the women to use the markets again." Three days later, FRK complained to the secretary of state for the colonies, Arthur Creech-Jones: "The Egba still maintain that we had been unfairly treated by the way Ademola was brought back and forced on us, the defenseless people, with the aid of the police, and we hope that those who were responsible for dragging the British government's integrity in the mud by this action will be called to question."[69]

The AWU continued to complain to local British officials as well, saying that the Alake was simply taking up where he'd left off and violating the conditions he'd signed in resuming office. The AWU, and particularly FRK, were convinced the Alake was pursuing a vendetta and attempting to keep her off the taxation assessment committee and from being reelected as one of the women representatives to the Central Council. They also accused the Alake of blocking FRK's nomination to the Western House of Assembly. Indeed, the Alake's candidate, Remi Aiyedun, did take FRK's place on the Central Council and later served in the Western House of Assembly.

On June 27, 1952, the AWU sent a letter to the council, stating their lack of confidence in it and that the women council members were traitors, presumably to other women. They asked that the council be dissolved and reconstituted. Ṣolanke, who had previously counseled patience, wrote to FRK:

> Re: Our Alake and Yourself
>
> I am still anxious that you should be reinstated as the Representative for women in the Central Council. I want to appeal to you to start now to go on making him [the Alake] feel as though you have forgiven him for all his past actions against you. As soon as we succeed in getting you to be accepted and reinstated then I want you to trust me that I shall start presenting to you from time to time ways and means whereby you together with your Women's Union rule not only Abeokuta but also the whole of Nigeria.[70]

With her direct and assertive personality and her strict adherence to principle even in the face of defeat, FRK was simply incapable of carrying out such a deception. Moreover, the public posture of her running battle with the Alake would have made such behavior incredulous. For his part, the Alake publicly expressed anger that FRK did not show him the traditional obeisance (falling to one knee) or respect by rising when he entered the room (*Daily Service*, July 11, 1952). Though there was "no love lost" between FRK and the Alake, the fact is that she did not show the traditional obeisance, falling to one knee or bowing down, to *anyone,* including her husband to whom it would have been her first duty to show it.

The AWU pursued other grievances against the Alake. As discussed earlier, in 1948 women had been exempted from paying water rate taxes. However, in April 1952 the issue resurfaced when the council faced the need to raise revenue to pay for extension and improvement of the water supply. The council therefore voted to reinstate the water rate tax on women. Three of the four women representatives on the council opposed the decision, saying that they represented women's interests and men could not decide this issue without consulting women directly (the fourth, Remi Aiyedun, the Alake's choice, said nothing during the debate). The women were overruled and the water rate tax took effect (*West African Pilot,* Apr. 16, 1952).

Almost immediately the AWU submitted a petition to the Central Council protesting the water rates. In part, the petition accused the Alake of hostility toward women's interests and informed the council that the water that women used was as much for their husbands and children as for themselves. The petition also recommended sinking new wells rather than extending the water supply, at least until the latter could be afforded. FRK sent copies of the petition to Britain, including copies to Creech-Jones and Sorensen. The Majeobaje Society supported the women's campaign against the water rates, asking why only women in Abeokuta and Ijebu had to pay them.[71]

In March 1953, FRK and several other women were arrested for non-payment of the water rate tax. FRK once again wrote to her friends in England, including Sorensen and Fenner-Brockway, also a member of Parliament. Sorensen raised the issue in the House of Commons and Fenner-Brockway initiated inquiries. In April 1953, Oliver Lyttleton, then secretary of state for the colonies, addressed the issue in the House of Commons. The following month, Lyttleton also wrote letters to Sorensen and Fenner-Brockway, indicating that the colonial secretary's office decided that it was a local issue and therefore up to the Western Provincial Government in Nigeria to decide. However, Lyttleton offered to continue to inquire whether it was lack of funds that prevented the women from appealing the tax.[72]

Although levying of the water rate was subsequently taken over by the Western Regional Government, only women in Abeokuta and Ijebu divisions continued to be assessed. As late as 1959, the AWU was still protesting the water rate, this time directly to the Western Regional Government. In that same year, FRK was arrested for inciting women to not pay the tax on water, but the charges were eventually dropped, and in 1960 the water rates on women were abolished. The official reason given for eliminating the rates was that "socially and economically, the earnings of the vast majority of women in the region are so intertwined with those of their husbands that accurate assessment of women for rates is impossible" — one of the women's own early arguments.[73]

In addition to the continual protests against the water rates, the AWU became involved in another fracas with the government. As mentioned earlier, July 29 to August 1, 1948, the AWU celebrated the fact that the Alake had left Abeokuta for the second time. Annually thereafter they celebrated what they considered a victory. In July 1952, with the Alake back on the throne, the AWU still applied to the police for a parade permit to continue to celebrate his former departure. The permit to parade was denied, although permission was granted for a celebration to take place at a site of the women's choice. The women considered this reaction as harassment due to their continued opposition to the Alake, the makeup of the Central Council, and the water rates. Therefore, they resolved to march anyway. Notably, they gathered at FRK's home to begin the march. The police attempted to stop them and used tear gas on the women. Forty-two women were arrested, including FRK, and as many injured. When the arrested women were jailed, hundreds of their supporters went to the British residency to maintain a vigil. The jail was nearby and the women sang to their sisters in jail who responded in song (*West African Pilot*, July 30, 1952). The women stayed until the next afternoon when those arrested were released on bail.

FRK once again wrote to her friends in Britain regarding the tear gassing of the women. On August 19 in the House of Commons, Sorensen questioned the use of tear gas. In early September, Lyttleton wrote to Sorensen, acknowledging the use of tear gas and supporting it as justified.[74] On September 3, forty-one of those arrested were fined £5 each; FRK was found guilty of collecting people for unlawful assembly and fined £10.

In 1958, FRK was once again elected to a seat on the council, representing Kemta district where she lived. By this time, she was very active in the National Council of Nigeria and the Cameroons (NCNC), a nationalist political party (chap. 5).

The AWU was not only involved in protest activities but also initiated a number of self-help projects targeted specifically at women. They operated a weaving corporation, ran a maternity and child welfare clinic, and continued to conduct literacy classes.[75] FRK also started to publish a small newspaper, *Nigerian Woman*, but only a few issues seem to have appeared between 1951 and late 1952.[76]

As a result of the campaign against the Alake and the SNA system, FRK became a national and international heroine in the struggle for women's rights. As early as 1948 she received a request from a group of women in Kano (a very old and major city in northern Nigeria) to aid them in founding a branch of the AWU there.[77] Another Kano resident (a male), Alhaji Alibabaru, wrote to FRK, congratulating her on her work with the Abeokuta women and soliciting her help in organizing Hausa women in the North.[78] One author has remarked that the women's wings of the two political parties in the North, the Northern People's Congress (NPC) and the Northern Elements Progressive Union (NEPU), "drew inspiration from Mrs. Ransome-Kuti."[79] At its second annual conference in July 1958, the women's wing of NEPU resolved to "affiliate with the NWU under the leadership of Mrs. Funmilayo Ransome-Kuti."[80] FRK was committed to struggle for the enfranchisement, education, and political representation of women in northern Nigeria, who due to early differences in the colonial structure, as well as a more restrictive practice of Islam, often fell behind their southern sisters when it came to the rights of women.[81]

In May 1949, the AWU resolved to go national to increase support for its long-term objectives of the enfranchisement of all women in Nigeria and their equal participation with men in the political process. At an AWU meeting on May 15, 1949, FRK proposed the founding of the Nigerian Women's Union (NWU). The proposal passed and the executive committee of the AWU became the executive committee of the NWU, Abeokuta branch. FRK took primary responsibility for organizing branches of the NWU all over the country. Thus began her foray into the organizing of women on a national basis.

Notes

1. The Majeobaje Society was formed secretly in 1947 by Western-educated men who sought progressive change in Abeokuta. Its president was Rev. I. O. Ransome-Kuti. The Ogboni was a traditional secret society that was comprised mostly of men and exercised considerable political influence and power (chap. 1).

2. Rev. O. A. Oke, speech, Centenary Hall, Abeokuta, Aug. 22, 1948, quoted in Aloba, *Fall of a Ruler*, 10–22.

3. FRK, interview, Abeokuta, Apr. 3, 1976. See also "The One and Only Mrs. Ransom-Kuti," *Women's World*, June 1973.

4. Soyinka, *Ake*, 181.

5. For more information, see Oyemakinde, "Pullen Marketing Scheme"; Johnson-Odim, "Female Leadership during the Colonial Period"; Mba, *Nigerian Women Mobilized;* Tamuno, *Nigeria and Elective Representation*.

6. Soyinka, *Ake*, 199–200.

7. Quoted in Odugbesan, "Béère."

8. FRK, interview, Abeokuta, June 23, 1976.

9. For more information on Tinubu, see Biobaku, *Eminent Nigerians.*

10. Much of the information on Ademola's succession comes from FRK's sixteen-page handwritten memoir, FRK Papers.

11. Alake Ademola II, interview, Nigerian Broadcasting System, Feb. 1, 1954. We located this interview in the Abeokuta Archives in 1976.

12. Adebesin, *Egba History and Life Review,* 59.

13. Oluwole Coker, interview, Lagos, June 16, 1989.

14. Ibid.; Ebenezer Taiwo Thomas, interview, Lagos, June 15, 1989; Oluremi Adebayo, interview, Lagos, June 10, 1989.

15. R-K to Ṣolanke, May 19, 1932, box 1, file 1, no. 6, Ṣolanke Papers.

16. FRK to Ṣolanke, box 2, file 6, nos. 18 and 19, Ṣolanke Papers.

17. Ajisafe, *Abeokuta Centenary,* 24. In 1930, the Alake was the proud owner of a Rolls Royce. See *Daily Times,* Oct. 22, 1930.

18. "Important Societies in Abeokuta," file no. 49, Egba Council Archives.

19. Chief Secretary's Office, 23 61 o/s.55, vols. 1 and 2, Nigerian National Archives, Ibadan.

20. Soyinka, *Ake,* 185.

21. AWU, *Constitution.*

22. "Analysis of the Audit," FRK Papers.

23. Aloba, *Fall of a Ruler.*

24. Files on Dipeomu, 254351, Egba Council Archives.

25. Annual Report, Abeokuta Province, 1936 and 1947, Egba Council Archives.

26. "A.W.U.'s Grievances," FRK Papers.

27. Iṣola, "History of Ifo," 33.

28. Aloba, *Fall of a Ruler,* 13.

29. Ibid., 21.

30. Makinde, interview, *Vanguard,* Oct. 1, 1985.

31. Copy of Charter Rules of the AWU, FRK Papers.

32. FRK, interview, Abeokuta, July 7, 1976.

33. Over two hundred songs are in the FRK Papers. On the women's evidence, see also, Minutes, Lagos Town Council meeting, Nov. 23, 1947.

34. *Vanguard,* Oct. 1, 1985.

35. FRK, interview, Abeokuta, July 7, 1976.

36. R-K to Ṣolanke, box 8, file 3, no. 31, Ṣolanke Papers.

37. Oluremi Adebayo, interview, Ibadan, June 7, 1989. He retired in 1950 (unrelated to Ademola's return) and relocated the family in Ibadan.

38. Document, file 40, FRK Papers. See also, FRK, diary, Aug. 21, 1946, FRK Papers.

39. Annual Report, Abeokuta Province, 1947, Egba Council Archives.

40. Files, no. 22706, Ministry of Local Government, Ibadan.

41. Ashabi was allegedly the Alake's mistress. She later joined the women's section of the Egbe Atunluse, which opposed FRK.

42. FRK never did find out what "good soul" paid her tax but suspected it was the British resident himself or the Alake.

43. FRK, interview, Abeokuta, July 12, 1976; Bekolari Ransome-Kuti, interview, Lagos, June 15, 1989. Beko was a young boy at home at the time. See also Aloba, *Fall of a Ruler.*

44. None of those discussing this incident, including the male informant who described Oro, would consent to be identified. We learned of this in 1989, too late to ask FRK herself.

45. Soyinka, *Ake,* 213. Interestingly, this seems to have set a precedent. A September 20, 1964, article in the *Nigerian Tribune* reported that women members of the Action Group and the NCNC danced at Emeko to an oro drum beaten by a rival party that had hoped it could be used to scare the women away.

46. All of the songs are in the FRK Papers.

47. *Funmilayo Ransome-Kuti v. E. N. Mylius,* suit no. 1943, Supreme Court of Nigeria, Ibadan Judicial Division, copies in FRK Papers.

48. Soyinka, *Ake,* 211.

49. Soyinka reports that during the demonstrations one woman gave birth to a baby girl, which the women considered profoundly propitious because the child was a girl. See *Ake,* 217.

50. FRK, interview, Abeokuta, July 12, 1976; Amelia Osimosu, interview, Abeokuta, July 17, 1976.

51. AWU, "Abeokuta Women's Union Grievances," FRK Papers.

52. Madam O.X.Y.A.Z.A. to FRK, Apr. 30, 1948, biography box, FRK Papers.

53. Annual Report, Abeokuta Province, 1948, Egba Council Archives.

54. "Ademola's Temporary Abdication", file 47, and minutes, Egba Native Administration Council meeting, file 47, Egba Council Archives.

55. Nora Majekodunmi, interview, Lagos, June 10, 1989.

56. Poster (2' × 18"), Egba Council Archives. See also Milburn speech, Aug. 1, 1949, transcript, FRK Papers.

57. FRK to Sorensen and FRK to Creech-Jones, FRK Papers.

58. Annual Report, Abeokuta Province, 1948, Egba Council Archives.

59. FRK, interview, Abeokuta, July 7, 1976.

60. See papers, box 73, file 8(g), Solanke Papers.

61. "Ademola's Temporary Abdication," file 47, Egba Council Archives; Little, *African Women in Towns,* 72.

62. See for instance, *Daily Times,* Oct. 14, 1978; *Nigerian Herald,* Oct. 14, 1978; *New Breed Magazine,* May 1975.

63. Little, *African Women in Towns,* 72.

64. A questionnaire was circulated among Egba men in Abeokuta and sur-

rounding districts in which 32,590 respondents favored women's representation on the council while 47,874 were against it. Chief Secretary's Office, file 2623521 on ENA reorganization, National Archives, Ibadan.

65. Schofield, speech to Egba Central Council, Sept. 28, 1950, Egba Archives, Abeokuta; "Agreement" (signed by Ademola), box 8, file 4, no. 47, Ṣolanke Papers; "Agreement" also in IORK Papers; *Daily Times,* Oct. 14, 1950. See also, R-K to Ṣolanke, Feb. 5, 1951, box 8, file 4, no. 47, Ṣolanke Papers.

66. Rev. Ransome-Kuti was also isolated from secret discussions about Ademola's return. His good friend Rev. E. O. Alayande, a member of the AG, recalled a time when there was an NUT meeting at Alayande's house where Rev. Ransome-Kuti was present. Ademola drove up to the house, wishing to speak with Alayande, who didn't want the reverend or Ademola to be aware of one another's presence. Alayande phoned Awolowo and arranged for Ademola to go elsewhere. Rev. Ransome-Kuti was identified as being supportive of the AWU's position and opposed to Ademola's reinstatement.

67. Ṣolanke to Rev. R-K, Mar. 24, 1950, and Ṣolanke to Rev. R-K and FRK, Feb. 13, 1951, box 8, file 3, no. 31a, Ṣolanke Papers.

68. "Agreement," Jan. 15, 1951, box 8, file 4, no. 47, Ṣolanke Papers.

69. FRK to Creech-Jones, Mar. 31, 1951, FRK Papers.

70. Ṣolanke to FRK, Sept. 29, 1952, box 73, file 8 (w), Ṣolanke Papers. See also box 13, files 8 and 9, Ṣolanke Papers.

71. Petition, FRK Papers.

72. General correspondence, FRK Papers.

73. This is a quote from the then Western Region premier, Samuel Akintola. See *Daily Times,* Mar. 18, 1960. In 1959, Obafemi Awolowo, head of the AG, accused FRK of retarding the progress of the Egba people by campaigning against the water rates and challenged her to go to Ijebu where women paid them and where he thought she would not receive support for her campaign against the water rates. See *Daily Times,* May 1, 1959.

74. FRK to Sorensen and FRK to Creech-Jones, copies in FRK Papers. She also wrote to the Women's International Democratic Federation (WIDF), which sent letters of support and helped in publicizing the incident (chap. 6).

75. Little, *West African Urbanization,* 127–28.

76. FRK, interview, Abeokuta, Aug. 10, 1976. See also application for license to publish and correspondence with O. Adeneye, a Nigerian journalist resident in London; biography box, both in FRK Papers; FRK to Ṣolanke, Oct. 29, 1952, box 73, file 8, Ṣolanke Papers.

77. Letter dated Apr. 5, 1948, FRK Papers.

78. Alibabaru to FRK, Mar. 6, 1948, FRK Papers.

79. Little, *African Women in Towns,* 63–64.

80. Sklar, *Nigerian Political Parties,* 419.

81. Ibid., 402.

"A True Citizen": The National Arena

Funmilayo Ransome-Kuti was a nationalist who neither exhibited nor tolerated ethnocentrism in her personal or public life, and she discouraged it in all the organizations she headed or was affiliated with. She demonstrated an extraordinarily vigilant civic consciousness by which she judged traditional, colonial, and independence political authorities and found them wanting. Her citizenship was informed by her feminism and socialism, not by mere partisan politics, and definitely not by ethnicity. For instance, she was consistently critical of the Northern People's Congress (NPC) Party government in northern Nigeria not because of its control of the federal government nor its interference in the government of the Western Region but because it disenfranchised and discriminated against women and because it oppressed and neglected the masses.

Her feminism included a nationalistic element. Despite her genuine commitment to international feminist solidarity (chap. 6), FRK recognized a priority of nationalist feminist allegiance, evident in her comments on the lyrics of the Nigerian national anthem, which had been composed years earlier by Lady Flora Lugard (née Shaw), a well-known colonial correspondent and author and the wife of Lord Frederick Lugard, former governor of Nigeria: "It is most surprising that it was not possible to find a person within 30,000,000 people capable enough to compose our national anthem. We as women are proud to see that the anthem had been composed by a woman. But we would have wished her to be a Nigerian woman. We hope she will pardon us for this expression. It is only natural that we should feel that."[1]

We have seen how in 1949 the Abeokuta Women's Union (AWU) had moved into Ijebu Province to support women there in their campaign against the SNA system and poll tax on women. By the end of 1949, the SNA system had been abolished throughout Abeokuta and Ijebu Provinces, and the AWU had become the Nigerian Women's Union (NWU). Branches of the NWU had been established in Ijebu-Ode, Ijebu-Remo, Ilaro, and Egbado areas. Thus, the NWU was ready to move further afield. As a result of her successes in Abeokuta and Ijebu, FRK had achieved national fame and was invited to visit a number of organizations and communities. She visited Benin, Ibadan, Calabar, and Aba (all in Nigeria) in 1948–49; in each of these towns she asked to speak to the women, calling on them to organize their own unions. Subsequently, branches of the NWU were formed in these four towns.

In Aba, FRK was welcomed by Margaret Ekpo, who had already done some preliminary work by organizing an Aba Women's Association. During a reception for FRK, Ekpo gave a purse (i.e., money collected by the members) to her. FRK handed it back as her contribution to the Aba Women's Association, stating that women leaders must place themselves on the same level as the poorest women. FRK's visit encouraged Ekpo to continue her work among Aba women. She wrote to FRK:

> I cannot explain to you what new spirit you have poured into me. I am now 100 times stronger than before. I have printed our constitution [NWU Aba branch] into English, Efik and Ibo. I want to surprise the women [in Aba] on the 14th January to tell them of the wonderful inspiration I have derived from you.[2]

FRK visited Enugu with an NWU delegation in December 1949, just after a violent confrontation between Enugu coal miners and the police, in which some miners were killed. FRK's delegation was received by the Enugu Women's Association (formed in 1945) by Janet Okala, G. I. Okoye, and Madam Peter Okoye. In honor of her visit, the association changed its name to the Nigerian Women's Union, Enugu branch. The NWU's visit was hailed by both the *Daily Times* and the *West African Pilot* on December 18, 1949, as a sign of women's nationalist solidarity. The Enugu women were apparently very impressed and inspired by FRK. As Okala put it: "Before that time women at Enugu had no right to probe into the affairs of their country. Mrs. Kuti on her arrival educated us."[3]

By 1950, NWU branches were established in Enugu, Aba, Benin, Ijebu-Ode, Ikare, and Onitsha. From 1950–53 many more branches were founded, especially in the North (Zaria, Kaduna, Jos, Kano, Jebba, Kafanchan, Funtua, and Ilorin) but also in the West (Ekiti, Ilesha, and

Ade-Ekiti) and East (Asaba and Abakaliki). In effect, the NWU was a federation of autonomous branches: each branch was concerned primarily with the interests of the women in its area, with a national executive committee that focused more concern on national issues affecting all Nigerian women. FRK was the president of the NWU, as well as of the Abeokuta branch; Ekpo served as national secretary while remaining president of the Aba branch.

The specified political objectives of the NWU were (1) the achievement of the franchise for women, (2) the abolition of electoral colleges, and (3) the allocation of a definite proportion of political representation to women, with women being allowed to nominate their own representatives on the local councils (which should not be headed by traditional rulers). The union disclaimed affiliation with any political party—rather it saw itself as nonpartisan.[4]

In 1953, FRK, as NWU president, invited all women's organizations in Nigeria to a two-day conference in Abeokuta (Aug. 5–7, 1953). The conference was attended by four hundred delegates from fifteen provinces and from several organizations as well as the NWU, including the Women's Movement, founded by Elizabeth Adekogbe in Ibadan in 1952.

Participants at the conference, which FRK described "as a parliament of the women of Nigeria," resolved "that this assembly be known as the Federation of Nigerian Women's Societies [FNWS], where the voice of all Nigerian women will be heard and known." As FRK explained: "This organization is a combination. . . . It does not debar anyone from carrying on with her own private organization." In the elections to the executive, care was taken to ensure that offices were distributed among representatives from various areas of Nigeria.[5] There was a battle of wills between Adekogbe and FRK, who won, and the Women's Movement of Ibadan, which Adekogbe had founded, withdrew from the FNWS. Subsequently, Adekogbe's group affiliated with the Action Group (AG) Women's Association.

The conference passed several resolutions. First, women should be represented in all local councils, with a proportion of the seats in all legislative houses allocated to them and with the women selecting their own candidates. Second, there should be universal adult suffrage, with symbols introduced in elections for the benefit of illiterate voters. Third, whenever a law was to be introduced, the FNWS should be informed and its opinion sought.

These resolutions embodied the federation's main political platform,

which was essentially identical to that of the NWU. After the conference, FRK wrote the federation's constitution; it stated that some objectives of the FNWS included (1) to encourage the womenfolk of Nigeria
to take part in the political, social, cultural, and economic life of their
country, (2) to create facilities for female education, and (3) generally,
to raise the status of women and to win equal opportunities for women.

At the second annual conference (July 30–31, 1954, Enugu), the
FNWS congratulated the Eastern Region government for introducing
universal adult suffrage on a nontaxation basis and demanded that the
other regions follow suit. In August 1954, FRK undertook a tour of the
North to campaign for the franchise for women.

In her spoken and written addresses to the NWU and FNWS, FRK
propounded a feminist consciousness and ideology. She acknowledged
that women were victimized by their social conditioning, which led
them to internalize a negative self-image and to be passive and apathetic:
"As women we still feel that we are inferior to men, we inherited this
feeling from our mothers whose spirits had been subdued with slavery
and we have to join hands together to shake off this feeling so that the
forthcoming Independence may be of reality to us." Believing that certain marriage customs, such as polygyny and "bride price," worsened
the situation for women, FRK wrote in reference to men in polygynous
marriages: "They smile while their wives weep. Women . . . were created with blood and flesh like men. I wonder how a man could tolerate
any of his wives should have a male friend. . . . I think this attitude of
disrespect to women's feelings was caused by the fact that the purchase
price had been paid on the women."[6] The NWU (and FRK personally)
opposed polygyny and the system by which a man paid a "bride price"
(in money or in kind) to the family of his wife, which entitled him to
sole custody of the couple's children. While the bride price did *not* signal
that he actually "bought" or "owned" his wife, in practice it often reinforced male domination in the marriage; since the bride price would
have to be returned in whole or part in the case of divorce, it also often
operated to discourage women from leaving unsatisfactory marriages.
In one speech, FRK appealed to women to put their gender solidarity
before political party allegiances. This, of course, is a universal feminist
ideal that is—equally universally—seldom achieved in reality.

In a June 2, 1957, article in the *Sunday Times,* FRK called for full self-
government for Nigeria by 1959 and further stated: "Adequate representation of women in all legislatures should be guaranteed. . . . I am appeal-

ing to every woman in Nigeria to realize the importance and urgency of the need for the emancipation of our womanhood. We should be awake and accept our responsibilities by intensifying the contributions we are making toward the progress of Nigeria." FRK's feminism was way ahead of her time in Nigeria; it appears that only a handful of the members of the NWU and FNWS were in a position to support fully and articulate these ideas.

Like the NWU, the FNWS was not affiliated with any political party, even though most of its leaders were members of the NCNC (e.g., FRK, Ekpo, Mrs. Fashina, Mrs. G. I. Okoye, and Felicia Obua). This inevitably created tension because the NCNC headquarters pressured some of the NCNC members of the federation to affiliate it with the NCNC. Indeed, at the second annual conference of the FNWS, FRK felt it necessary to issue a policy statement on the issue: "The FNWS is independent . . . ready to cooperate and support any political party that works for the uplift and progress of womanhood and for the happiness of Nigerian citizens as a whole."

This did not satisfy the NCNC, and the pressure by the party head-quarters on its women members continued. On August 4, 1959, the NCNC National Executive Committee called on all women members of the party to withdraw immediately from the FNWS (*West African Pilot,* Aug. 5, 1959). At the same time, Ekpo resigned from the federation on the grounds that the "union (NWU) was originally founded on a cultural basis but later embarked on political functions."[7]

The directive to withdraw was not well received by the NCNC women in Onitsha, Enugu, and Aba, who at first refused to believe it. Immediately thereafter, the Enugu NCNC Women's Wing received a letter from the Lagos headquarters, signed by Kolawole Balogun, order-ing the NCNC women to withdraw from the FNWS. Perplexed, Mrs. G. I. Okoye of the Enugu branch wrote to FRK on August 17: "We want your advice on the way to do it because they told us to take ourself [*sic*] out and we like your organization."[8]

Not only did the NWU and the FNWS remain steadfastly indepen-dent of the NCNC, despite political pressure from the party, but both organizations consistently criticized NCNC policies toward women, while ignoring similar policies by the Action Group (AG)—for ex-ample, the failure to nominate women candidates. As president of the NWU and FNWS, FRK wrote frequently to Nnamdi Azikiwe and other NCNC leaders, appealing for women to be nominated as candidates for local, regional, and federal elections. Since this was the party to which she belonged at the time, she showed integrity in criticizing her own party. For example, in 1958 the NWU petitioned the NCNC headquarters about the refusal of the branch in Sapele to sponsor Felicia Obua as a candidate for the Western Regional local elections. This may be why, not long after (see below), the NCNC refused to back her candidacy.

From 1956–59, FRK was at the same time president of both the NWU and FNWS and of the Western Region NCNC Women's Wing. While she maintained that the roles were completely separate and insisted that the NWU and FNWS remained politically independent, there is little doubt that the roles overlapped. The NWU may not have been affiliated to the NCNC, but it was certainly sympathetic to it. That confusion arose over FRK's dual roles is attested to by a letter from Obua to her: "Surely I did meet you as the president of the Western Region N.C.N.C. Women's Wing and not of the N.W.U."[9]

In 1958 at a conference on women in the North (Jos), the FNWS formed an alliance with the Women's Wing of the Northern Elements Progressive Union (NEPU), a socialist-oriented party based in the North that was allied with the NCNC. Following the conference, on August 19, 1958, FRK led a joint delegation of the FNWS and NEPU women to the office of the Northern Region premier at Kaduna. The delegation demanded that unless the franchise was given to women in the North, the Northern Region should agree to a reduction in the number of its seats in the federal House of Representatives. The women argued that since representation in the House was supposed to be proportional to the voting population, if the women in the North were not allowed to vote, they should not be included in the population count in the North. This politically explosive argument was totally unacceptable to the North because, if based only on its male population, the Northern Region's representation at the national level would be cut in half. The delegation also complained that NEPU women were discriminated against in education and employment and were harassed by the police.

Another FNWS delegation—this time to the governor general—composed of these same members, along with representatives of the Western and Mid-Western Region women, was undertaken in August 1959 (*West African Pilot*, Aug. 21, 1959). Once again, the main issue was the franchise for the Northern Region women. The delegation informed the governor general that if the Northern Region women were denied the franchise the FNWS wanted him to advise the constitutional conference that the number of seats allocated to the Northern Region in the enlarged House should be drastically reduced and that seats should be reserved for women in both legislative houses. At a press conference held by the delegation after the interview with the governor general, FRK declared that if the constitutional conference still rejected their demand for the franchise, "We have friends among [British] MPs. We can write to them to see what they can do for us." However, neither external nor internal pressure was sufficient to affect the North's rigid attachment to an exclusively male franchise, a position unchanged until 1977.

The alliance between the FNWS and the NEPU Women's Wing was further cemented by the close personal relationship between FRK and Mallama Sawabo Gambo, the NEPU Women's Wing leader. They exchanged visits and letters and supported each other's political activities. In 1959, when FRK sought the NCNC nomination for the federal election, Gambo wrote to her: "We Northern women have made a decision on this matter and we have forwarded a letter to the National President to the effect that Mrs. Ransome-Kuti must be nominated for election; any decision by the National Election Commission (NEC) to the contrary would be vehemently opposed."[10] When Funmilayo Ransome-Kuti lost the NCNC nomination in the 1959 federal election, some speculated that she would contest as an FNWS candidate (*Daily Service*, May 29, 1959). Although this did not materialize, she ran as an independent (see below). With her consequent expulsion from the NCNC, she lost some of the politicized members of the FNWS and the active support of Gambo.

The shrinking membership of the movement was furthered by the emergence in 1959 of a new rival women's organization, the National Council of Women's Societies (NCWS). The initiative for the NCWS's formation was taken by several of FRK's rivals and political opponents: Elizabeth Adekogbe, Mrs. T. Ogunlesi, and Mrs. Wuraola Esan — all active in the AG Women's Association. Also among active NCWS members were Oyinkan Abayomi and Kofoworola Ademola (daughter-in-law of Alake Ademola II). Partly because of the influence of its high-status members and partly because the NCWS defined itself as nonpolitical, the organization received an annual government subvention and was regarded by government as *the* organization representing women. The group was far less active in either articulating women's interests or attempting to influence the government than was the NWU or FNWS. Moreover, its leadership lacked the mass appeal of the charismatic FRK. The NWU and FNWS had first identified and articulated the interests of women in a way in which they had never been nationally represented or articulated. The NCWS simply built on the foundation laid by FRK. Although the FNWS continued to operate, after 1959 its scope gradually shrank to Abeokuta, and it ended up as a basically one-woman movement.

FRK was one of four female members of the Abeokuta Urban District Council (AUDC), which was created in 1950. She represented the Egba Alake section of Abeokuta. Women there were among the first to be involved in local government in Nigeria.[11] But from 1952 she was not appointed to the council—a situation that she blamed on the Alake. Instead, her position on the council was filled by Remi Aiyedun who also was nominated to the Western House of Assembly in 1953 (chap. 4).

On June 27, 1952, the AWU sent a letter to the council protesting FRK's exclusion from the council and expressing their lack of confidence in the female council members. Yet one of those councilwomen was Amelia Osimosu, formerly one of the top leaders of the AWU but one who had become very critical of FRK. Moreover, by 1952 Osimosu was an active member of the AG and later an AG organizing secretary. Since FRK was affiliated with the NCNC, political party differences clearly encouraged a split between the two women.

As an index to change in political alignments, it is interesting to note that one of the most constant and vociferous critics of FRK was Chief J. O. Kashimawo, who had accused the AWU of financial improprieties (*Daily Service,* Sept. 9, 1949). Osimosu had answered these charges in a lengthy detailed letter published in the *Daily Service* on September 22, 1949. But by 1952 both Osimosu and Kashimawo were members of the AG and political opponents of FRK.

On July 9, 1952, FRK presented a petition to the AUDC in which she accused the Alake of being responsible for her not having been selected as the Egba Alake section women's representative. The sectional Oba held a special meeting with Ademola to discuss the issue. Ademola rejected the charges, insisting that the sectional council members alone selected their own representative (*Daily Service,* July 11, 1952).

FRK regularly seized opportunities to criticize the council. For instance, she attacked the council's ban on drumming by societies as a means of summoning meetings; she saw the ban as a way of curtailing the Majeobaje Society, which was no longer viewed as supportive of her after her husband's death in 1955 (chap. 7). In the petition, she claimed that most of the council members were illiterate and under the thumb of the Alake. This criticism was understandably resented by the councillors, who included a number of highly literate members of the Western House of Assembly, such as D. Adegbenro and A. Adedamola, *and* by the illiterate councillors, such as Alhaja Ejuwura who pointed out that she personally was surprised that FRK did not exclude the female members from her attack (*Daily Service,* July 8, 1952). In addition, both FRK and her husband were involved in drawing up and supporting the Egba Constitution when provisions were made for illiterate members. The only explanation for FRK's attack seems to be her desire to confront the Alake, who was positioned to thwart her efforts, and did so, often in ways that could not be traced directly to him.

The fact that FRK was not selected by her section reflects the opposition to her from the Ogboni and other chiefs, who supported Ademola's reinstatement (chap. 4). Nonetheless, when the Western Region Local Council election was held in 1958—and women voted—FRK was elected on the NCNC platform to represent the Kemta ward.

Within the council, as in the Western House of Assembly, the AG constituted the majority party and the NCNC the minority. FRK was appointed by the NCNC members as their leader, that is, the opposition leader. She was an active hardworking member of the AUDC. She was a member of the Assessment, Tenement Scheme, Education, and Finance Committees. Eniola Soyinka and Amelia Osimosu (relatives of FRK and former members of the AWU executive committee) were also on the AUDC, elected on the AG platform, and though the three women served together on some committees their political differences often became quite bitter. Thus, party allegiance obfuscated female solidarity.

In 1956, just before the Western Region elections, FRK and Osimosu clashed publicly. In Ogunmakun, a village on the boundary between Ibadan and Abeokuta Provinces, FRK had mobilized traders who were NCNC supporters to leave the traditional market site sanctioned by the local council and create a new market. AG women traders complained to Osimosu that this was disrupting their business. Osimosu reported the matter to the Alake but his intervention failed to change the situation so she traveled to Ibadan, reporting to Ayo Rosiji, who was the federal legislator for the area, Egba East, and AG general secretary. Rosiji then called on the regional representative, Hon. S. O. Ṣogbein and advised him to get the local council to move the market to the new site, thus taking the steam out of FRK's gesture. This was done and the AG retained its seats in the election.[12] At a meeting on August 7, 1958, Osimosu berated the AWU members who had gathered in support of FRK, shouting: "You worthless women, if you continue to follow Mrs. Ransome-Kuti, when she receives the bullet you will all scatter."[13]

At this time, as discussed in chapter 4, the AWU was campaigning against the payment of water rates and taxes by women and thus incurred the opposition of the AG government, legislators, and council members. FRK frequently complained of harassment by Egba AG legislators such as Adegbenro, Kotoye, and Ṣogbein, and reported such instances to the police. In addition, the NWU sued Adegbenro and Ṣogbein in the Ake grade "I" native court for interrupting their meetings and verbally abusing them. The case was later dismissed (*Southern Nigerian Defender*, Jan. 19, 1958).

There is no doubt that such politically inspired harassment operated within each region against its minorities, ethnic and/or political. In 1959, the AG chairman of the AUDC, Chief Toye Coker, asked "the government of the Western Region to institute an inquiry into the AWU" (*West African Pilot*, May 11, 1959). Coker's motion referred specifically to FRK's visits to communist countries and to the financial affairs of the AWU. According to the *West African Pilot*, this move was an act of reprisal following Obafemi Awolowo's (AG leader) threat that if the Eastern Region government insisted on probing the affairs of the Calabar Ogoja Rivers State (COR) Movement (an AG-supported non-Igbo organization in the East where Igbos were one of the majority populations, and the AG was primarily identified with the Yoruba people of the Western region) in Eastern Nigeria then he would institute inquiries into the activities of the NCNC. Since FRK was an NCNC leader in Abeokuta and equated with the AWU, the AWU was vulnerable to such harassment. On the day of Coker's motion, FRK was absent and the nomination was dismissed; it never came to a vote. Not long afterward, FRK was expelled from the NCNC (see below), and in the subsequent local government election she lost her seat, never regaining entry into the AUDC.

While FRK was very active in the politics of Abeokuta in 1949, she was also well aware of political developments on a national scale. Careful not to repeat the mistakes of the Richards Constitution, the colonial government insisted on convening constitutional conferences at which Nigerian leaders, "traditional" and "modern," were invited to express their views on the proposed new constitution. There were regional conferences at Ibadan, Enugu, and Kaduna in 1949 and an all-Nigeria conference in Ibadan in January 1950.

FRK was invited to the Ibadan conference as one of the representatives of Abeokuta Province. She was the only woman present at the conference and must have been chosen as acknowledgment of her leadership role in Abeokuta, though she saw herself as a representative of all Nigerian women. She spoke on the right of women as well as men to vote. In this demand, she received more support from the Eastern Region delegation than from the Northern and Western delegates. She also criticized the proposed system of indirect election through electoral colleges as undemocratic. On the question of the creation of a House of Chiefs, she was more in sympathy with the Eastern delegates than with those from her own region: she argued that traditional rulers had no role in a modern democratic Nigeria and that there should not be a House of Chiefs in the East. This was a particularly sticky historical point because many of the chiefs in the East were in fact creations of the colonial hierarchy and had not existed in the traditional system, unlike in the West and North. This view was also, however, fully consistent with her fierce opposition to the SNA system in Abeokuta, which had distorted the powers and scope of the traditional office of Alake.

The 1951 Macpherson Constitution that emerged from the conferences instituted two political parties in addition to the NCNC: the Action Group (AG) in the Western Region and the Northern People's Congress (NPC) in the Northern Region, both of which contested in the 1951 election.

The elections for the new regional Houses of Assembly and Chiefs under the new constitution took place between August and September 1951. In 1951, Nigerians, except for a relative few in Lagos and Calabar, had no experience in voting. The constitution gave only a limited chance to increase this experience, by restricting popular participation to voting in the primary electoral colleges of a three-tiered system (primary, intermediate, and final electoral colleges). At the primary college level, there was taxpayer suffrage in the West and East, though in the North only male taxpayers could vote. This meant, as FRK pointed out, "that the majority of women were eliminated from the whole show as there were only very few women who paid income tax."[14]

FRK had the distinction of being the only female candidate in the 1951 election. She contested on the NCNC platform for the primary college in Kemta ward, Abeokuta, Egba Division.[15] Her opponent was Ayo Rosiji, an Egba lawyer based in Ibadan running on the AG platform. Rosiji was one of those whom FRK described caustically as "the professional sons of Egbaland, with good posts elsewhere [who] thought themselves a bit more highly enlightened and civilized than their fathers, brothers, and sisters at home . . . who besieged Egbaland [in] luxurious cars . . . to offer their services in different places for the House of Assembly and to preach party politics not easily accepted by the Egbas" (*West African Pilot*, Nov. 3, 1951).

Rosiji had been active in the political maneuvers that reinstated Ademola as Alake, which indeed the AG supported as a matter of policy because at that time it identified with the traditional rulers of the Western Region. Therefore, FRK received support for her candidacy by categorizing Rosiji as one of those who wanted to sell Egbaland.[16] FRK was much better known in Abeokuta than Rosiji, who had been overseas during the women's protests. She won the primary college election on August 13, 1951.

After that, in her own words, "corruption began to creep in . . . because of the government announcement on August 23 stating the allowances for representatives in the new Houses of Assembly and the House of Representatives. . . . The thought of money had a big influence on the minds of many farmers."[17] FRK was defeated at the intermediate electoral college on September 10, observing cynically, "There was an interval of a fortnight between the voting in the intermediate and the final colleges during which period a great deal happened. The talk of the hour was 'since the successful candidates will receive £300 pounds a year those who were nominated must pay for our votes.'" The result, according to FRK, was that "far too many of the candidates were unworthy of the Egba people's representation at home and abroad."[18] While there may be an element of "sour grapes" in her judgment, she repeated the same criticisms of the electoral system years later in a letter to M. A. Majekodunmi: "I know it is bad all over Nigeria but the wickedness and the corruptions started from the West in [the] 1951 [election]."[19] In her analysis of the 1951 election, FRK declared what would become the guiding principle of the rest of her political career: "Many people felt that if women could have played a prominent part in voting, things would have been much better done, and there would have been no disappointment in choosing the right candidates. Women are earnestly praying for the day when there will be universal adult suffrage so that once again they can assist the men to do things properly."[20]

Since it was obviously not feasible to transform the Nigerian Women's Union into a political party, it seemed to FRK, with justification, that the NCNC was the most sympathetic to women's participation and thus the most appropriate party for her to associate with in the electoral sphere while simultaneously working with the NWU.

As mentioned in chapter 1, both Ransome-Kutis were founding members of the NCNC. In 1945 when the NCNC organized a nationwide campaign of protest against the Richards Constitution, FRK was the only woman present at the rally in Abeokuta (*Daily Service*, June 16, 1945), and at a later reception she presented the Abeokuta community's purse to the NCNC delegation (*West African Pilot*, Dec. 24, 1946). It was partly because she was well known as an articulate supporter of the party that she was selected to join the NCNC delegation to London in 1947 (chap. 6).

The NCNC had provided full support to the AWU'S campaign in Abeokuta, which was extensively publicized in the Azikiwe-owned newspaper, the *West African Pilot* (Azikiwe was the leader of the NCNC). Furthermore, Nnamdi Azikiwe personally spoke out in favor of universal suffrage, and the *West African Pilot* editorials argued in support of the AWU slogan, "no taxation without representation" (e.g., Mar. 31, 1948). The NCNC continued to press for extension of the suffrage during the succeeding years of partial, then complete self-government. The colonial administration extended the limited franchise of the 1951 election in stages. There was universal suffrage for the first time in the 1954 federal elections in the NCNC-governed Eastern Region, while in the West there was a taxation requirement for women. In the 1959 federal elections, there was universal suffrage in the South but only male taxpayers could vote in the North. When it came to the issue of the franchise for women in the Northern Region, both the NCNC and AG backed down when confronted with NPC intransigence. This was due to the need for conciliation with the North in order to ensure consensus for the timetable for independence. For FRK, this pragmatic position on northern woman suffrage was a source of great disillusionment with the NCNC.

Long before FRK broke with the NCNC and was expelled, she had publicly criticized the party's position on women, in cases where she felt it was no better than that of other parties. For instance, during the 1957 London Constitutional Conference, FRK wrote an article that attacked the three parties for officially excluding females from their delegations: "The three women on the delegations are unofficial advisers and observers; they are not even allowed near the hall. They could not express the views of women. Government should guarantee adequate representation of women in all legislatures. We should not be contented with being used as mere symbols and tools only at the polling stations."[21] Regardless of FRK's reservations, the public identified her as an NCNC member from 1950. This explains why, even though she was then the most famous and publicly assertive woman in the Western Region, she was not nominated as the special woman member to represent women in the Western House of Assembly in February 1953 by the Western Regional government, whose leader was Obafemi Awolowo, leader of the AG. Instead, Remi Aiyedun, an AUDC member, was nominated. Aiyedun herself believed that she was chosen on the recommendation of Alake Ademola (who was very close to Awolowo, since the AG had supported his reinstatement in 1950).[22] Indeed, Ademola and Awolowo were quite unlikely to nominate FRK. In 1955, when a second special member was appointed, another AG woman was appointed, Oyinkan Abayomi. Neither Abayomi nor Aiyedun was outspoken on behalf of the rights of women or the poor, as FRK would have been.

Funmilayo Ransome-Kuti fought resolutely to win the NCNC nomination in the next election. In the 1954 federal election, the Egba division of the NCNC at first proposed to nominate her. However, she traveled overseas shortly before the election and in her absence, unsure of her priorities, the party instead nominated J. A. O. Akande, who had been a clerk at the Abeokuta Grammar School when Rev. Ransome-Kuti was principal. When FRK returned, she contested the election as an independent but received only 334 votes to Akande's 2,575, which was enough to win him the Egba North seat in the House of Representatives.[23] When the 1956 Western Region election occurred, FRK half-heartedly applied for the NCNC nomination but again her stronger commitment was to her involvement in the Women's International Democratic Federation (WIDF). She was at a weeklong conference in China at the time the nominations were processed and therefore her name was not submitted (chap. 6).

The fact that FRK was not "on the ground" for possible nomination in the 1954 federal and 1956 regional elections meant that it was possible for the NCNC to temporarily evade the potentially contentious issue of nominating a female candidate. Before 1959 the NCNC had not nominated any women for any election. Margaret Ekpo had canvassed for support for nomination for the 1957 Eastern Region election but had been advised by Azikiwe that the election was too crucial to take the additional risk of presenting a woman candidate.[24] The same handicaps for women existed in the AG—no women were nominated for any election prior to 1959, when only two women were nominated for the federal election, Wuraola Esan (Ibadan) and R. T. Brown (Port Harcourt), and both lost.

In the 1959 federal election, the confrontation between FRK and the NCNC over the nomination of women could not be evaded. From 1956–59, FRK's involvement with the NCNC had strengthened. She was elected treasurer of the Western Nigerian Working Committee of the NCNC, the only woman member of the committee. As she noted: "The NCNC in Egba division elected me as treasurer after they felt I was a smart woman and I had the integrity to look after their funds."[25] As we have seen, she received the NCNC nomination for Kemta ward in the 1958 Western Region local government election and was elected leader of the NCNC opposition in the AUDC. It was reasonable therefore for her to expect the party's nomination for one of the Egba constituencies in the 1959 federal election.

This time FRK made sure she was "on seat" for the nomination process. She paid her £100 deposit in 1958, and in March 1959 the Egba Divisional Selection Committee nominated her as a candidate for the Egba Central constituency (i.e., Abeokuta). There were three other Egba constituencies: North, East, and South.[26] The incumbent member for Egba North, J. A. O. Akande, protested this decision and campaigned for his renomination. The chairman of the Egba division of the NCNC since 1957, G. S. Odunlami, happened to be Akande's father-in-law. Odunlami had competed against FRK in the 1951 election for nomination. He supported Akande's nomination and overruled the Egba Divisional Selection Committee. FRK protested against this flagrant partisanship, and a bitter dispute ensued. The matter was referred to the Western Region Working Committee of which FRK was a member. This notwithstanding, the chairman of that committee, A. M. F. Agbaje, a friend of Akande, supported Akande's nomination. This decision prompted a further dispute, with various sections of Abeokuta petitioning and counterpetitioning the committee. FRK refused to accept Agbaje's judgment.

On May 8, 1959, she telegramed Hon. J. O. Fadahunsi, first vice president of the NCNC, protesting against the May 3 decision of the working committee in favor of Akande: "Agbaje's unilateral decision unacceptable by us. State categorically now whether NCNC is Ogbonism or political party. Your immediate action requested to avoid complete NCNC destruction Egbaland."[27] The reference to "Ogbonism," which reflected FRK's parochial concern, probably was prompted by the fact that the organization of Egba Ogboni in the NCNC had sent a memorandum to the Egba Division Secretariat supporting Akande and accusing FRK of being uncooperative.

Fadahunsi wrote to Agbaje urging a meeting of leaders to settle the dispute, but this intervention achieved nothing. At this juncture, Agbaje was fighting to retain his position as chairman against T. O. S. Benson and E. A. Adisa, the latter like Agbaje an Ibadan man who belonged to a different faction of the Mabolaje Alliance of the NCNC. In the end, Agbaje lost to Benson in July 1959, but the committee upheld Agbaje's choice of Akande.

The dispute was referred to the NCNC National Executive committee, which set up an appeals committee for the Western Region, headed by Jaja Wachukwu. Memoranda and petitions were submitted to that committee in support of each contestant. One dated August 2, 1959, from the Strangers Elements Egba Central constituency (i.e., from the non-Egba and likely non-Yoruba residents in Abeokuta) highlights FRK's national appeal: "In the last registration we promised to abstain considering AG oppression till we heard that Mrs. Ransome-Kuti was nominated. Then we held a meeting and resolved to register: 20,886 women registered because of Mrs. Ransome-Kuti."[28] The memo also urged the committee to endorse FRK as the official candidate because of her popularity and past services for the NCNC. There was even a letter from a member of another Egba constituency, Egba East, that praised FRK for "the many registrations she did" (for the NCNC) and gave the example of a village called Ibafo where there had not been a single member of the NCNC before FRK converted them all.[29] There is no doubt that FRK had been extremely active in the registration campaign throughout the Western Region. As late as August 1958 she was a delegate to the NCNC Ondo provincial conference, where she delivered a speech and opened the floor to dance with the Hon. J. M. Johnson.[30]

FRK campaigned on her own behalf as well. She wrote to Azikiwe, expressing the hope that the Wachukwu team would come to Abeokuta and observe the situation for themselves. She complained that the AG was using chiefs brought into the NCNC by Odunlami (Akande's father-in-law) and that the AG was using the Alake to influence voters against her. She repeated that Agbaje was biased in favor of Akande.[31]

The Wachukwu team did not investigate. Even the national secretary of the NCNC, F. S. McEwen, conceded, "All they did was to send in a report that the Hon. Akande had refused to cooperate, and as such they were unable to proceed with the investigation they were asked to carry out." McEwen criticized the committee for its failure, saying the committee "showed neither initiative nor enterprise." Even though he thus acknowledged that Akande was uncooperative, McEwen called on FRK to be submissive and loyal to the local branch, asking her to "forgo what you believe to be your legitimate rights and to stand for Owode [Egba East] rather than Egba Central." McEwen recognized the danger that FRK might pose if she decided to stand as an independent. The party had already had such an experience in Ibadan where a faction led by E. A. Adisa had severed its relationship with the NCNC and contested the election independently. The NCNC feared FRK might even join up with the Ibadan group. McEwen appealed to her not to do so and promised that "the party will in turn do everything to signify its gratitude for your loyalty."[32]

Nonetheless, FRK regarded her existing "legitimate right" as more important than any future rewards from the party, which had so far not given her any appointment outside the party organization. The NCNC, which was a far less disciplined party than the AG or NPC, demanded strict discipline from FRK yet admitted that it had not been able to control its own committee. Herself a strong disciplinarian at home, at school, and in the AWU and NWU, FRK would have appreciated consistent and rational discipline but these actions seemed unfair and partisan. She believed that she was denied a fair hearing by the Wachukwu committee because, first and foremost, she was a woman, and second, because she was not a protégée of Azikiwe's, who preferred to keep such an outspoken critic out of the House of Representatives. Thus, she decided to contest the election as an independent.[33]

A similar situation arose at the same time when Margaret Ekpo contested the NCNC candidacy for Aba North constituency against Felix Okoronkwo, chairman of the Aba branch of the NCNC. The resultant dispute was arbitrated by the party's national executive committee, which selected Okoronkwo because (according to Ekpo) she was a woman and Okoronkwo used bribery and political pressure tactics. In Ekpo's case, because she was a more loyal and committed party supporter, she did not stand as an independent. She continued to campaign extensively for the NCNC and believes it was as a reward for her rejection as a candidate that she was later appointed to the Eastern House of Chiefs. In the 1961 Eastern Region election, the NCNC nominated Ekpo and a second woman, Janet Mokelu, and they both won seats in the Eastern House of Assembly. In the 1959 election, FRK used the symbol of the hand on the ballot boxes, which was the same symbol being used by Adisa in Ibadan (he gave his permission for her to use it). In an interview, FRK said she chose the hand symbol because the only person she could really trust was her own hand. Akande's followers tried to affix a sketch of a palm tree (symbol of the AG) to her posters to give the wrong impression that she was switching parties rather than running as an independent.

In the election for the Abeokuta (Egba Central) constituency 36,739 persons registered as voters. The tally is given in table 1. The AG won by a slim majority of 688 votes. The AG also won the Egba South and Egba East constituencies comfortably while the NCNC won Egba North by a very narrow lead of 109 votes.[34] FRK had the satisfaction of seeing the NCNC lose its seat in Abeokuta and believed this was due to her part in splitting the vote. She issued a spirited press statement: "I feel very grateful to the Egba electorate for showing that they believe in the leadership of a woman and resented the insult levied on Mrs. Ransome-Kuti by voting the NCNC out of Abeokuta."[35]

The scholar Kenneth Post agreed with FRK's assessment: "In Abeokuta (the NCNC) was admittedly unlucky since Mrs. Ransome-Kuti split its vote by standing as an independent and gave the AG a minority victory."[36] After she stood as an independent, the NCNC might have reabsorbed her as it did in 1954 when she stood as an independent and as it did with a number of other erstwhile NCNC independents all over Southern Nigeria—had FRK so desired. But she, who had never been as obedient or disciplined a party follower as, for example Margaret Ekpo, refused to go through the usual face-saving motions for readmission into the fold. No doubt her pride was hurt at the shabby treatment that she, as an NCNC founding member and officeholder, had received. In addition, she decided that one of her reasons for supporting the NCNC in the first place—namely, its support for the enfranchisement and empowerment of women—no longer existed. Since there was no existing political party in Nigeria that did support women's enfranchisement, the solution seemed to be to form a feminist-oriented party. In addition, her other political options were limited.

Her fellow ex-NCNC rebel, Adisa, had been very successful in the

Table 1.

	Number of Voters	Percentage
Abeokuta		
NCNC	9,755	37.25
AG	10,443	39.90
FRK as Independent	4,665	17.80

Source: Post, *Nigerian Federal Elections.*

election, with his breakaway group winning six of the seven seats in Ibadan division. His group, the Mabolaje Grand Alliance Party, had secured the defeat of their common foe Agbaje, who lost his own seat in the election. FRK decided to ally herself with Adisa but only on the basis of an equal partnership. To do so, she needed her own party organization. Thus, she set about forming a party. As she said at the time, "Although we are young we hope to fight for the emancipation of the women of this country" (Lagos *Sunday Times,* Aug. 28, 1960). Moreover, FRK reported she formed the party because the NCNC did not want to support women and only used women for its own benefit, a view expressed in a 1961 article: "Men do not want women to take part in our legislation; they want women as mere voters, ordinary election tools."[37] Years later she recalled, "My status as a woman made me unwanted in the political circle then largely dominated by men and this made me unhappy and I decided that I would fight to force the men to change their attitude towards women."[38] However, the name she first chose for her party, Funmilayo Commoner's Party, did not live up to her sweeping feminist ambitions since it so blatantly identified the party with her. She soon changed the name to the Commoner People's Party (CPP).

As expressed in its constitution, the objectives of the CPP were not expressly feminist but populist in a rather nebulous way:

To cater for [*sic*] the interests of the common people.

To cater for [*sic*] the sound education and the health of the children of the common people.

To see that the common people are no longer victimized and oppressed.

To fight for and protect the natural rights of all people, irrespective of creed, tribe, and sex.

FRK was the president and a man, E. O. Agunbiade, was the party's secretary.[39] No information is available about the membership though it was apparently very small.

The CPP allied with Adisa's Mabolaje Grand Alliance Party; when that party affiliated to the NPC in 1960, the CPP followed suit. This alliance sponsored candidates in the 1960 Western Region election. However, the alliance broke down in August 1960 during the Western Region election campaign, due to a dispute between FRK and Adisa, oddly enough over the use of the hand symbol. It seems Adisa was willing to let FRK use it when she ran as an independent but not as a symbol for a new party, the CPP. The CPP never really gained steam, remaining very much a one-woman organization, and FRK suffered a resounding defeat in the election. Later, Adisa's group left the NPC alliance and returned to the fold of the NCNC. FRK, however, never returned to the NCNC. She continued her association with that part of the Mabolaje Grand Alliance Party headed by K. O. S. Are, which remained affiliated to the NPC, and she corresponded and met with Are and NPC officials. At the same time, she sought an alliance of her Commoner People's Party with another "maverick" party, the Dynamic Party, led by Dr. Chike Obi, another NCNC rebel and an old friend. Obi wrote to FRK in October 1960: "We are perhaps aiming at the same subject of ridding this our dear fatherland of the pests which eat up the results of the sweat and toil of the common people."[40]

Obi was invited to speak at the first annual conference of the CPP on November 6, 1960. The meeting was advertised in circulars and posters in Abeokuta. One flyer announced: "Hear Chike Obi—the Truth Speaker politician—you will be convinced why you should join the CPP."[41] The Dynamic Party, which was quite well organized and had won the Onitsha seat in the House of Representatives in 1959, was not really interested in an alliance with a fledgling one-woman party in Abeokuta. Although the CPP conference attracted some media attention, after that it disappeared from the public eye.[42] The Commoner People's Party never took off as a political party or developed a large or loyal membership or articulated ideology; by 1962 the CPP had completely disappeared.

Given the overwhelming predominance in the Nigerian political scene of the three major political parties (NCNC, AG, NPC), each controlling the government in its home region, there was little chance of success for a nonconformist, radical, independent party—let alone for a tiny populist and feminist party. The same fate had befallen another independent and unorthodox woman, Adunni Oluwole, who had formed a political party, the Nigerian Commoners Party in 1954 to campaign against self-government and which had also entered into an alliance with Obi.[43]

Had the CPP been able to carry with it the support of women, even just those in Abeokuta, it would have carried some weight, at least in Abeokuta, but in fact FRK had lost her commanding influence over Egba women when it came to national politics. Most of the AWU leaders had joined first the AG and then the Nigerian National Democratic Party (NNDP), likewise the majority of the membership aligned with one or the other of the parties. The Egba women, as was happening all over Nigeria with women and men, were voting according to ethnic and party allegiance. The NWU members outside of Abeokuta, as we have seen, were also following the line of their region's controlling party. The prospect of imminent independence saw the common bond of gender fall by the wayside as political parties—based on ethnicity and region and led by middle-class Western-educated people who stood to inherit the mantles of power—campaigned furiously for support. Feminist consciousness was not the only loser: class consciousness was also obfuscated by the drive for independence. Thus, FRK lost two of her main constituencies: women and the poor. Abeokuta, where she had her greatest amount of support, was drawn into the AG network as that was seen unofficially as the party of the Yoruba. Nonetheless, if FRK had stayed in the NCNC, she would have retained a political base and likely would have gained a seat in the Western House of Assembly in 1960 (as happened with Ekpo)—but she would have had to abandon her wider feminist causes and connections. FRK was more effective in the politics of protest against the colonial regime than in the ethnicized party politics of independent Nigeria.

Thus in 1962, when the Western Regional government was dissolved and a state of emergency declared, FRK no longer held a political base other than her legendary name. A number of politicians and members of the Western House of Assembly were detained but it is an index of her alienation from the political scene that she was not included. She was no longer directly involved in the dramatic turn of events, but remained a commentator on them through her many influential friends in government and the private sector.

For instance, the federal government appointed Dr. M. A. Majekodunmi as Minister of Health. As the administrator of the Western Region, Majekodunmi, an Egba man, was well known to FRK. His father, Chief J. B. Majekodunmi, was the Otun of the Egba, a very high chieftaincy, under Alake ̀Ademola. FRK had found Chief Majekodunmi reasonable and sympathetic and had turned to him for support during the AWU days, when the Otun of the Egba had defended the women against the Alake in council meetings. M. A. Majekodunmi's sister, Amelia Osimosu, had been one of the leaders of the AWU and had been on its executive committee. M. A. Majekodunmi, who had studied medicine at Trinity College, Dublin, so impressed Rev. Ransome-Kuti that he decided to send his son Koye to the same university. In addition, FRK had asked M. A. Majekodunmi to speak to the AWU on health matters when he visited his father in Abeokuta and he had done so. FRK also got on well with his Irish wife, Nora, who recalls that FRK "put her teeth, her hands and all her energies into causes and was bloody marvelous in her fearlessness and her folly." Nora Majekodunmi also recalled: "Mrs. Kuti allowed me to be myself. She did not set about advising me to be a good Yoruba wife as did so many others, because she would have had a great dislike of anyone who wanted *her* to be a good wife."[44]

So FRK welcomed the appointment of M. A. Majekedunmi as Minister of Health and wrote to congratulate him on his successful administration. She praised his nonpartisan approach and concern for efficiency and order. She deplored the abuses committed by politicians and expressed her shock at the financial improprieties found by the commission of inquiry set up to probe the former regional government.

After the emergency administration, which lasted approximately seven months (May to Dec. 1962), the federal government empowered Samuel L. Akintola to act as premier; his newly formed United People's Party (UPP) constituted the government. Subsequently, the UPP merged with part of the Western Region of the NCNC to form the Nigerian National Democratic Party (NNDP), which allied with the NPC in the 1964 election. The federal election in the Western Region was fought bitterly and in some areas violently. In Abeokuta, FRK's erstwhile critic and opponent in the AUDC, Alhaji Adegbenro, was the AG leader and premier designate in the Western Region while her former NCNC colleagues in Abeokuta had largely joined the NNDP. FRK was out of sympathy with both camps and deplored the way the region was being torn apart. Earlier, at a meeting of the FNWS in Abeokuta she had issued a press release that called on the prime minister to release the leader of the AG, Obafemi Awolowo, who had been jailed for "treasonable felony." She said his release was necessary in the interests of "peace, unity, and solidarity" (*Daily Times,* Feb. 16, 1964). The 1965 Western Region election and its aftermath heightened the violence and insecurity in the region and brought the entire country to the brink of collapse.

When the political crisis was terminated by the military coup of January 15, 1966, FRK was among the majority of Nigerians who welcomed it as a resolution to a terrible impasse. She wrote to the Soviet Women's Committee: "We did not expect that the solution would come as quickly and the way it came but everyone in our country was very happy that it had come." [45]

The federal military government appointed Lieutenant Colonel Francis Adekunle Fajuyi as the military governor of the Eastern Region. FRK wrote a letter of congratulations and reiterated her satisfaction that the politicians had been dismissed: "Different politicians in different regions had been used to drive fear into the women of Nigeria and many of us had had to dance to the tune of these politicians against our will." [46] She also appealed to the military government to do what the civilian government had refused to do, namely, enfranchise women in the North. Whether the government was military or civilian, FRK never abandoned her mission to gain the franchise for women in the North.

The promise of the January coup was unfulfilled. A backlash in the Northern Region led to a counter coup in July 1966, during which the head of state, Brigadier A. Ironsi and Col. Fajuyi, among others, were assassinated. It would appear that from that event dates FRK's growing disillusionment with military government, which now revealed itself as no improvement on the First Republic government.

The civil war between the secessionist Biafra (in the East) and the Federation of Nigeria (divided in 1967 into twelve states) raged from July 1967 to January 1970. It was a source of great distress to FRK who had always been a fervent, genuine nationalist. While based in Abeokuta, she had a nationwide network of friends, had taught many children from Eastern Nigeria, and both she and her husband were well known for their rigid rule that non-Yoruba students should be freely integrated and treated fairly. Olisa Chukura, an Igbo from Asaba, who was first a student and then a teacher at the Abeokuta Grammar School, recalled that there was simply no question of ever being made to feel different or alienated.

The civil war cut FRK off from her close associates like Margaret Ekpo and Felicia Emodi, both residents of the East. FRK's grandnephew

Wole Soyinka was imprisoned for most of the war for being an outspoken opponent against it. Her former political colleagues Chike Obi and Margaret Ekpo were detained on the Biafran side.

On behalf of the FNWS, FRK made speeches and sent telegrams calling for an end to the war. When the Nigerian and Biafran negotiating teams met in Kampala in 1968, she sent an identical telegram to Anthony Enahoro of the federal government and Sir Louis Mbanefo of Biafra: "Nigerian women implore you find a solution to our country's problems, may peace and love reign again."[47] Unfortunately, the war ended not through diplomacy but through the collapse of Biafra in January 1970, after great loss of life. The war had not solved Nigeria's fundamental problems of establishing good governance and promoting the welfare of all its citizens, and the successive military governments have likewise failed to solve those problems. FRK and her family continued to criticize the policies of the military governments as will be seen in chapter 7. But while FRK had become less of a political factor in national politics, she still remained a political figure and was active on the international scene, explored in the next chapter.

Notes

1. FRK, speech, FNWS Third Annual Conference, Aug. 29, 1959, copy, FRK Papers.

2. Ekpo to FRK, Dec., FRK Papers; Mba, *Nigerian Women Mobilized*, 172.

3. Okala to FRK, FRK Papers; see also Mba, *Nigerian Women Mobilized*, 172.

4. NWU, "Demands for Political Democracy," FRK Papers.

5. FRK was elected president general; vice presidents were Janet Okala (Onitsha), Elizabeth Adekogbe (Ibadan), Alice Obafor (Benin, the Erelu of Lagos), and G. I. Okoye (Enugu). Assistant secretaries were Felicia Emodi (Onitsha) and Keziah Fashina (Lagos); the position of "entertainer" was held by Abiedun Ogundimu (NNDP, Lagos). All information on the FNWS was found in FRK Papers.

6. FRK, speech, Aug. 29, 1959, copy, FRK Papers.

7. *West African Pilot*, Aug. 5, 1959.

8. Okoye to FRK, Aug. 17, 1959, FRK Papers.

9. Obua to FRK, May 10, 1958, FRK Papers.

10. Gambo to FRK, Aug. 24, 1959, FRK Papers.

11. A couple of women had been appointed to councils in Eastern Nigeria after the 1929 Women's War. The first woman elected to a council was Esther Adesigbin to the Port Harcourt town council in 1949, followed by Ekpo Young

to the Calabar Urban Development Council in 1952. See Mba, *Nigerian Women Mobilized,* 276.

12. Amelia Osimosu, interview, Lagos, June 17, 1976; Ayo Rosiji, interview, Lagos, June 14, 1990.

13. FRK Papers.

14. FRK, "Women Should Play a Bigger Part," 1015.

15. Egba division had to elect five candidates through the three levels of electoral colleges. Egbaland was composed of about 3,500 villages and 143 townships. The villages were grouped into 340 primary colleges with major villages as voting centers. Towns were grouped into 96 primary colleges. Four-hundred-sixty-eight candidates were to be elected from all these primary colleges: these, with 153 members of the Native Authority, were to form the 16 intermediate colleges, from which 169 candidates were to be elected for the final colleges; this was to meet in only one center, and from it the five Egba members of the Western House of Assembly were to be elected.

16. Ayo Rosiji, interview.

17. FRK to M. A. Majekodunmi, Nov. 16, 1962, Majekodunmi Papers in his possession, Lagos. See also FRK, "Women Should Play a Bigger Part," 1015.

18. Ibid.

19. FRK to M. A. Majekodunmi, Nov. 15, 1962, private papers of Dr. Majekodunmi.

20. FRK, "Women Should Play a Bigger Part," 1015.

21. FRK, "Women Are Used as Tools at Elections," 7.

22. Remi Aiyedun, interview, Lagos, Oct. 6, 1976.

23. Mba, *Nigerian Women Mobilized,* 285.

24. Ibid., 240.

25. FRK, interview, *African Woman* no. 4 (April/May 1976).

26. For the 1959 election, Egba division was given an extra seat, Egba Central or Abeokuta, which had been part of the Egba North constituency.

27. FRK to Fadahunsi, telegram, May 8, 1959, FRK Papers.

28. Strangers Elements Egba Central constituency to NCNC Appeals Committee, Aug. 2, 1959, FRK Papers.

29. Egba East constituency to NCNC Appeals Committee, Aug. 10, 1959, FRK Papers.

30. FRK, interview, Abeokuta, Aug. 12, 1976.

31. FRK to Azikiwe, Aug. 12, 1959, FRK Papers.

32. McEwen to FRK, Dec. 11, 1959, FRK Papers.

33. FRK, interview, Aug. 12, 1976.

34. Post, *Nigerian Federal Elections,* 360–61.

35. FRK, press statement, copy, FRK Papers.

36. Post, *Nigerian Federal Elections,* 361. Although FRK never rejoined the NCNC, she remained on cordial personal terms with some of its leaders, such

as Festus Okotie-Eboh, Minister of Finance, even though earlier she had accused him (without justification) of giving financial support to Akande in 1959.

37. FRK, "Women Are Used as Tools," 7.

38. FRK, interview, *African Woman* no. 4 (April/May 1976).

39. Agunbiade seems to have been a professional political organizer. In 1959 he was in the Egba NCNC; during the dispute over FRK's nomination, he wrote to Azikiwe in her support, calling her a "leader and redeemer of the NCNC to the last." In 1964 he was the Egba division administrative secretary of the NNDP. He was also associated with FRK's educational activities, but a dispute over that led her to take him to court (chap. 7).

40. Obi to FRK, Oct. 1960, FRK Papers.

41. Poster, FRK Papers.

42. One of Azikiwe's pro-NCNC newspapers carried an editorial in advance of the conference and praised the points listed in the preconference press release: "It will call on government to dissolve all customary courts in the Western Region because they are being used as a weapon to punish political opponents. Amend the constitution so government can dissolve any regional government found guilty of maladministration. We may not see eye to eye with CPP--but common suffering or adversity can produce agreeable bedfellows if only for a brief moment" (*Southern Nigerian Defender*, Oct. 27, 1960).

43. Mba, *Nigerian Women Mobilized*, 284.

44. From the private papers of M. A. Majekodunmi; Nora Majekodunmi, interview, Lagos, June 10, 1989.

45. FRK to Soviet Women's Committee, Feb. 7, 1966, FRK Papers.

46. FRK to Fajuyi, Feb. 2, 1966, FRK Papers.

47. FRK to Enahoro and to Mbanefo, telegrams, Aug. 7, 1968, FRK Papers.

Souvenir montage (1950s) from Federation of Nigerian Women's Societies (FNWS). Photos labeled in montage.

Opening of Nigerian Women's Union textile showroom in Abeokuta, 1952.

Memorial service for Rev. Ransome-Kuti. FRK in headtie and glasses. To her left are Beko and then Fela.

FNWS executive committee, 1953.

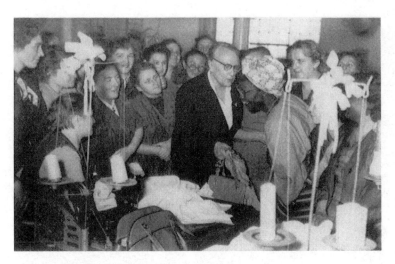

FRK at a factory in Łodz, Poland, 1956.

Same factory in Łodz, Poland, 1956.

Ransome-Kuti homestead in Abeokuta, 1989.

Reverend Ransome-Kuti Memorial Grammar School, Abeokuta, 1989.

FRK shaking hands with Prime Minister Tafawa Balewa (of Nigeria), late 1950s.

6   "For Their Freedoms":
The International Sphere

One of the features that makes Funmilayo Ransome-Kuti a unique woman in the Nigerian context is the extent and diversity of her international connections. No other Nigerian woman of her period had the same international exposure. In West Africa, only Adelaide Caseley-Hayford and Constance Cummings John, both of Sierra Leone, and Mabel Dove of Ghana had any comparable international links.

Though Funmilayo Ransome-Kuti had gone to school in England from 1919–22, there is no evidence that she made any political contacts then that shaped her later radicalism. The one slim piece of evidence about her political life in England—that she dropped Frances (her Christian name) and chose to use Funmilayo (her Yoruba name)—seems to have been a personal reaction to some racial or ethnic slight more than a considered political decision (*Nigerian Tribune,* Apr. 14, 1978; chap. 2). Though her first overtly political sojourn out of Nigeria was in 1947 as the sole female member of the Nigerian delegation to London to protest the Richards Constitution, she had been involved in international issues long before that. Chapters 4 and 5 document her rise as a leader of women in Abeokuta and in national politics, including the direct and indirect ways these struggles involved an understanding of and response to international issues.

Yet the real starting point of her awareness of international women's organizations and British anti-imperialistic circles was likely the close friendship between Ladipo Ṣolanke and the Reverend I. O. Ransome-Kuti. Ṣolanke was born in Abeokuta in 1884, attended Oyo Training Institution (later known as St. Andrews), and taught for some years before going to Fourah Bay College in Sierra Leone where he obtained a bachelor's degree in 1921. Ṣolanke and the reverend knew each other as boys and young men in Abeokuta and were close friends. From Fourah Bay, Ṣolanke went to England where he qualified as a barrister at law. He then settled in Great Britain, though he traveled to Nigeria at irregular intervals. Ṣolanke experienced many hardships and frustrations as a young self-financed West African student in England and resolved to improve the conditions of other students. This led him to form an association of West African students in London in 1925.

The West African Students Union (WASU) developed into far more than a students' self-help association. It promoted nationalist, anticolonialist movements of British West Africans in England and acted as a kind of liaison between such movements and the British Colonial Office, on the one hand, and the anticolonial movement in England, on the other. The WASU aimed at generating an anticolonial consciousness both in British West Africa among the traditional and educated elite and among West African students in Great Britain. To raise funds for the WASU and for setting up a hostel, Ṣolanke toured British West Africa from 1929–32, holding meetings with traditional rulers, lawyers, doctors, teachers, and journalists. As already mentioned, among the founding members of WASU in Nigeria were the Reverend I. O. and Funmilayo Ransome-Kuti, then residents of Ijebu-Ode. Indeed, the reverend founded a branch of WASU in Ijebu-Ode in 1929. The Ransome-Kutis were in illustrious company, as early WASU supporters included the Alake of Abeokuta, the Emir of Kano, and the Asantehene of Ghana.

The Ransome-Kutis later became lifetime members of WASU, along with Dr. Nnamdi Azikiwe, Chief H. O. Davies, and Dr. Akinola Maja in Nigeria, H. A. Korsah of Gold Coast, and Dr. E. A. Taylor-Cummings of Sierra Leone (the latter two were later appointed to the Elliot Commission, along with Reverend Ransome-Kuti [see below]).

From the ranks of educated elite, the WASU recruited members who later became the leaders of the nationalist movements in West Africa. As the Nigerian historian G. O. Olusanya points out: "When the Nigerian Youth Movement was formed in 1934, most of its foundation members were members of the various branches of WASU. It is therefore obvious that the union had contributed significantly to the stimulation of political consciousness in West Africa."[1]

In England, the WASU served to bring together West Africans in a West African association. Kwame Nkrumah and Joe Appiah were vice presidents of the WASU in 1946. Indeed, this may have been Nkrumah and FRK's first knowledge of one another. Later, as president of Ghana, Nkrumah invited her to a meeting at Flagstaff House to discuss the formation of a Ghanaian women's organization. FRK attended its inaugural meeting, and Nkrumah credited her with helping to inspire its creation.[2] The WASU also attracted support from blacks in the diaspora who believed in a "renascent" Africa, such as the world-famous African American actor and singer Paul Robeson. In addition to his work with the WASU, Ṣolanke identified closely with the diverse network of anticolonial movements in England, such as various Indian organizations, and with the left wing of the Labour Party, the Fabian Society, and the Fabian Colonial Bureau.

In October 1940, the Fabian Colonial Bureau was formed as a special department of the Fabian Society. Arthur Creech-Jones and Rita Hinden were the founding chairman and secretary, respectively. The bureau's aims were to formulate proposals for self-government in the colonies, to prepare data for members of Parliament for debates on colonial issues, and to propagate an anticolonial philosophy. When the Colonial Development Council was formed in 1948, three members of the bureau were members. Creech-Jones had been a trade unionist, then a member of Parliament (1935–50); in 1950, he lost his seat by 81 votes but regained it in 1954. He was deputy secretary of state for the colonies from 1947–50. Reginald William Sorensen observed that in his administratioon Creech-Jones implemented much of what he had decided when chairman of the bureau.[3]

One of Ṣolanke's closest associates was Sorensen, who was later the chairman of WASU Limited. They met in 1930 and maintained a longterm friendship. Sorensen was the godfather of one of Ṣolanke's children.[4] As Sorensen explains, "My West African activities led me to join the Fabian Colonial Bureau."[5]

Sorensen first entered the British House of Commons in 1929 as the member of Parliament for West Leyton, which he represented on and off until 1964, when he was made a life peer and moved to the House of Lords. Sorensen was deeply committed to the cause of freedom for the British colonies and was active in Indian nationalist organizations in Great Britain. In 1946 he was a member of the British parliamentary delegation to India. In 1949 Sorensen and Dr. Rita Hinden were invited to Nigeria by the Nigerian Youth Movement, which recognized their valuable contributions to Nigeria's nationalist movement.[6]

Another of Ṣolanke's close associates was Archibald Fenner-Brockway.

He was also a left-wing Labour Party member of Parliament and in 1948 the first chairman of the Congress Peoples against Imperialism. In 1954 Fenner-Brockway was elected chairman of the Movement for Colonial Freedom. He was also made life peer in 1964.

Ṣolanke built up a network of contacts with such left-wing Labour people as Sorensen, Fenner-Brockway, Creech-Jones, and Hinden, who gave moral and at times financial support to the WASU. Ṣolanke introduced these people to West African students and visitors. One such visitor from May to September 1939 was Ṣolanke's very close friend, Rev. Ransome-Kuti, president of the Nigerian Union of Teachers (NUT), which was affiliated with the National Union of Teachers in England. When Rev. Ransome-Kuti proposed to the Nigerian government that he visit Great Britain to look at schools and the teachers' union, the NUT in England endorsed his request and assisted in the arrangements. Ṣolanke spent a lot of time with the Reverend Ransome-Kuti on his tour, and through Ṣolanke the reverend met many British activists who sympathized with the WASU and anticolonialist movements. Later, when the reverend was appointed to the Elliot Commission on Education he was able to renew many of these contacts (see below).

The Reverend Ransome-Kuti seems to have made a very good impression. One of the teachers he met in this tour, Sir Ronald Gould, later became the secretary of the National Union of Teachers in England. When Gould visited Nigeria in 1959, he laid a wreath on Rev. Ransome-Kuti's grave, commenting: "When he attended a meeting on education with us in England he rose with dignity and spoke with conviction and understanding."[7]

While in Great Britain, Rev. Ransome-Kuti had an hour-long interview with the Colonial Office, at which time he submitted a memorandum on the difficulties under which teachers in Nigeria labored. As a result of his trip, in March 1940 several questions were raised in Parliament about the urgent need to improve the conditions of service for mission teachers in Nigeria.[8]

Long before his visit to England in 1939, the Reverend Ransome-Kuti and Ṣolanke engaged in extensive and regular correspondence, both personal and about the WASU. Later, Rev. Ransome-Kuti brought his wife, Funmilayo, into the correspondence, which developed into a three-way exchange that was generally very warm and intimate.[9]

Ṣolanke called Oludotun Kuti (the reverend) "my constant comrade" and Funmilayo Ransome-Kuti "my wife." Ṣolanke's first son by his first wife (Aduke Phillips), Oladipo, attended "Mrs. Kuti's class" (kinder-garten), beginning in 1944. In the 1940s they corresponded frequently about Oladipo's school fees, performance, and character. In addition, Rev. Ransome-Kuti was the godfather of one of Ṣolanke's other sons, Ladipo, born December 14, 1949. Thus, the relationship between the Ransome-Kutis and Ṣolanke was extremely close.

Ṣolanke asked the Ransome-Kutis to undertake (in Nigeria) a num-ber of tasks in support of the WASU. For example, Ṣolanke sent artificial pansies to FRK, asking her to sell them to raise funds for WASU. The Ransome-Kutis' eldest son, Olikoye (Koye), remembers clearly being sent around the "European quarter" of Abeokuta selling those pan-sies to eager buyers. In a letter to Ṣolanke dated January 19, 1934, the reverend noted that "the British Resident has bought a pansy for one guinea. . . . Here is an officer of the British Empire doing his duty to the dark-skinned members of that Empire. I am convinced there are more like him."[10]

Between 1933 and 1942 Ṣolanke sent copies of the WASU newsletter to FRK to sell. He asked the Ransome-Kutis to appeal on the WASU's behalf to prominent persons in Abeokuta and Lagos, which they did. The reverend even persuaded the Alake to pay for the cost of furnishing one room in the WASU hostel in London.[11]

Ṣolanke also maintained a close relationship and regular correspon-dence with Alake Ademola II. A lot of the letters were concerned with the welfare of the Alake's first son, Adetokunbo, a law student at Cam-bridge University. In the 1930s, there seems to have been very cordial re-lations among Alake Ademola, the Ransome-Kutis, and Ṣolanke, which is evident in the correspondence.

There was also a close connection between the NUT and WASU, reflecting the close working relationship between the reverend and Ṣolanke. The 1941 annual conference resolutions of the WASU mirrored the NUT's major concerns. In 1943 Ṣolanke submitted a memorandum from the NUT executive committee to the West African Parliamen-tary Committee with the request that the committee discuss it with the secretary of state for the colonies in Parliament. The memo included demands for improved conditions of service for Nigerian teachers, for Nigerianization of the teaching staff, and for more scholarships, more schools, and universal education.

Another way in which Funmilayo Ransome-Kuti was involved in international activities and persons was through her husband's activities

in British colonial education policy. Oliver Stanley, the colonial secretary, visited Nigeria in September 1942. The NUT held an audience
with him, after which the government announced Rev. Ransome-Kuti's
appointment to the Commission of Higher Education in West Africa
(usually referred to as the Elliot Commission). The Elliot Commission
was "to report on the organization and facilities of the existing centers
of higher education in British West Africa and to make recommendations regarding future university development in that area." Three West
African members were appointed: Kobina Korsar from Gold Coast,
H. H. Taylor-Cummings from Sierra Leone, and Rev. I. O. Ransome-
Kuti from Nigeria.

On Rev. Ransome-Kuti's nomination, the acting director of education wrote to the chief secretary: "He is energetic and if he were
nominated to serve on the Committee I believe that it would prove
a popular appointment with the general public."[12] Apparently, Rev.
Ransome-Kuti's appointment was seen by some as being "staged" by
the British, that is, as appointing someone the British thought would
be a pushover and not cause any trouble. A Nigerian student, E. Babalola, who was at Fourah Bay College, Sierra Leone, recalled meeting the
Elliot Commission members on their visit to Fourah Bay and talking
to Rev. Ransome-Kuti "till the small hours of the morning." Babalola
recorded the prevalent belief that Rev. Ransome-Kuti "was mistakenly
chosen by British officials for they thought him a simpleton. I reliably
learnt that later when the British were thinking of the representative for
Nigeria, someone said the 'smiling clergyman' would be alright. But to
their dismay the smiling clergyman turned out to be an uncompromis-
ing fighter."[13]

Another Nigerian student at Fourah Bay at the same time was
Emmanuel O. Alayande, who later became Rev. Ransome-Kuti's colleague as the principal of Ibadan Grammar School. Alayande recalled
how deeply impressed he was by the reverend during the Elliot Commission's visit to Fourah Bay. Thereafter, the reverend became Alayande's
hero on whom he modeled his own life and work. Indeed, Alayande was
one of the very last people to speak to him a few days before he died.[14]

Another member of the commission was Arthur Creech-Jones, a
Labour Party member of Parliament, who subsequently became deputy
colonial secretary and then colonial secretary. The renowned zoologist,
Julian Huxley, also a member of the commission, recorded his rather
acerbic recollections of the commission's West African tour, describing

Rev. Ransome-Kuti as a "Nigerian headmaster who was rather a buffoon."[15] In this comment he was probably referring to the reverend's
well-known love of jokes and storytelling, which were often accompanied by his deep rollicking laugh. But to call him a "buffoon" was
a biased and uninformed distortion. The Reverend Ransome-Kuti was
held in great esteem not only by his fellow Nigerians but by such well-
regarded Britons as Creech-Jones and Walter Elliott. Undoubtedly, the
fault lay with Huxley's jaundiced perception. Indeed, Huxley actually
did develop jaundice on the trip, ironically near Abeokuta, so he "had
to be put in Mrs. Kuti's bed at Abeokuta and later taken to Lagos hospital."[16] The kindness the Ransome-Kutis showed to Huxley was hardly
repaid by such a remark.

Huxley was one of the commission members who submitted a minority report that recommended a single university for all British West
Africa. Rev. Ransome-Kuti, the other two African members, the chairman, and the members of the Conservative Party submitted the majority report that recommended three universities, one in each colony.
Huxley later admitted, "I was soon proved wrong. . . . So great was the
demand for higher education that not only did these three flourish but
many more."[17]

The Nigerian Union of Teachers also protested the idea of a single
university. Partly as a result of this, another delegation, led by Sir William
Pyfe, visited West Africa, and its report influenced the new secretary of
state, Creech-Jones, to decide that there should be a second university
in Gold Coast.

The reports of both commissions were placed before Parliament in
June 1945. In the next month, the elections were won by the Labour
Party. No decision was made on the Elliot Report for a year; then in
July 1946 the secretary of state recommended proposals in line with
the minority report (the proposals were signed by Creech-Jones). Both
Sierra Leone and Gold Coast found the proposals unacceptable. In 1947,
Creech-Jones advised establishing two university colleges, one at Achi-
mota (Ghana) and one at Ibadan (Nigeria).

During the Elliot Commission's tour of Nigeria, the Ransome-Kuti
family was much involved in its itinerary and activities. The commission
visited Abeokuta, including the Abeokuta Grammar School, and had
lunch with the Alake on February 15, 1944. In addition, Rev. Ransome-
Kuti's younger brother, A. O. Ransome-Kuti, held a party for the commission on February 17, 1944, at his residence in Military Street, Lagos.[18]

Funmilayo Ransome-Kuti was one of twenty-three people who gave evidence to the commission in Abeokuta. Before the visit of the commission, the Alake had held a meeting with the Abeokuta branch of the NUT on February 2, 1944, to discuss the commission's reception. FRK was one of the NUT members present. She advised the Alake to convene a public meeting to discuss the program "lest people might say they knew nothing about it."[19] This is a revealing anecdote because her democratic, open-minded approach is contrasted with the Alake's mode of "closet" decision making.

At the reception at the Afin (palace) the Alake offered an area of land sufficient for the site of the university. Creech-Jones replied (Elliot was not present) that this was a "good gesture but that the commission could not be expected to commit itself."[20]

A few days later, Elliot and the Reverend Ransome-Kuti called on the Alake. In his address, Elliot carefully stressed that Africans and Europeans in the commission were on equal terms. At lunch, Rev. Ransome-Kuti described Elliot as "a godly man of unbiased mind, not a time-server."[21]

Undoubtedly, a cordiality existed in the relations among Rev. Ransome-Kuti, Elliot, and Creech-Jones that extended to Funmilayo Ransome-Kuti. Twelve years later when Elliot visited Nigeria as the leader of a Commonwealth Parliamentary Association delegation, he wrote to FRK that he would visit her in Abeokuta (although whether he did or not is unknown). Sufficient cordiality and closeness were established in 1944 between Creech-Jones and the Ransome-Kutis that FRK maintained a correspondence with Creech-Jones and his wife from 1945.[22] FRK congratulated Creech-Jones on his appointment as colonial secretary in 1947, for instance. In the same year, she made her political debut on the international stage when she was invited by the NCNC to join its delegation to Britain to protest the Richards Constitution.

Funmilayo Ransome-Kuti's connection with the formation of the NCNC is discussed in chapter 5. The NCNC was very critical of the Richards Constitution and organized meetings to discuss it. FRK attended the meeting in Abeokuta where she spoke against the constitution (Daily Service, June 16, 1945). Once the NCNC made the decision to send a delegation to Great Britain, party officials toured the country for several months gathering petitions to present to the colonial secretary. The choice of members for the delegation also occupied the minds of NCNC leaders. The party's leader, Nnamdi Azikiwe, was an obvious choice; after his selection, it was agreed that each region and the Cameroons should be represented. Thus, P. M. Kale (Cameroons), Chief Nyong Essien (Eastern Region), Mallam Zanna Bukar Dipcharima (Northern Region), and Prince Adeleke Adedoyin (Western Region) were appointed. Lagos, which occupied a special status, was represented by its mayor, Dr. A. B. I. Olorun-Nimbe.

In 1947, the NCNC was a mass movement with a very loose organization that derived its financial support from subscriptions. There was no women's association as such. However, at its inception the NCNC had formed an alliance with Herbert Macaulay's Nigerian National Democratic Party (NNDP) and many Lagos market women were strong supporters of the NNDP. During the NCNC tour of the country in 1946, the leader of the Lagos Market Women's Association, Alimotu Pelewura, had chaired the Lagos reception for the tour. Moreover, the market women had contributed generously to both the NNDP and NCNC (*West African Pilot,* Oct. 25, 1946). In light of this, the *West African Pilot* (owned by Azikiwe) published an editorial suggesting that since women played such an important role in the anticolonial struggle they should be represented in the NCNC delegation. This suggestion accorded with party thinking. The first obvious choice of a woman was Pelewura, but the elderly Pelewura was ill and could not travel (*West African Pilot,* July 25, 1947).

The next choice was also fairly obvious. Funmilayo Ransome-Kuti was one of the first members of the party, she had attended the NCNC meeting in Abeokuta, and she had received considerable media coverage during the activities of the AWU in Abeokuta, especially in the *West African Pilot.* Moreover, it was known that she and her husband knew Creech-Jones from the Elliot Commission three years earlier. Also, unlike Pelewura, FRK was well educated and articulate in English. She herself stated that she was chosen partially due to her contact with Creech-Jones.

The delegation that left for England on June 26, 1947, was not well briefed and its itinerary was not properly organized. The NCNC's position on the constitution was not discussed beforehand, even on the ship (the *Almanzora*) where only one meeting was convened by the secretary, Adedoyin.

In Great Britain, press releases were not prepared properly or distributed in a timely manner to the press and members of Parliament. According to FRK, in a prepared commentary on the NCNC delegation given to a meeting of the party at Kirsten Hall, Lagos, on October 17, 1947:

> Azikiwe . . . never liked to receive suggestions from any other member of the delegation and whenever an opinion was expressed by any other member which might be contrary to his, he would charge that member with an attempt to usurp his position as the leader. The members of the Home Front will be sorry to know that the draft memorandum and constitution that was sent to the Secretary of State were drafted and signed by Dr. Azikiwe alone and was therefore termed and commonly referred to as one man's constitution.[23]

When the members were touring the British provinces, Azikiwe did not accompany them. When the delegation returned to Lagos, the media, especially the *West African Pilot,* treated them as returning heroes but many felt very disappointed at the poor showing of the delegation. A number of erstwhile admirers of Azikiwe began to change their opinions of his leadership. Samuel L. Akintola observed that FRK had gone further than any other member of the delegation in her criticisms of its performance: "She told me she was going to address personal letters to various political leaders and organizations in Nigeria appealing to them for unity and cooperation. Without unity and cooperation she said we are doomed" (*Daily Times,* Sept. 5, 1947).

The *Daily Times* editorial of September 8, 1947, stated dryly that "NCNC funds could have been better utilized with more credit to the NCNC in relieving some of the conditions so graphically depicted by Mrs. Ransome-Kuti." In Glasgow, when the members were to receive money, the bank withheld payment because of suspected mishandling of a check by the treasurer. Two members, Kale and Dipcharima, returned to London in disgust. The police were called in, which FRK regarded as "a great disgrace on the delegation and Nigeria and the Cameroons as a whole."[24] The delegation reached Britain during the summer recess of Parliament, which meant little lobbying could be effected. However, through Şolanke, FRK arranged a meeting with Sorensen that she and Azikiwe attended. When Sorensen asked how the delegation had apportioned the tasks among themselves, Azikiwe replied that he was the only one qualified to deal with all matters. FRK reported to the *Daily Times* that she objected to this claim and later told the other members and complained bitterly about Azikiwe's attitude (Dec. 17, 1947). The *Daily Worker* of August 14, under a photo of FRK, reported that the colonial

secretary told the delegation that there was no question of the Nigerian constitution of 1945 being changed until "experience had shown in
what way it needed amendment." Also, according to Azikiwe, Creech-
Jones advised them to return to Nigeria and cooperate in working with
the constitution that they were in Britain to discredit.[25] Azikiwe conveyed to Lagos the opinion that the British attitude was hostile; therefore, the NCNC recalled the delegation in August. FRK urged that they
stay until the resumption of Parliament in October, but Azikiwe insisted
they leave. The NCNC condemned the colonial secretary for his response to the delegation, "which would put a strain on British-Nigerian
relations" (*West African Pilot,* Aug. 27, 1947). FRK's frank, bold criticisms
of Azikiwe's leadership and of the organization of the delegation created ill feeling toward her on the part of Azikiwe and his followers. She
believed that Azikiwe was never again comfortable with her.[26]

During the delegation's two-month stay in England, FRK seized the
initiative to contact women's organizations and women factory workers.
Violet Creech-Jones lined up engagements for FRK and the secretary
of state himself assigned a woman from his office to arrange an itinerary. FRK had already begun to make her own plans. She contacted the
director of the British Broadcasting Corporation to attempt to arrange
an interview but was informed that they had just concluded a series on
the lives of women around the world.[27] She was, however, invited to
address the London Women's Parliamentary Committee.[28] She also addressed a group of women journalists, the London National Federation
of Young Farmers Club, the National Federation of Women Institute,
and the National Union of Townswomen's Guilds. She visited several
factories and day-care centers, the Association of Country Women of
the World, and the National Council for Maternity and Child Welfare. At one factory in Surrey, Mitcham Works Limited, she arrived at
11:00 A.M. to address the workers and stayed until closing at 5:00 P.M.[29]
At a special reception held by the Lord Mayor of Manchester on September 20, 1947, she was asked, by special request of the mayor, to talk
about the problems of women in Nigeria and the Cameroons (*West African Pilot,* Sept. 20, 1947).

Before the delegation left London, one of the left-wing women's
groups asked FRK to write an article on the condition of Nigerian
women. Her article, which appeared in the *Daily Worker,* the newspaper
of the British Communist Party, on August 18, 1947, argued that under
colonialism women had lost more than did men: "Before the British

advent in Nigeria . . . there was division of labor between men and women; . . . women owned property, traded and exercised considerable political and social influence in society. . . . With the advent of British rule . . . instead of the women being educated and assisted . . . their condition has deteriorated." This thesis has been thoroughly documented by feminist scholars since the mid-1970s, so FRK was way ahead of her time in making this point in 1947. She argued that under colonialism Nigerian women had lost their traditional economic and political power and that they were oppressed by the colonial system and its agencies, such as the Sole Native Authority in Abeokuta. Not only were they denied suffrage and any voice in the government but in Abeokuta they were forced to pay taxes that they could not afford and in return did not receive even basic amenities, such as medical services. She maintained that women were poverty-stricken, disease-ridden, and malnourished. She held Britain responsible for this state of affairs and appealed to British women to help free the women of Nigeria from "slavery—political, social, and economic."

The article, reproduced in Nigerian newspapers, caused a stir in Abeokuta and Lagos. The Alake of Abeokuta issued a statement denouncing the article (*West African Pilot,* Sept. 13, 1947). The Nigerian Woman's Party, an organization of elite women in Lagos, led by Oyinkan Abayomi, held a meeting to discuss the article and passed a resolution expressing its disagreement with it (*West African Pilot,* Sept. 22, 1947).

On the other hand, the Lagos Market Women's Association met at Pelewura's residence on September 23 and declared its support for her arguments and that she had spoken on the organization's behalf in England (*West African Pilot,* Sept. 24, 1947). The Abeokuta Women's Union (AWU) issued its own statement distancing itself from the Alake and fully supporting the arguments in her article (*West African Pilot,* Sept. 2, 1947). In fact, the AWU, with the support of Rev. Ransome-Kuti, organized a rousing reception at the Abeokuta Grammar School for FRK's return to Abeokuta from Lagos.[30] Several months later, FRK defended her position by arguing that "the true position of Nigerian women had to be judged from the women who carried babies on their backs and farmed from sunrise to sunset . . . not women who used tea, sugar, and flour for breakfast" (*West African Pilot,* Jan. 9, 1948). (These sentiments, inherently a class analysis, are some of the lyrics of the song "Mushin," written many years later by her son Fela.) At a reception for the NCNC delegation in Lagos in October, FRK thanked the ruler of

Lagos, Oba Falolu, and the women activists Charlotte Obasa and Madam Pelewura for their cooperation while she was in London (*Daily Times*, Oct. 10, 1947).

The controversy created by the article was in turn covered by the *Daily Worker* on September 30, 1947. The headline read, "Mrs. Kuti Was Quite Right"; the subheading stated, "Women of Nigeria Refused to Have Their Conditions Misrepresented." The correspondent, Derek Kartun, reported on the ENA Council meeting at which the resolution condemning the article was passed. Kartun's article inferred that the women present who spoke against FRK's article had to be "prodded" to do so and were wealthy traders, one of whom, Alice Dada from Ifo, "has developed such methods in her salt trade that the AWU had made inquiries on behalf of their members." The resolution was forwarded to Whitehall where shortly afterward it was delivered, under Colonial Office seal, to the *Daily Worker*. The AWU, however, had also sent its resolution that praised and agreed with FRK to the *Daily Worker*.[31]

While the delegation was in England, India and Pakistan became independent states. This, for FRK, showed the model for Nigeria. As she wrote to Sorensen on February 6, 1957 (after Ghana emerged as an independent state), "I saw how particularly happy the members of your organization were. Now Ghana—should be Nigeria."[32] Clearly, her goal was independence for Nigeria, not reform of colonialism.

On the trip to England, through her contact with women in the Labour Party, such as Violet Creech-Jones and Freda Grimble, FRK first came into contact with the international women's organization, the Women's International Democratic Federation (WIDF). One of the many Soviet-inspired international organizations propagating communist and socialist philosophies set up in the aftermath of World War II, the WIDF was founded in Paris on December 1, 1945. Its aims were to "unite women regardless of race, nationality, religion and political opinion, so that they may work together to win, implement and defend the rights of children to life, well-being and education; win and defend national independence and democratic freedoms, eliminate apartheid, racial discrimination and fascism; [and] work for peace and universal disarmament."[33]

From 1946–53, the WIDF was run by a council secretariat, headed by a general secretary. In 1953 the federation convened the World Congress of Women in Copenhagen which then constituted the congress of the WIDF. Thereafter, the congress elected a council and the council elected a bureau consisting of a president, vice president(s), general secretary, and other members. Meetings were open to observers and guests by invitation. The WIDF sought to associate with their work prominent women and organizations and groups, including national organizations of women in many countries. The organization published newsletters, documents, brochures, informational leaflets, congress reports, and books.

In postwar Britain under the Labour Party government, thousands of British Socialists, Labour Party supporters, liberals, pacifists, and anticolonialists joined these organizations. Only after 1950, when the cold war really set in, were these organizations described as "communist fronts" and their members suspected of being "dupes." For students and visitors from the British colonies, their anti-imperialistic posture and support for national independence obviously made these organizations very attractive. A number of West African students joined the World Congress of Youths, for instance, and other international socialist organizations. They also clustered around the WASU, the Fabian Colonial Bureau, and people such as Sorensen and Fenner-Brockway, who had demonstrated their sympathy for West African nationalism. In this context, it is not surprising that FRK, given her contacts with the left-wing Labour Party and radical women's groups in Britain, should also meet members of the WIDF and find its objectives in sympathy with her own aims for the AWU and her ideology on gender and socialism as articulated in the *Daily Worker* article.

Just a month after FRK left Britain, the executive committee of the secretariat of the WIDF met in Stockholm and decided to set up a special commission to examine the conditions of women in Asia and Africa. Undoubtedly, this new direction was related to the publicity that FRK had generated while in Great Britain. The commission included Dr. Pat Miles of the British WIDF coordinating committee, Zelma Brandt of the Congress of American Women, Simone Bertrand of the French Union, and several members from the USSR and its republics. The commission visited India, Malaya, and Burma and compiled information on Vietnam and Indonesia, where they were refused visas. It also compiled reports on other Asian countries and countries in the Middle East and Africa. The reports were submitted to the Second World Congress of Women for Peace, held in Budapest in December 1948, and then published as a book, *The Women of Asia and Africa: Documents*. The book includes a report on Nigeria that had been published in the WIDF

Information Bulletin, no. 33, in November 1948. With data provided by FRK, most of the one-page report focused on the agitation in Abeokuta against taxation. There was also a brief reference to the women's demonstrations in Mbawsi, Eastern Provinces, against the introduction of pioneer oil mills. The book included reports from Francophone Africa and South Africa and concluded its survey with a call for women worldwide to work for national independence.

Thus, very soon after her visit to Great Britain, FRK was in regular correspondence with the WIDF. In early 1948, the WIDF wrote asking if she would be willing to participate as a Nigerian delegate to an international exposition of women planned for May of that year. In addition, they requested delegates from the women's wing of the NCNC. FRK declined on behalf of the NCNC on the grounds that she felt the organization "ill prepared" at that moment but added, on behalf of the AWU, "We are anxious first of all to have our union affiliated to WIDF as soon as we are qualified to do this."[34] Later (see below), she rescinded the AWU's offer to affiliate but did join the organization as an individual. It is not clear why she felt the NCNC "ill prepared" to send women delegates. Perhaps she believed that fallout from her recent disagreement with Azikiwe over the organization's delegation to England would have militated against such cooperation. Or possibly she felt that the WIDF's socialist orientation would have caused the NCNC to rebuff any such invitation.

Obviously, the WIDF was eager to recruit FRK as one of the very few radical, feminist, women leaders in Africa at the time. She, however, was somewhat disconcerted by the intensity and speed of WIDF contacts with her; she turned to Solanke for advice, because he was one of the intermediaries through whom these contacts were first made and because he was well acquainted with the international scene. When she received an invitation to attend the WIDF congress in China in 1949 she again sought Solanke's advice: "Now some people here say that we must not attend the congress because it is a communist organization and some say it is not. I really don't know what it really is. I will be very grateful if you could please write immediately to let me know what to do."[35] He replied via cablegram, counseling her "to ignore that particular invitation or write them a diplomatic letter rejecting the invitation because it is Communists that govern China."[36] Apparently Solanke already had doubts about the WIDF's communist orientation, though FRK appears more curious than discouraged.

Even Ṣolanke was sometimes confused by the plethora of organizations. In October 1950, FRK wrote to Ṣolanke about an invitation from
the People's World Convention to meet in Geneva 1951. She asked, "On
what would you advise me to speak? Could you please send me a draft of
what I should say?"[37] Ṣolanke replied, "There are so many world conventions or international organizations out here in Europe and I am not yet
well acquainted with them. But I believe that the one your letter refers
to is nice enough and I am therefore opining that [you] may accept."[38]

Ṣolanke took his role as advisor seriously. On September 23, 1948, he
wrote, "I am anxious that Funmi should attend the WIDF conference in
India. I have discovered since my return that the whole world particularly India is very much interested in Nigeria. Suggest cablegrams, 1 to
Nehru, 1 to Mrs Couturier. Should read as follows: Have sent the cablegram to Nehru as directed. Like very much to attend the conference but
no money for travel. Could any help be given me in the latter."[39]

FRK also corresponded with Ṣolanke about woman suffrage in Great
Britain. She especially wanted to know whether all voters were taxpayers.[40] She used this information, which Ṣolanke supplied promptly,
in her speeches and lobbying on behalf of the NWU's pro-woman suffrage position.

In addition, Ṣolanke served as a direct intermediary between women
in Great Britain and FRK: "Please tell our Funmi that she will soon get
a letter from a certain British Women's International Association. Their
delegate came to see your Iyawo [Okikiolu Ṣolanke, Ṣolanke's wife] for
advice on how to get in touch with her."[41] After her initial doubts, by
1952 FRK had decided to accept the WIDF invitations. She attended a
WIDF conference on the "Defense of Children" in Vienna on April 9,
1952. At that conference, information was obtained that was later presented to the first WIDF World Congress of Women in Copenhagen,
June 5–10, 1953. At this congress, FRK was elected as one of the vice
presidents of the WIDF.

The reports of the two conferences were then published in 1954 as
a book, *That They May Live: African Women Arise.* The book contains
reports on women's conditions and activities in various African countries. The one-page report on Nigeria was authored by FRK. There was
an inset photograph of her and a picture of delegates to the National
Conference of Women held at Abeokuta in August 1953. The write-up
described the meeting and the aims of the Nigerian Women's Union. It
also referred to the Abeokuta women's agitation against the water rate

tax. The caption accompanying FRK's photograph states, "She conducts tireless action in defence of women's rights and against the arbitrary administration."[42]

En route back to Nigeria from Vienna, FRK spent a few weeks in Great Britain. She visited her son Olikoye in Dublin and her daughter Dolupo and granddaughter Frances in England. She held her usual meetings with Sorensen and Fenner-Brockway and also met Dr. Edith Summerskill, a Labour Party member of Parliament and a well-known feminist activist. FRK also met two women journalists from the *Daily Worker*, Sheila Lynd and Joyce Hunter, who had written an article on her involvement in the abdication of the Alake in 1949.[43]

Sheila Lynd did another article about FRK after this meeting. Entitled "Nothing Dismays Mrs. Kuti," it appeared in the *Daily Worker* of May 14, 1952. After an account of the activities of the NWU, the article quoted FRK's views on the Vienna conference that she had recently attended:

> Surely it will help towards peace and understanding for so many to meet without thinking of colour, religion and position and pool ideas about the welfare of children. When I go back I shall tour Nigeria reporting what I saw and heard there. Then I shall call the leaders of the movement together and we shall draw up our proposals to the government based on the resolutions about the child's rights to health and education at the conference which were completely in accord with what we have all along been working [toward].

Lynd's article reported that FRK would be one of the speakers at the first big public meeting to report on the Vienna conference at Caxton Hall, London. While FRK was in Vienna, another attempt had been made to collect the water rate tax in Abeokuta. She received the news in London and made several protests to the Colonial Office.

The reference to the collection of water rates is to the incident described in chapter 4 when on April 16, 1952, the Abeokuta Urban District Council (AUDC) had decided to impose a water rate of three shillings per annum per woman. This was in spite of the opposition of the AWU representative on the AUDC. The AWU's petition against the water rates was sent to FRK in Vienna. While in London she raised the subject in her discussions with Sorensen and Fenner-Brockway. This is a clear instance of the way in which she used her international contacts and experience to create political pressure on the British colonial administration in Nigeria regarding its policies toward issues concerning Nigerian women.

During the colonial period, ultimate power lay with London: therefore, FRK regarded London as a legitimate arena in which to fight the Alake and the Western Region government. She carried the fight both to the inner caucus—the Colonial Office—and to the opposition, the then Conservative government and the Labour Party, especially its left wing. She thus used her international experience to support her national and local agenda and tactics.

When FRK returned to Nigeria from Europe and was embroiled in the agitation against the payment of water rates (chap. 4), she continued to try to mobilize international pressure. After the tear-gassing incident on July 29, 1952 (chap. 5), she wrote to Madame Couturier, president of the WIDF. The WIDF sent cablegrams to British officials in Nigeria to protest the use of force against the AWU women. The WIDF newsletter of March 1953 also contained an article demanding the abolition of the water rate. The WIDF sent a telegram to the president, Abeokuta magistrate's court, urging the dismissal of a charge against a woman for leaving the body of her dead child at the house of the president of the court. The woman believed her child's death was due to ill treatment during the demonstration.[44]

FRK also contacted G. R. McGregor-Wood, a leader of the British Women's International Association, a women's union in England, to whom she had been introduced by Solanke. McGregor-Wood was initially suspicious of FRK's affiliation with the WIDF, which she saw as a communist organization, but Solanke assured McGregor-Wood that FRK was not a communist: "It was not true because from the beginning I did all I could to make you [FRK] assure me [Solanke] that you have nothing to do with communist organizations."[45]

Solanke asked FRK to write to McGregor-Wood, explaining that she was not a communist and that the AWU was not affiliated with the WIDF. Apparently, FRK responded in a way that caused Solanke to write that McGregor-Wood was satisfied "that neither you personally nor your women's union has anything to do with communists."[46] FRK never wrote to Solanke or McGregor-Wood explaining the distinction—that she was personally involved with the WIDF but had not committed the AWU to any involvement.

In the context of the cold war, the WIDF was undoubtedly seen in the West as a communist front, and FRK must have been fully aware of this perception. When she wished to have the help of anticommunists in the West, her political maneuvering was characterized by its pragmatism. Undoubtedly, she also felt herself to be extremely vulnerable. In a time when so much public and governmental support in Nigeria was aligned against communism, she felt some need to tread gingerly on the issue of her political affiliations with communists. In her struggles she sought support from diverse ideological sources and often performed a delicate balancing act in order to maintain her right to independent political thought and action. She pursued this same policy in the crisis over her passport (see below). When she felt her cause was just, she asked for help from those who may have considered themselves one another's enemies—but not her enemy. She did not consider herself to be abandoning her principles with such action but rather behaving pragmatically. During this period, for instance, both the WIDF and McGregor-Wood responded to FRK's solicitations and lent support to the women's cause.

Funmilayo Ransome-Kuti was not a member of the Communist Party. She was not frightened or repelled by communism either, as evidenced by her travel, and often admired what she perceived as the greater flexibility of gender roles in certain communist countries. FRK was a democratic socialist, meaning that she believed a government should be duly elected by all adult citizens and that from communal funds (graduated income tax) the government should provide free education and health care for all and guarantee the basic necessities (food, clothing, shelter) for the poorest of its citizens. She was also a feminist in that she believed men and women were equal in their abilities and advocated equal treatment and opportunities for both genders. In her real-life political activity, though, she was a pragmatist. That is to say that though she did not compromise her principles, she was willing to accept help from diverse ideological sources, though unwilling to be controlled by any of them. When she felt herself greatly in need of external support, such as in the tear-gassing incident—she was not beyond a certain level of political ambiguity.

McGregor-Wood, once satisfied that FRK was not a communist, then wrote to the Colonial Office protesting about the tear gassing of women. To the editor of *West Africa* magazine, she sent a letter entitled "Affair at Abeokuta" that was published in the September 20, 1952, issue:

> Sir, for the past month I have been combing the papers for information about the events reported to have taken place at Abeokuta, Nigeria, on August 4 this year. It is alleged that tear gas was used by police on a party of women

belonging to the Women's Union who were going for a "picnic." It appears that their previous plan to hold a procession had been altered in deference to official requests and that they understood no permission was necessary for a "picnic." I have in my possession photographs which seem to prove the use of tear gas—surely a somewhat more drastic remedy than the offence called for if indeed offence there was.

Perhaps if all women in Nigeria were voters, milder methods would have been used as more indicative of the defence supposedly due to those possessing the franchise. In any case we should like to hear more about what happened on August 4.

Yours faithfully,
G. R. McGregor-Wood
Hampstead

The editor of *West Africa* added a postscript: "As a result of the incident referred to by Mrs. McGregor-Wood, Mrs. Ransome-Kuti was found guilty at the magistrates' court at Abeokuta of collecting an unlawful assembly and was fined ten pounds. Forty-one other women were found guilty of taking part in an unlawful assembly and were each fined five pounds."

As the cold war conflicts hardened in the early 1950s, the British government became extraordinarily apprehensive of communist infiltration into the colonies. In Malaya, the British engaged in suppressing a communist insurgency; at the same time, the Korean War had ended with the communists consolidated in North Korea. In Nigeria, therefore, the British administration was very suspicious of organizations like the WIDF. This fear and suspicion were conveyed to Nigerians. By the 1950s, those who had been radical or socialist students in Great Britain in the 1940s no longer identified themselves with international socialist organizations. Nigerian political parties adopted goals of social welfare and democracy but their main concern was the struggle for political power within Nigeria. FRK was one of the very few of the Nigerian political elite who was consistent in her attachment to socialist internationalism and, in addition, to international radical feminism.

The government placed a ban on communist literature in July 1954, including that of the WIDF (*West African Pilot,* Aug. 4, 1954). The WIDF sent a formal protest to the government of Nigeria about the banning of its publications. The All Nigerian Trade Union Federation passed a motion declaring itself opposed to communism and determined to exterminate it in the trade union movement (*West African Pilot,* July 15,

1954). The government announced that it would not employ communists in strategic branches of the public service (*West African Pilot*, Oct. 15, 1954).

In July 1954, the secretary general of the WIDF, Mollie Mandel, visited Nigeria and spent a couple of days in Abeokuta, staying in FRK's home.[47] In May 1955, FRK and two FNWS members planned to attend a meeting of the World Assembly of Peace at Helsinki, Finland. She applied for her passport to be endorsed for Finland, Russia, and China. She was asked to see the chief secretary of the government and "was told of the State of Policy towards communism issued jointly by the Federal and Regional governments. . . . It was . . . explained to her that the WIDF and the World Assembly of Peace were Communist-dominated organizations. At the end of this meeting, FRK was told that, if she persisted in attending communist controlled conferences abroad, serious consideration would have to be given to withdrawing her passport."[48]

In April 1956, the WIDF invited FRK to attend a meeting of their council in Peking. When she again applied for her passport to be endorsed, she encountered opposition and reluctance. Nonetheless, it was endorsed and she went to China for three weeks where, in her own words, "I spoke about Nigerian women and children. I sang Yoruba songs and showed them various customs and traditions of my country. I traveled to many parts of China. Delegates came from every part of the world to attend the Chinese May Day celebration, even from Britain. I wonder if attending independence celebrations of other countries means social communism to our Prime Minister who cries wolf when there is none to come."[49]

The visit to Peking attracted international attention. Shortly after, the London *Times* of May 28, 1956, carried an article on "Indoctrination of Africans." It cited the WIDF as a communist international front organization and FRK as an example of an African being subjected to indoctrination. The *Daily Worker* of June 12, 1956, also had an article and photograph of FRK at the WIDF meeting in Peking.

The *Nigerian Sunday Times* of June 17, 1956, referred to the London *Times*'s article of May 28 and included an interview with FRK. She denied the accusation that she went to China to show Nigerian women how much better off women were in communist countries, saying her sole interest was to work for the enfranchisement and celebration of Nigerian women by seeing what "other races had done to achieve similar results." She acknowledged that she had brought back a copy of the famous Chinese film *The White-Haired Girl,* which she planned to show to the public.[50] In a June 17, 1956, interview in the *Nigerian Sunday Times,* FRK insisted she was not "indoctrinated" in her trip to China but that she was working to find strategies aimed at the "improvement and liberation of Nigeria women."

In June 1957, she submitted her passport for renewal in order to attend another WIDF conference, but after repeated procrastination the prime minister (Tafawa Balewa) announced in December that the government refused to renew her passport. An NWU delegation called on Balewa. They addressed him as their "son" and registered him as an honorary member of the NWU, then asked him to renew FRK's passport. The women denied that FRK had any communist connections and demanded that the government "halt the tendency to deny Nigerians their democratic civil rights in the name of 'Red Hunting.'" Balewa told the women's delegation that he would reconsider the government's decision, but on December 31 he wrote a letter to the NWU explaining, "I still do not find myself able to recommend the renewal of Funmilayo Ransome-Kuti's passport. I wish to make it quite clear to the members of the union that I have no quarrel with them, and I readily believe that they are actuated by the most worthy motives. It was, indeed, a most interesting meeting."[51]

The NWU gave an impassioned reply:

> Mr. Prime Minister, remember that you are only a man, born of Nigerian womanhood. As a religious man with fear of God in you, I must point it out, that you are doing this nation injustice by restricting the movement of her citizens. Thou Oh man made of clay, born of woman, you are assassinating the Nigeria Women's Union Liberties. You sincerely promised the Nigeria Women's deputation stating that as the servant of the public, the servant of God, as an Alhaji, you will reconsider the renewal of Mrs. Funmilayo Ransome-Kuti's passport, communicate this union a favourable answer. Remember, you asked for your old women's prayers to help you never to be confused and your office was turned into a Mosque with prayers on the lips of the ten women delegation including the Federal Prime Minister himself. Remember our sitting was that of [a] mother with her son. You requested the union to guarantee Mrs. Funmilayo Ransome-Kuti's movements in Europe which the union feels holds no water in the fundamental principle of human rights but we promised to inform the government of her movements to any part of the world outside Nigeria.[52]

The refusal to renew FRK's passport provoked considerable controversy. Editorials and articles in the *Daily Service,* the *Daily Times,* and the

West African Pilot argued that as an individual she had the right to travel at her discretion and that the government's action was "an unnecessary restriction of civil liberties" (*Daily Times,* Jan. 2, 1958). However, the editorials also warned her about being a tool of the communists and importing foreign ideas into the country. The general secretary of the All Nigerian Trade Union Federation criticized the government, and the Nigerian Union of Students protested the "violation of the principles of fundamental rights" (*West African Pilot,* Dec. 30, 1957). Fenner-Brockway cabled his protest to the British secretary of state for the colonies.

Finally, on March 3, 1958, Balewa made a statement in the House of Representatives explaining the government's position in answer to the questions of J. A. O. Akande, member for Egba North. Balewa listed the number of communist countries that FRK had visited. Quoting a statement she allegedly made in China—that women in Nigeria had never ceased fighting for their rights in the last ten years—he observed that "in the past when it was thought that Mrs. Kuti might be the innocent victim of Communist schemes, she was informed officially . . . but now it can be assumed that it is her intention to influence the various Nigerian women's organizations, with which she is connected, with Communist ideas and policies."[53] On those grounds, the government would not renew her passport.

FRK issued a public statement denying Balewa's charges and ridiculing his assumption that because she visited communist countries, she was a communist intent on making Nigerian women communists. She asked if Balewa's visits to Egypt and Saudi Arabia made him an Arab out to Islamize Nigeria and suggested that "it can also be assumed that the governor general of the Federation, once of the Sudanese government, is out here to make Nigerians Sudanese" (*Daily Service,* Mar. 4, 1958).

She also wrote a letter of protest to the prime minister in which she complained bitterly of what she felt was the racism exhibited by the expatriate senior assistant secretary of immigration, Mr. Roberts, who had tried to get her to sign a "confession" that she had not traveled to communist countries for health reasons, as she had claimed. Of him she said: "Ill-treated as I felt, a European who signed his name 'Mr. Roberts' presented this insulting statement to me. . . . I am so sorry to note that because of my colour, Mr. Roberts should take it upon himself to have me insulted." She demanded an apology and the renewal of her passport. She also sent the letter to the British secretary of state for the colonies and to the United Nations. The rest of the letter charged that the prime minster played a dirty political game of the NPC under the direction of expatriates. . . . The rights of Nigerian women are now being assassinated by virtue of the federal prime minister's high office. A woman shall succeed him one day as prime minster. Because we demand the franchise for Balewa's North, women are called communist. Because Nigerian women are used as tools in this country by various political parties, Balewa's speech was greeted by cheers. This organization [NWU] will continue to champion the freedom of Nigerian Womanhood. We [women] need a place in the federal House. We demand equality with northern male politicians. . . . [We] tell nothing but the truth to the Nigerian oppressed inhabitants, women ask the ministers to cut down their salaries, that they should copy the prime minister of Ghana, who brought the feelings and comfort of his people always first to his heart, and lived in a room and parlour till after Ghana's independence, and never in a thirty thousand pounds' paradise, because Nigerian women's organizations demand franchise for Alhaji Tafewa Balewa's North, women all over the Federation of Nigeria have been declared communists by the prime minister with his team of expatriates and his council of ministers."[54]

These protests, however, did not succeed in changing the government's decision, and FRK's passport was not renewed until after independence. She then continued her association with the WIDF, attending a conference in Budapest in 1961 and visiting Moscow, Prague, and Warsaw in 1962. In 1963 she and Margaret Ekpo, a Nigerian feminist and political activist from the Eastern Region who regarded FRK as her mentor, attended the World Congress of Women in Moscow.

In 1958, FRK had applied to the United States for a visa to attend a women's conference in San Francisco to which she had been invited. Her visa application was denied on the grounds of her alleged communist connections.[55] In 1975, she once again applied for a visa to the United States to speak at a UN-sponsored conference on International Woman's Year. She did not receive the visa although the reason is unclear (*Nigerian Sunday Times*, Apr. 9, 1977).

FRK was also involved with the Women's International League for Peace and Freedom (WILPF). A branch of the WILPF had been organized in Nigeria as early as 1950 under the initiative of a Nigerian woman, C. A. O. Essien.[56] Shortly after this branch was established, there were ideological and personal problems between the main organization and the Nigerian branch, which apparently became defunct sometime in the 1950s. By the early 1960s, the WILPF reappeared in Nigeria, this time spearheaded by FRK, who had apparently been introduced to the organization by Sam Enwerenzu, who had been a student at Pennsylvania's Lincoln University, a historically African American university. The WILPF had a very active section in Philadelphia, which is where he may have encountered it. The organization had asked him for contacts with African women and FRK's name was one of those he suggested. In 1960 FRK responded to WILPF literature by writing the organization and saying she wished to organize a section of the WILPF in Abeokuta and, in fact, "We hope to spread all over the country. The members will be composed of teachers, workers, traders and housewives—of all creeds."[57]

By October 1961, the WILPF was referring interested persons in Nigeria to FRK.[58] On February 12, 1961, FRK wrote to the WILPF's Geneva section, "The branch in Abeokuta was inaugurated on November 14th. Meetings have been held monthly since, even when I was away from home (in Egypt and UK). Ibadan branch is not well fixed yet; it needs my supervision a bit. Ibadan is 48 miles from Abeokuta, so it is not very easy for me to be present at their meetings."[59] A WILPF representative, Emily Simon, visited Nigeria in February 1961 at FRK's invitation and was hosted by her in Abeokuta. FRK drove Simon to Lagos, and on the return trip to Abeokuta she had a car accident in which she broke her wrist and ankle and suffered head injuries. A few months later in June 1961 she attended a WIDF meeting in Berlin, and she stayed to receive medical attention for the injuries suffered in the car accident. By 1963 the WILPF was listing FRK as president of its Nigeria section, yet it is unclear how active this section was. It is apparent that FRK's affiliation with the WILPF was never as active as that with the WIDF, and given the WILPF's anticommunist orientation, the apparent lack of a paper trail of criticism of FRK's travels seems odd. FRK's affiliation with WILPF and even her efforts on the organization's behalf in Nigeria seem to have been sporadic and uninspired. Given the attitudes expressed by a number of WILPF organizers regarding the need to "lead" and "teach" particularly African women, it is not hard to imagine a personality conflict with a woman of FRK's character and experience. According to the scholar Anene Ejikeme, by 1970 the WILPF seems to have again become defunct in Nigeria.[60]

In addition to her WIDF and WILPF activities, FRK was actively engaged on the African continent, though there is far less information available (at least in Nigeria) on these connections than on those in Britain. She visited Ghana several times and greatly admired its prime minister, Kwame Nkrumah. In 1953 Nkrumah invited her, along with a number of male Nigeria political activists including Obafemi Awolowo, Nnamdi Azikiwe, and Aminu Kano, to attend a conference of West African Nationalists in Ghana.[61] In 1954, following closely on the electoral success of his Convention People's Party, she invited Nkrumah to speak at the annual conference of the FNWS. After some preliminary remarks on other issues, he expressed his sorrow at being unable to attend due to a conflict:

> I am sorry it will not be possible for me to speak at the Conference of Nigerian Women's Organizations owing to the forthcoming opening of the Legislative Assembly. I had planned to send Miss Mabel Dove as a representative, but unfortunately, she is expected to be occupied by Assembly duties just about the same time your Conference takes place. Would you like me to send someone else?
>
> >   Wishing you continued good health,
> >   Kind Regards,
> >   Yours very sincerely,
> >   Kwame Nkrumah[62]

A month earlier she had received a letter from Mr. Tadamafio, general secretary to Nkrumah's Convention People's Party, in which he stated: "I am directed by Dr. Nkrumah to acknowledge with thanks the receipt of your esteemed telegram of congratulations which he very much appreciates. Your visit to this country at the time of the West African Nationalist Conference and your several public addresses at the time have doubtless contributed to this signal success."[63] On that same trip, she had also attended women's conferences in Algeria, Dahomey (now Benin), Guinea, Liberia, and Togo. She was an invited guest at the inauguration ceremony of the Ghana Women's Movement in September 1960 and is credited with having played a role in its founding. Among her personal papers are a number of letters and reports on women's political activity in the Cameroons, Liberia, South Africa, and Sierra Leone. She maintained a long correspondence with Constance Cummings-John of Sierra Leone and visited Freetown in 1960 at the invitation of the Sierra Leone Women's Movement.

After the Sharpeville incident in South Africa in 1960 (in which a number of women pass-law protesters were killed), FRK received a letter from Leah Maphalthe of Mafeking, Basutoland, asking for her help. In April 1960, FRK sent a telegram to Queen Elizabeth in which she appealed to the queen's maternal feelings to guide her in helping to "relieve South Africans from inhumanity."[64]

In 1949, she also wrote to Marcus Garvey's (the well-known Jamaican Pan-Africanist leader who died in 1940) United Negro Improvement Association's womens' corps, proposing some contact between it and the Nigerian Women's Union.[65] On May 22, 1947, Garvey's widow, Amy Ashwood Garvey, had visited Abeokuta. She spoke on the position of women and championed their equality, urging that the title of Iyalode of the Egba be revived. This may have prompted FRK's 1949 query.[66] There is no correspondence to indicate the outcome.

Moreover, there are bits and pieces of correspondence from Trinidad, the Korean Democratic Women's Union, the All China Women's Democratic Federation, the Committee of Bulgarian Women, the National Federation of Indian Women, and the Vietnam Women's Union, some but not all of it clearly channeled through the WIDF. Through contacts made in her travels, her WIDF associations, and her association with the WILPF, FRK appears to have been well informed on women's issues worldwide.

Although she could likely have lived elsewhere if she wished, she chose to remain in Nigeria—in fact, in Abeokuta. Yet, right up to her death, she continued to be the recipient of various kinds of information, requests, and invitations from women's organizations around the world. A year before her death a Nigerian newspaper profiled FRK in a two-page spread, saying in part, "Like 76-year-old Mrs. Vijayalakshmi Pandit of India, who this year campaigned against Prime Minister Indira Gandhi . . . our woman political pundit, Mrs. Anikulapo-Kuti, is most likely to ride again" (*Nigerian Sunday Times*, Apr. 9, 1977).[67] Funmilayo Ransome-Kuti did not "ride again" after 1977, but she surely left her mark on Nigeria and on the history of women's struggles for equality.

Notes

1. Olusanya, *Second World War and Politics*, 42.
2. *Lagos Headlines*, no. 49, Apr. 1976.
3. Sorensen, autobiography, House of Lords Record Office, London, 305.
4. Ṣolanke to FRK, Mar. 1, 1943, box 73, file 8 (g), Ṣolanke Papers.
5. Sorensen, autobiography, 304.
6. Ibid., 305. In the course of their tour, Sorensen and Hinden visited a number of towns in Nigeria including Abeokuta where they met again the Reverend and Mrs. Ransome-Kuti. During a meeting with "local notables" at which the reverend was present, FRK suddenly entered, declaimed rapidly in Yoruba to the astounded company, and as suddenly withdrew. Shortly afterward, the

team left the meeting, entered an adjoining courtyard, and encountered an angry confrontation. One of the supporters of the Alake had flung a stone at one of FRK's women followers. The angry women had seized the culprit and were tearing off his clothes. Sorensen recorded: "The Rev. Kuti plunged his burly weight into the crowd, snatched off a headgear from a woman to enwrap the battered almost naked man and banged from the culprit's hand a magical bone juju. A police van appeared, the badly bruised wretch was bundled in, the van departed, the women cheered and we went our way to discuss the future of Nigeria." Sorensen does not reveal what he felt about FRK except to describe her as an "intrepid feminist agitator." Dr. Oladipo Maja, who (as Sorensen himself wrote, "frequented my home as a London student" [313]) was a longtime close personal friend of the Sorensen family, suggested that Sorensen regarded FRK as a "rabble rouser" and that he much preferred the company of the Reverend Ransome-Kuti.

7. Quoted by Rev. (later Canon) J. S. Adeniyi in a three-page typescript biography of Rev. Ransome-Kuti, Aug. 10, 1960, IORK Papers.

8. Smyke and Storer, *Nigerian Union of Teachers,* 65.

9. Some of this correspondence has been preserved in the Ṣolanke Papers. The letters from Ṣolanke are very detailed and effectively briefed the Ransome-Kutis about WASU activities, contacts like Sorensen, and so on.

10. R-K to Ṣolanke, Jan. 19, 1934, box 2, file 1, no. 24, Ṣolanke Papers.

11. R-K to Ṣolanke, Jan. 7, 1933, box 1, file 6, no. 6b, Ṣolanke Papers.

12. Fajana, "Evolution of Educational Policy," 243.

13. Babalola, *My Life Adventures,* 134.

14. E. O. Alayande, interview, Lagos, Feb. 12, 1991.

15. Huxley, *Memories,* 366.

16. Ibid., 271.

17. Ibid., 278.

18. Elliot Commission file, Abeokuta Archives.

19. Ibid.

20. Ibid. Abeokutans were disappointed that Ibadan was chosen as the site instead of Abeokuta, just as the people of Onitsha were disappointed that Nsukka was chosen as the site for the University of Nigeria in 1960. It is unclear what recommendations Rev. Ransome-Kuti made for Abeokuta as the site but it has been suggested that the Alake was very disappointed that Ransome-Kuti failed to get Abeokuta named as the site.

21. Ibid. Elliot had visited the Afin sixteen years earlier with his father, and he was glad to find his father's signature in the Alake's visitor's book. On July 9, 1954, FRK wrote to Elliot, then a member of the House of Commons, asking him if he could help find a hospital for her son Koye's internship year.

22. In the IORK Papers are copies of the letters FRK sent to the Creech-Joneses, which also refer to letters from them. In the Creech-Jones Papers, how-

ever, there is only one letter from FRK to Mr. and Mrs. Creech-Jones (dated Mar. 15, 1950). It reads: "I congratulate you on behalf of all the women in Nigeria and myself for all that you have done to help them towards their emancipation, for what you have done to further the progress of Nigeria socially, politically, and educationally. . . . I am not at all sorry that you have lost your seat in the Parliament during this term, because I feel you really need a rest the way you were both working. . . . It is certain that the government cannot go without you and we hope you will try to take sufficient rest. We all send you our thanks for all you have done for us and we hope that Mr. Griffith will also do his best for us."

23. FRK, speech entitled "Mrs. Kuti's Observation of the NCNC Delegation to London," Oct. 17, 1947, copy, FRK Papers.

24. Ibid.

25. Sklar, *Nigerian Political Parties,* 63.

26. FRK, interview, Abeokuta, July 12, 1976.

27. Mary P. Ussher to FRK, Sept. 4, 1947, FRK Papers.

28. Freda Grimble to FRK, Aug. 29, 1947, FRK Papers.

29. FRK, speech, Kirsten Hall, Oct. 17, 1947, copy, FRK Papers.

30. Soyinka, *Ake,* has a wonderful description of this reception (194).

31. The *Daily Worker* had paid more attention to the NCNC delegation than other British papers and particular attention to FRK. For instance, the Aug. 14, 1947, front page carried a photograph of FRK and the headline "Nigerians Plan Meeting Here." The short write-up did not refer to FRK but stated that the delegation announced its plan to tour six provincial cities.

32. FRK to Sorensen, Feb. 6, 1957, FRK Papers.

33. WIDF, Constitution, Northwestern University Library.

34. FRK to Madam Courtier, Mar. 21, 1948, FRK Papers.

35. FRK to Ṣolanke, Oct. 3, 1949, box 73, file 9K, Ṣolanke Papers.

36. Ṣolanke to FRK, cablegram, Sept. 17, 1949, box 8, file 3J, Ṣolanke Papers.

37. FRK to Ṣolanke, Oct. 1950, box 8, file 4, no. 23, Ṣolanke Papers.

38. Ṣolanke to FRK, Nov. 9, 1950, box 73, file 9, 1p, Ṣolanke Papers. There is no evidence that FRK went to Geneva in 1951 or that Ṣolanke sent her the draft speech.

39. Ṣolanke to FRK and Rev. R-K, Sept. 23, 1948, box 73, file 8, Ṣolanke Papers.

40. FRK to Ṣolanke, Apr. 1949, box 8, file 2, Ṣolanke Papers.

41. Ṣolanke to Rev. R-K, Aug. 2, 1949, box 73, file 9f, Ṣolanke Papers. The delegate referred to was probably G. M. McGregor-Wood (see below).

42. WIDF, *That They May Live.*

43. FRK, diary, 1952 entries, FRK Papers.

44. Correspondence with WIDF, FRK Papers.

45. Ṣolanke to FRK, Aug. 20, 1952, box 73, file 8i, Ṣolanke Papers.

46. Ṣolanke to FRK, Sept. 10, 1952, box 73, file 8i, Ṣolanke Papers.

47. Correspondence with WIDF, IORK Papers.

48. Balewa, speech, House of Representatives, Mar. 3, 1958, Column 710, copy in University of Lagos Library.

49. FRK, press release, Mar. 5, 1958, in response to a criticism of her travel, FRK Papers.

50. Years later, FRK applied to the Board of Film Censors to have the film uncensored so "that the public may have the privilege of seeing it." It had been shown in Obiesesan Hall on June 26, 1960, to friends, and it was liked and favorably commented upon. FRK to Board of Film Censors, Sept. 7, 1960, FRK Papers.

51. Balewa to NWU, Dec. 31, 1957, FRK Papers.

52. NWU to Balewa, FRK Papers.

53. Balewa, speech.

54. FRK to Balewa, FRK Papers. See also, *Daily Times,* Dec. 21, 1957.

55. FRK, interview, Abeokuta, Aug. 10, 1976. See also *Daily Times,* May 2, 1973.

56. The information on WILPF in Nigeria is from Ejikeme, "Core-Periphery Relations in an International Women's Organization."

57. WILPF Circular Letter, no. 8, 1960, reel 29. WILPF Papers are available on microfiche at the main library, Ohio State University, Columbus, Ohio.

58. Eleanor Fowler (assistant to the administrative secretary of WILPF, Philadelphia) to Mr. Umo of Eket, Oct. 3, 1961, WILPF Circular Letter, 1961, reel 53.

59. WILPF Circular Letter, no. 2, 1961, reel 29.

60. See Ejikeme, "Core-Periphery Relations in an International Women's Organization," for several references to these attitudes on behalf of WILPF organizers.

61. Nkrumah to FRK, Aug. 17, 1953, FRK Papers.

62. Nkrumah to FRK, July 3, 1954, FRK Papers.

63. Tadamafio to FRK, June 23, 1954, FRK Papers.

64. FRK to Queen Elizabeth, telegram, Apr. 1960, FRK Papers.

65. FRK to UNIA Women's Corps, Aug. 9, 1949, FRK Papers.

66. Ake 2/1 box 10, file 30, Abeokuta Archives.

67. In the early 1970s, FRK dropped Ransome from her name and instead used Anikulapo (chap. 7).

7 "Virtue Is Better than Wealth":
Death and Legacy

The last three decades of Funmilayo Ransome-Kuti's life were fraught with tragedies and defeats but relieved by recognition of her contributions to the local, national, and world communities and by the attention from and successes of her children. In addition, she remained a focal point for the concerns of local market women, who frequently descended on her house to gather advice and have her settle disputes. Of this time her daughter Dolu said, "Every morning was just like a little court in her house . . . just like the Alake's house."

Perhaps it was advancing age in conjunction with the existence of a military government with which she often disagreed that gave her an increasing sense of vulnerability. Whatever it was, she kept a will in her possession at all times, constantly altering it.[1]

The consuming passions of these decades, though, were her desire to continue her role as an educator (and to immortalize her husband's contributions to education), to manage and control the family's resources (especially those involving land), and to exercise civic rights she considered "natural," such as free speech, even under a military regime. This chapter discusses her husband's death, her role as a school proprietor, the complex land cases generated by her inheritance from her father and the investments she made with Rev. Ransome-Kuti, the awards she accrued, and her children's lives. Her response to the challenges of these decades sheds a particular light on her personality as she aged. The chapter also chronicles the circumstances of her death and her legacy as seen in the eyes of others.

In 1952, Rev. Ransome-Kuti became seriously ill and was diagnosed with prostate cancer. FRK was traveling often during this time, particularly abroad, and her children believe she was unaware of the gravity of her husband's illness. Rev. Ransome-Kuti had always enjoyed robust health, and initially he too had a stoic attitude toward his illness, hoping to recover.[2] He remained supportive of his wife's political work and understanding of her absences from home. In June 1952, he wrote several letters to her at her various destinations, with "Love" as the salutation and signed himself as "Your Own, Dotun"—and never referred to his illness.[3] FRK herself may have felt overwhelmed during this time. In reference to a dream she had on her birthday the previous month, on November 14, 1952, she recorded in her diary that she had seen insects coming out of pieces of cake that she was eating. She later expressed guilt and regret at not having stayed more closely by her husband's side during his illness.[4]

By 1953, the reverend's health had deteriorated. In addition, the board of governors was pressuring him to retire as principal of the Abeokuta Grammar School (AGS), due to his age. His AGS staff wrote to the board, asking that he be allowed to stay on another year until "conditions" would be right for his retirement. It is not clear how much the staff knew about his illness. Staff from other secondary schools also wrote letters of support, pointing to the reverend's distinguished career and contributions as an educator.[5] Relenting due to the public outcry, the board allowed him to remain. He retired voluntarily at the end of December 1954 but continued as president of the Nigerian Union of Teachers (NUT).

The Reverend Ransome-Kuti's illness and his increasing need for his wife's attention presented her with a dilemma. Should she place her political activity, in a formal sense now at its height, on hold in order to devote her time to her husband? She seems to have decided against that, though there is evidence she experienced much anguish in making decisions to travel.[6]

During one hospital confinement in Ibadan, the reverend was visited by Christine Groves, a member of the NUT executive committee. She asked him if his wife was visiting him daily and he replied: "My wife is eaten up with her concern for women's affairs and I leave her to do it." She reported that this was said not with bitterness but in resignation.[7] There is little doubt, however, that the marriage was under great strain during this time.

In 1954 the reverend was to attend an NUT meeting in Ibadan where the organization wished to honor him. He stayed with his friend and fellow NUT activist, Reverend E. O. Alayande, in whose home he collapsed. He was hospitalized for two days in Ibadan and later transported to the General Hospital in Lagos. In her diary for October 16, 1954, FRK recorded that her husband had been transferred to Lagos in an ambulance.

On April 6, 1955, the Reverend Ransome-Kuti died. There was a large memorial service in Abeokuta, and many sent letters of condolence, including Fourah Bay College and the Nigerian Federal Advisory Committee on Education. There were also memorial services in Ijebu-Ode and Ibadan. In 1957, the University of Ibadan memorialized Rev. Ransome-Kuti by naming a men's residence hall after him. All of his physical property was jointly held by with his wife so she inherited the bulk of his estate. He left most of his money, £800 each, to his sons Beko and Fela, because they had not yet completed their educations. Much smaller sums were left to his children Koye and Dolu, his brother A. O., his niece Eniola Soyinka, and his wife.

FRK experienced a great sense of loss at her husband's death. Fela maintains that on the day of his father's burial his mother sobbingly accused her political colleagues of having taken her away from her husband. He also alleges that his parents had not slept together for years before his father's death.[8] There is no corroborating evidence for this and testimony of the other children contradicts it. It may be that by the early 1950s the cancer made physical intimacy impossible and, as already noted, the illness and FRK's activity undoubtedly caused tension in the marriage.

In 1956, FRK composed a prayer that she often read at her husband's gravesite in ensuing years.[9] After his death she also visited Fourah Bay College, his alma mater. In a poignant retrospective, Davidson Nicoll of Fourah Bay recalled her visit, remembering her as courteously and quietly impressive and as looking introspective in a pair of steel-rimmed spectacles. He said she mentioned that Fourah Bay had meant a lot to her husband. He told her that many people said how well the Reverend Ransome-Kuti spoke of her and the important part she played in his life. FRK later reported that she would forever miss her husband's "sense of humor, his big and roaring laughter, his sympathy and his constant companionship."[10] In a June 1973 interview with *Woman's World,* she reflected: "When a woman suddenly finds herself a widow, particularly if she and her husband had been very close as mine and I were, it will be then that she will need something to help her keep her balance from the sorrow that often springs from that loss." [11] Though she outlived her husband by twenty-three years (almost to the day) and was only fifty-four when he died, informants, family, and other available evidence concur that she had no romantic liaisons after his death. Rather, she rededicated herself to their dream of founding schools and to her political activities.

After her husband's death, she undertook to establish a large and diverse educational complex through a series of personal investments, partnerships, and mergers. In her strong-willed, determined way she maneuvered to exercise control over both her partners and her staff. Because she was constantly on the verge of bankruptcy and absorbed in national and international politics, it was even more difficult for her to exercise effective educational administration. Still, her belief in the critical importance of literacy and her lifelong role as an educator led her to try to create a viable Ransome-Kuti educational complex in Abeokuta. In the last twenty years of her life, this was sometimes done with spit and glue.

After Rev. Ransome-Kuti's retirement in December 1954, his family had to leave the principal's living quarters at the AGS. Earlier in the year FRK's father, Daniel Thomas, had died, and she inherited a large piece of land along Iṣabo road, Igbein, Ake (Abeokuta). The land was divided into sections. On what became Nos. 11–13 Iṣabo Road, she built Thomas Hall as a place to establish her own school. On No. 15 Iṣabo Road she built a two-story house that was not quite completed when the family moved into it in January 1955.

In 1955 four men, three of them ex-AGS students and teachers—I. O. Oduntan, Mr. Akinboro, E. O. Agunbiade, and E. S. Oduniyi—rented Thomas Hall where they established an evening school known as the Reverend Kuti Memorial Evening School. FRK was appointed a member of the school board. By July 1956 the school, now a full-time day school, was approved by the Ministry of Education to operate up to the school certificate level (the end of secondary school). By this time, FRK was listed as one of the proprietors of the school.

By 1962 FRK had become chairperson of the school board and appears to have been acting as sole proprietor, which strained relations between her and her co-owners. For instance, in 1963 her co-owner Agunbiade was arrested on her accusation that he stole £12 from the school. He was charged and found guilty. In 1964, he and Oduntan sued FRK over the ownership of the school (Abeokuta suit No. AB/21/64 [*I. O. Agunbiade and I. O. Oduntan v. FRK*]). FRK won the case, though the details are unavailable.

Four years earlier she had purchased thirty acres of land just off Iṣabo Road. She used twenty-eight acres of that land for a new secondary school that opened in 1962 with the name the Reverend Ransome-Kuti Memorial Grammar School; two acres were reserved for an extension of her primary school.

In addition to her other schools, FRK also established a nursery school, provided for in the will of her very good friend, Modupe Moore (d. 1957). Moore was a wealthy trader and businesswoman who had been awarded the title of Iyalode of Egba Christians in 1936. FRK was one of the executors of Moore's will. Part of the estate was set aside for a nursery school to be called the Dupe-Ayeni Memorial Nursery school, under FRK's direction. It took FRK some time to execute this project. Her application for permission to open the school was rejected by the Ministry of Education in 1964 but approved in 1968. The nursery school was housed in what became an extensive Ransome-Kuti educational complex.

FRK received a little financial support for the schools from the Western Regional government; for example, in 1955 she received £1,200. Basically, however, her schools were self-supporting. By 1970 the Reverend Ransome-Kuti Memorial Grammar School encompassed twelve classrooms, chemistry and biology laboratories, a library, and six apartments for staff quarters. The student hostels were in the Iṣabo Road complex. The grammar school also had a van purchased by FRK. In concert with her and her husband's commitment to coeducation, the school accepted both female and male students. Indeed, the Ransome-Kutis had planned to set up such a school when the reverend retired from the AGS, but the action was postponed due to his illness and her travel schedule. The first set of students took the West African School Certificate O level exam (for ordinary level, secondary school) in 1967. The disappointing performance of students on this exam from 1967–71 can be seen in Table 2. The cause of such a disappointing performance is unclear, but it may have been related to the troubled financial status of the school and the ensuing lack of teacher commitment (chronicled below). In 1972, total enrollment was 367 students.

The grammar school was run by a board of governors consisting of FRK, her children, the well-known educator Dotun Oyewole, the social worker Mrs. B. A. Ojesina, the teacher Mrs. P. O. Fadayomi, and several clergy. FRK exercised a hands-on approach in her administration. She personally arranged educational visits for students to places such

Table 2.

Year	Number of Candidates	Passed	Failed
1967	18	10	8
1968	47	6	41
1969	35	8	27
1970	41	7	34
1971	33	16	17

Source: Education file, FRK Papers.

as the Nigerian Textile Mills, Lagos, and the Guiness Brewing Plant. Such exposure was a concrete expression of her belief that manual work had as much dignity as "intellectual" work and that Nigerians must learn to run all aspects of their country. Not surprisingly, she projected her own values in school policies. For instance, she insisted that students be known by their "native" (Nigerian) names and not "English" names. Teachers were not allowed to smoke or drink—at least on school grounds. Her husband had been known for running a tight ship when it came to discipline, and she continued this tradition. The library was stocked with over two thousand volumes, a testament to her commitment to literacy and knowledge.

FRK received additional support for the school from the Soviet Women's Committee, which donated science equipment, offered scholarships to graduates, and sent Soviet science teachers to the school. In the 1960s, a few graduates of the school were given Soviet government scholarships to study at Lumumba University in the Soviet Union. In 1970, two Soviet women science teachers were replaced by two men, but in 1971 there was again a Soviet woman teacher at the school. In that same year, the Soviet Women's Committee awarded two scholarships to female students to go to the Soviet Union to study early childhood education. In an April 1971 letter to the permanent secretary of the Western State Ministry of Education, FRK appealed for permission for the students to travel to the Soviet Union.[12]

Perhaps the Soviet assistance was a response to the tremendous financial difficulty in which the school found itself, for 1968 had been a particularly bad year. FRK confided in a letter to her townsman and ex-AGS student, Dotun Oyewole, acting senior deputy registrar, West African Examinations Council (WAEC): "November 12, 1968 — 'This year has been a troublesome one — a year in which I have experienced things that had never happened in my school since the 50 years I had had in teaching and in the running of schools. By the end of the first term 1968, the teachers had not prepared the students' report cards because their salaries had not been paid.' "[13]

Given the fact she was not well-disposed toward her principal, J. O. Owa, when he applied for permission to supervise WAEC exams at another school, FRK insisted she would not pay him for the time he was away even after Oyewole had interceded. In a memo to Owa, she stated: "Please do not allow any staff meeting to alter my arrangements for any plan laid down for the running of the school."[14] When the principal applied for the basic car allowance (a maintenance allowance), a benefit that normally accrued, FRK refused and instead offered him the use of the school vehicle from 7:30 A.M. to 7:30 P.M. In another memo to Owa, she observed tartly: "You had bought your car for your own pleasure long before you came to my school and there is no reason why I should ask you to jack your car up."[15] Indeed, her attitude toward allowances due to the teachers was included in a memo of June 2, 1968: "It can only be convenient for the school to pay any allowances due at the end of the year when we shall have collected all our fees."[16]

In some ways, it seems that as a school administrator FRK was guilty of the high-handed, parsimonious behavior toward teachers that the Nigerian Union of Teachers had campaigned against since 1931. Somewhat in her defense, the school was simply not paying its way. As a means of raising funds, she had even begun to insist that students pay 5 shillings 3 pence for the school magazine before receiving their grades. Perhaps in response to such policies, in December 1968 students rioted at the school, but the riot was soon quelled and classes had resumed normally by January 1969.

Some of the school's financial problems were relieved when on July 1, 1970, the school was admitted to the "public list," that is, it could receive funds from the Ministry of Education. Even after the government grant, the school had problems again in 1972. Students rioted once more and the government sent an inspector to investigate school conditions. The report observed that there had been nine principals since 1962 and noted:

"Most parents do not rate the school highly, therefore only poor quality students are admitted. This was borne out by the school's record at the West African School Certificate examination held after the fifth year."[17]

Why the school apparently lost its academic luster is unclear. It was likely a combination of several factors. FRK was getting older, and with increasing age seems to have come an even greater desire to control all aspects of the school. In the early 1960s, this was complicated by her frequent international and national travel and her continuing involvement in the political scene. Especially by the late 1960s, there was a much greater number of public government-run schools whose resources, particularly staff, outstripped financially strapped private schools, such as FRK's. She was also very much involved (see below) in land cases and other personal legal disputes that sapped her energy and time as well as her finances.

In 1974, the Western State government took over all schools owned by voluntary agencies and private proprietors in its area. It set fees to be charged by proprietors and withdrew subventions. Some compensation was to be paid to the owners. FRK protested against this government measure and decided to close the school. She made her stand clear in a notice published in the *Daily Times* of November 8, 1974.

In a letter addressed to the board of governors, she also chided the state government on their decision that education should not be a profit-making venture but "good food, housing, and clothing, which are even more basic for common people's existence were not included in this category [meaning that the government still supports people's right to make a profit on the provision of food, etc.]. . . . In a country which is being run on a Capitalist system and where some members of the ruling elite can boast of having several houses, ordinary people should not be forced to make sacrifices which their leaders are not prepared to make."[18] She concluded by thanking all those who had made various contributions to the school over the years.

Despite her protests and even after the takeover, FRK cooperated with the government for the good of education. For instance, the acting secretary of the Western State School Board wrote to her on September 12, 1974, to ask her help in solving the acute shortage of teachers: "In view of your possible contacts with overseas institutions and organizations, it will be appreciated if you would be good enough to supply this office with particulars of such organizations which might be interested in sending qualified personnel to teach in Western State."[19]

Shortly after receiving the letter, FRK wrote to the WIDF, saying in part, "As they know you had once come to my aid in supplying my school with teachers . . . please help."[20]

▲▲▲

Funmilayo Ransome-Kuti believed passionately in social and legal justice and throughout her life was ready to appeal to the courts to obtain redress for injustice either to others or herself. Although she alleged frequently that various court personnel were biased against her, she believed in the integrity of the judicial system. Like Gandhi in India, she criticized the British colonial administration by referring to British legal principles: she attacked the authoritarianism of colonialism by contrasting it with British democratic *ideals*. She used the law to attack actions that were deemed "legal" by the colonial code but that she considered unjust, such as the payment of an arbitrarily administered tax levied on a population without political representation. Her readiness to sue for the collective good during the 1940s and 1950s has been shown in chapters 4 and 5.

But she also took legal action to establish, confirm, and protect her individual rights, in both traditional (customary indigenous) and modern (British-derived) legal systems. An instance of the latter concerned her father's property. Daniel O. Thomas had assigned his property to members of his family when he died in 1954. This was done to ensure that, according to Yoruba principles, the children of one mother should be given shares equal to those for the children of another mother and that the first child of the deceased, on the principle of seniority, had additional rights. Thus, FRK, as the eldest child, was given the right to take care of the family house at Igbogun on behalf of all her brothers and sisters. Then FRK and her sister, Comfort Oluremi, "being children of the same mother and the children of the married wife [*sic*], were given the story-house [multistoried house] at Ago-Oko, Abeokuta, and the low house at Ifo where the Hausa man resides."[21] The two daughters were also given the Alego and Adejare farms.

The children of the second wife (Rebecca Olushade), Adebola and her brothers, though described in the document only as children of the same mother, were given the "story house at Ifo, the landed property at Ifo, and two farms." The full implementation of this division was frustrated because the youngest child, Bankole Thomas, refused to vacate the house in Ifo left to FRK and because he, who alone resided in Igbogun and knew the exact boundaries of the farmlands, would not cooperate with the partitioning of the farms.

In 1964, a financially pressed FRK appealed to the head of the village, the Bale, who used the traditional method of settling family disputes. The Bale convened a meeting of representatives of the children of the two mothers, elders of the village, and other family members. The Bale conducted everyone around the farmlands to show the correct boundaries of the four farms. The meeting then reconfirmed the division of property as laid down by Daniel Thomas. "At the conclusion, Mr. B. Thomas, on behalf of himself, his sister (Adebola), and brothers, gave the committee six bottles of beer and one guinea, Mrs. Funmilayo Ransome-Kuti gave them two pounds five shillings, one bottle of gin, and a basket full of *eko* and fish soup and *efo*. The ceremony ended by prayer at the grave of our father [Daniel Thomas]."

Thereafter, however, when the tenant of her house, the "low house in Ifo where the Hausa man resides," had not paid his rent, FRK appealed to the modern court to force him to pay the rent. Although the house had belonged to her father, the family had confirmed her inheritance of it and thereafter the property became subject to Nigerian law. On October 26, 1975, FRK finally sued the tenant (Alhaji Bala Yaro) for nonpayment of rent in the Abeokuta High Court.[22]

FRK also owned non-family-derived land in Abeokuta: in 1948 a piece of land between Iṣabo Road and the Afin (palace) was, according to FRK, given to her "free of charge by Salami Lojede and Madam Aje as per agreement, 21 October 1948." In 1951 the Western Region government acquired part of that land and built the Abeokuta High Court on it—ironically, in view of the fact that FRK was to become a frequent visitor to that court! In 1962, John Akintola, a clerical officer at the Afin, "squatted" on the land. FRK first took "customary action" by reporting him to the new Alake, Ademola's successor, Gbadebo II, who apparently ordered Akintola to leave. Only when that failed did FRK go to court (Suit AB/25/66 [*FRK v. John Akintola*])—the Abeokuta High Court. The second land case was heard in the same court the following year over a piece of land at Oke-Ijeun, Abeokuta (Suit AB/12/67). The outcomes of these cases are not known.

The most serious, controversial, and protracted of FRK's land cases concerned land in Lagos and was referred to the Lagos High Court and then the Federal Supreme Court of Nigeria, the highest court of appeal in the Nigerian judicial system. The Ransome-Kutis invested their meager savings in land. In February 1932, the couple attended an auction sale of land in Lagos and jointly paid for two plots. The receipts issued by the auctioneer to them are dated February 10, 1932, and February 25, 1932, and are for the plots labeled as "Land at Suru Lere" and "Suru Lere Ojuelegba." The land in question had belonged to the Oloto family, one of the extensive, traditional, landowning families in Lagos.

The purchase of land from communities or extended families in Lagos—indeed, in Nigeria—is a very complex undertaking fraught with hazards for the unwary because of the intersection of customary and English law; because extended families are so large that, even with titular heads, it is possible for some members to act independently without the knowledge of others; and because there may be divisions within the family. Therefore, it is quite common for purchasers to negotiate in good faith with one family member only to discover later that that person did not have the authority to act for the whole family; thus, the transaction is rendered invalid. Apparently, something along these lines happened to the Reverend I. O. and Funmilayo Ransome-Kuti. Totally unknown to them, the same land had been purchased from a representative of the Oloto family by Bamgbolu Amao for £30 in 1927. The land was not conveyed to him until 1956, by order of the Lagos High Court (Suits 362 and 363, 1952 [*in re the matter of Bamgbolu Amao*]). In January 1957, Amao sold the two pieces of land to J. B. Atunrase who took possession of the land.

The land purchased by the Ransome-Kutis in 1932 was conveyed to them in 1947 and the deed of conveyance was signed by Adekunle Shonibare, supposedly a member of the Oloto family (in court, FRK testified that the signer was Adekunle Bankole, the son of Bankole Shonibare, who arranged the conveyance, because Shonibare died before 1947). This deed of conveyance, the court decided in 1958, was "not worth the paper it is written on," partly because of the confusion over the identity of the signatory. Needless to say, though, as far as the Ransome-Kutis were concerned they had legal title to land they had purchased in good faith.[23]

The Ransome-Kutis did not do anything with the land before the reverend's death. About two years later, when FRK was trying to raise money to cover the costs of building classrooms for "Mrs. Kuti's class" and finishing up the house at 15 Isabo Road, she decided to do something about the land. In 1932 when the land was paid for and up to the time it was conveyed in 1947, the Suru Lere area was undeveloped and sparsely settled (although only about ten miles from Lagos Island where the city of Lagos was sited). By the mid-1950s, the area was growing rapidly with many new houses being built, especially because it was the site of the resettlement of thousands of residents from Lagos Island in a slum clearance scheme. Therefore, the land had become far more valuable and a commercial proposition. So in January 1958, FRK began to construct a building on the land, but she was confronted by J. B. Atunrase who claimed that he was the owner of both plots of land. The result was a court case (Suit LD/181/58 [*J. B. Atunrase v. FRK*]) in which Atunrase, the plaintiff, claimed that the piece of land lying along Ojuelegba Road and Modele Village Road, Suru Lere, was his property. The court agreed with the plaintiff. FRK appealed to the Supreme Court against the decision of the Lagos High Court (Suit 272/1962 [*FRK v. J. B. Atunrase and Total Oil*]), but in 1962 the higher court confirmed the decision of the Lagos High Court. Judgment was given by the chief justice of the federation, Sir Adetokunbo Ademola (the son of Alake Ademola II).

Not satisfied with this decision, FRK sued again (Suit LD/476/63 [*FRK v. J. B. Atunrase*]), this time for declaration of title of the second piece of land, £1,000 in damages for trespass, and an injunction against the defendant to stop further acts of trespass upon the land.

In the interval, Atunrase had sold the second piece of land to Total Oil Products (Nigeria, Limited); the company then joined Atunrase as party to the action. The presiding judge, J. A. Adefarasin, ruled in favor of the defendants and dismissed the case of the plaintiff, Funmilayo Ransome-Kuti.

She was still not satisfied. In 1965, FRK issued an appeal to the Supreme Court against the judgment. That appeal was also dismissed. The Ransome-Kuti family, spurred on by FRK, then decided on a different strategy. Since she had already gone to court in four suits, they thought that someone else should sue on the family's behalf. No one really wanted to, but FRK was insistent.

A. O. Ransome-Kuti, the reverend's brother, was one of the three executors of his estate (the other two being his son Olikoye and daughter Dolupo). Since Rev. Ransome-Kuti was a joint owner of the land, A. O. Ransome-Kuti could sue on behalf of his brother's estate. Once again, judgment was given in favor of Total Oil and costs were claimed against A. O. Ransome-Kuti (Suit LD 207/67 [*A. O. Ransome-Kuti v. Total Oil*]).

Even after this defeat in 1972, FRK would not abandon the fight. She next tried to persuade the other executors of her husband's estate (i.e., her children Olikoye and Dolupo) to initiate another legal proceeding using different legal grounds. The children were very reluctant in view of the previous judgments and the costs involved. They worried also that the protraction of the case was causing their mother great distress and becoming an obsession with her.[24]

FRK believed she was the victim in this land case. She and her husband had bought the land legally, kept the receipts, had it duly conveyed, and done nothing wrong. She refused to accept that the problem was that they had been tricked and cheated by the middlemen involved in the transaction. She regarded the loss of the land as one of her greatest disappointments in life and, indeed, related it to another great disappointment—the reinstatement of the Alake Ademola—because it was the Alake's son, Adetokunbo, who, as chief justice of the Federation of Nigeria, presided over the Supreme Court hearings of the two appeals cases. FRK was convinced that Sir Ademola was biased against her. However, a reading of the judgment indicates that the Supreme Court simply upheld the judgments of the lower courts, which were based upon the fact that the Ransome-Kutis never had proper legal title to the land.

There were a number of other litigations. Some concerning the schools have been referred to earlier; others concerned property and money. Particularly because this was a time of great financial stress, FRK pursued her various legal cases as far as she could. In doing so, she went through a number of lawyers, so much so that when her daughter, Dolu, was asked if FRK had any men friends after Rev. Ransome-Kuti's death, Dolu replied laughingly, "Her only men friends were her lawyers."[25]

These cases are evidence of FRK's determination once she believed she was in the right. She certainly did not accept losing well. As annoying as her tenacity may have been in these personal situations, it had its positive side politically. She never abandoned her principles or her struggle to see women in Nigeria become social and legal equals with men. She remained dedicated to educational pursuits and to the idea of social and economic justice for the poor and oppressed. She continued to express her political philosophy and to assert herself, without regard for conventions of gender, in both private and public.

Another of FRK's properties became a subject of such bitter controversy and the venue of such extraordinary events that it is one of the most famous sites in post–civil war Nigerian history and has acquired an almost legendary aura. The property was located at 14A Agege Motor Road in Lagos. The property belonged to the Ransome-Kuti family and the house on it had been occupied for several years by the well-known musician son of the Ransome-Kutis, Fela. Both Fela's music and his life-style were considered antiestablishment and in some quarters scandalous. His songs, often utilizing the patois known as "pidgin" English, were sharply critical of Nigeria's governments and often poked fun at the bourgeois lifestyle of the Western-educated elite. On his return from the United States in 1970, Fela, who considers himself a Pan-Africanist and a champion of "traditional" African culture, had founded a commune on the property. As previously mentioned, while in the United States Fela had fallen in love with an African American woman named Sandra Smith. She exposed him to the Black Power movement, which had a tremendous influence on the development of his political philosophy.[26]

Prior to 1977, Fela had already had several run-ins with both the army and police and, in addition to his non grata political ideology, he had been charged with drug use. After a short incarceration in the early 1970s, he had christened the home on Agege Motor Road and adjoining property as the Kalakuta Republic. "Kalakuta" referred to the name by which his jail cell had been known, and "Republic" signified his disdain for the authority of the Federation of Nigeria within his own com-pound.[27]

FRK was fiercely protective of Fela, who had often been abused by the authorities in a series of raids on his nightclub, the Shrine, and on his home.[28] She was a frequent visitor to the Kalakuta Republic, and she and Fela were extremely close. One Nigerian observed, "Fela be-came the darling of his mother towards the last stage of her life because she found in him a man who has a message for our oppressed people" (*Guardian*, Feb. 18, 1985). Though she never changed her name legally, in the early 1970s she had dropped Ransome and substituted Anikulapo, a Yoruba word meaning "warrior who carries strong protection" or alter-natively "hunter who carries death in a pouch."[29] She had done this at least partially at the suggestion of Fela, who had previously changed his own name to symbolize his disparagement of the neocolonial mentality he attached to the adoption of European names. As early as the 1920s she had dropped her European given names, Frances Abigail, and used only Funmilayo and, as shown earlier, also insisted that pupils at her schools use their African rather than European names.

On February 18, 1977, the Kalakuta Republic was surrounded by nearly a thousand armed soldiers. As usual, there were a number of people in residence, including FRK and Fela. This last raid was to be a particularly brutal one, as well as believed to have precipitated FRK's death. According to eyewitness accounts, the soldiers, armed with bayonets affixed and clubs, stormed the compound without warning. Ostensibly to arrest two young men who had committed a traffic violation, the soldiers broke down the door and began beating people inside. Bekolari Ransome-Kuti was bayoneted in the forehead and hand, tossed from a window, and then beaten. He was forced to march on a broken foot from the residence to the army barracks nearby. His medical clinic in the compound was destroyed. Clothes were torn off some of the young women in the house, and they were forced to go outside naked. Some claimed they were later raped. Fela himself was severely beaten and hospitalized. Soldiers pulled Funmilayo Ransome-Kuti, then nearly seventy-seven years old, by the hair and threw her out the window, severely injuring her leg and causing her to go into shock. A fire ensued that destroyed the entire property.[30]

Although the army blamed the fire on an explosion of the residence's generator, FRK later called that "a fantastic lie" (*Daily Star*, Feb. 25, 1977). Others present at the raid agreed with her and insisted that the army had deliberately set the fire.[31] The raid, popularly known as the "Kalakuta War," received tremendous publicity in two major newspapers and caused the military government to convene a public administrative tribunal to investigate the incident. Reportedly, the tribunal threatened to make international news when a *New York Times* correspondent attempted to attend hearings; the day following the first sitting of the tribunal, the correspondent was arrested and deported.[32] In the end, blame was apportioned both to "overzealous" unknown soldiers and to Fela. The Kalakuta Republic and surrounding land occupied by uninvolved citizens were destroyed. Neither these citizens nor the Ransome-Kuti family were compensated for their property loss. This is still a sore point for the them, and they continue to press their claims against the government for compensation for the destruction and confiscation of the property. Years later, a Lagos State secondary school was built on the site, and, in a rather gratuitous manner, the school was subsequently named the Reverend Ransome-Kuti Memorial School.

Family and other close observers concur that Funmilayo Ransome-Kuti was never the same after the raid. Not only was her physical recovery slow but her fighting spirit and will to live seem to have been shaken. She remained ill for an entire year. Her foot, injured in the fall from the window, did not heal well, and she was admitted to Lagos University Teaching Hospital and treated by an orthopedic surgeon. Her family and doctors felt she was very depressed. Just prior to the Kalakuta raid she had gone (with her son Fela) to Ghana for an operation for glaucoma. After the raid, the fluid pressure in her eye increased again and she was once more admitted to the hospital in Lagos. According to the accounts of close family members, she remained withdrawn and refused to take her medicine. The family arranged to have her transferred to Lagos General Hospital where one of her sons, Dr. Bekolari Ransome-Kuti, was the medical officer. She continued to refuse to talk or eat; her daughter Dolupo (a nurse) slept on the floor next to her bed. In her last days, she was constantly attended by her children. In February 1978 the family suit for damages from the Kalakuta raid was dismissed, and she is said to have moaned, "Why are they doing this to us?" Shortly after, Funmilayo Ransome-Kuti lapsed into a coma-like state (*Punch,* Feb. 17, 1978), and on April 13, 1978, she died.

Several of the major Nigerian newspapers carried lengthy eulogies. The headlines ranged from "Defender of the Rights of Women: Eulogy on the Soul of Funmilayo Ransome-Kuti" to "The Voice of Woman Is Dead: Fela's Mum Passes Away." Several eulogies were full-page spreads and chronicled the importance of FRK's life as a political activist, her special concerns for women, children, and the poor, and her legacy to future generations. One *Daily Times* article stated in part, "She is still admired even after her death as a heroine by the generality of womenfolk in Egbaland who regarded her as 'our leader'" (May 5, 1978). A few days after her death, the *Nigerian Sunday Times* quoted a prominent Lagosian who hailed FRK "as a progressive revolutionary whose immense contribution to the continued crusade for the educational emancipation of this country will never be forgotten" (Apr. 16, 1978). Yet another article called her a Pan-African visionary who was an anti-imperialist and recalled that "in pre-independence days Mrs. Kuti was one of the handful of nationalists in this country who were sought out by Nkrumah" (*Daily Times,* Apr. 18, 1978).

Several important traditional leaders of the Western Region, including the Alake of Egbaland and the Olubadan of Ibadan, praised her work on behalf of the interests of women and the nation, as did many other prominent citizens (*Nigerian Sunday Times,* Apr. 16, 1978; *Daily Times,* Apr. 14, 1978). The newspaper *Punch* did a full-page tribute replete with quotes from FRK in which she stated much of her personal philosophy: The happiness of ordinary women was her happiness (and because women knew that they followed her); she did not consider herself an agitator but a defender of human rights to which cause she would be dedicated as long as she lived; and on religion, "I believe in my God. You could be a pagan and be godly. As far as I can see, if you don't think of cheating people you are godly and I think if there is any paradise you will get there. Many pastors as I see them will end up in hell. I will see God in the sort of life I lead, not because I go to church every Sunday" (May 5, 1978).

Though the wife of an Anglican minister, her religious views were clearly her own. In a May 2, 1973, interview in the *Daily Times,* she had described herself "as a worker claiming the rights of human beings to fight against exploitation wherever it might rear its ugly head."

On May 5, 1978, a motorcade bore the body of Funmilayo Ransome-Kuti from Lagos to her hometown of Abeokuta, the site of most of her family life and of the political activity that catapulted her into the national and international arenas. Her body laid in state in the Reverend Ransome-Kuti Memorial Grammar School Assembly Hall. Services were held later at St. John's Anglican Church, Igbein, Abeokuta. Thousands of mourners were present, including a large contingent of market women shouting "Bèèrè, Bèèrè" and other women traders who together had closed all the markets of Abeokuta and many shops for the day. Bishop Seth I. Kale, a former NUT activist and longtime friend of both Funmilayo Ransome-Kuti and Reverend I. O. Ransome-Kuti, conducted the funeral services. The *Nigerian Sunday Times* reported that a "series of praises were showered on the great Egba woman leader at the gravesite" before the final burial where she was interred in a vault with her husband of nearly thirty years, with whom, she had more than once commented, she shared dedication to the causes of women's equality and justice for all the exploited and dispossessed (*Sunday Times,* May 7, 1978; *Sunday Punch,* May 7, 1978).

One year after her death, her three sons and hundreds of sympathizers staged a protest march to commemorate the first anniversary of her death. They carried a mock coffin that they deposited at the 14A Agege Motor Road property (*Sunday Observer,* Apr. 15, 1979). On the second anniversary of the Kalakuta incident, the family took out a full-page advertisement in February 18, 1979, issue of *Sunday Punch:*

NO JUSTICE

KALAKUTA AFFAIR

★★ 2ND ANNIVERSARY ★★

Armed Nigerian soldiers marched on our family
house at 14A, Agege Motor Road

They burnt it completely to the ground.

It was a 5-hour long military assault.

Scores of people were severely wounded and some
of us have been permanently maimed.

Properties worth millions of naira were
destroyed and hundreds of people were later rendered
homeless.

Our dear mother eventually died from the
shock she received from this inhuman
assault on her personal self-esteem.

Today, two years after, we still have not
heard any word of remorse or apology; nor
have we had any reparations for these atrocities
and all our immense losses.

Yet we know for certain that other victims
of less but similar calamity have been
treated with speed and generosity.

The question on everybody's mouth is:

What is our crime to deserve this
oppressive treatment in our own country
where we are supposed to be free citizens?

Kuti Family.

▲ ▲ ▲

In May 1948, early in FRK's political career, a Nigerian woman had written to her in support of her initial action aimed at ending the taxation of
women and reforming the Sole Native Authority system in Abeokuta.
The letter stated: "Even the veiled children in their respective mothers'
wombs, though inarticulate, nod approval of your deeds."[33] Propheti-
cally, during the same time period, among the songs the market women
who followed FRK into battle against the Alake and SNA sang was one
that said: "Your life is beneficial to us, Olufunmilayo, your life is beneficial to us. . . . You will certainly live to a good old age, Funmilayo, you
shall not die young. . . . Béére shall not die young."[34] At seventy-seven
years old, Béére had not died young, nor had she lived an unfulfilled life.
Even though the imposition of military rule in 1966 (except for a brief

period of civilian rule from 1979–83) would characterize all Nigerian governments to the present day and severely circumscribe all civilian political activity, she continued to receive awards and to espouse her political beliefs in many newspaper and magazine interviews.

In 1965, she was awarded the national honor of membership in the Order of the Niger for her contributions to her nation. The award was conferred by the elder statesman and well-known nationalist Nnamdi Azikiwe with whom FRK had worked (and often differed) in the NCNC. In 1968, she received an honorary doctorate of laws degree from the University of Ibadan, where the Ransome-Kuti name was already memorialized in the naming of a hall after her late husband. After accepting the honorary degree, FRK wrote to the vice chancellor of the university, saying that the honor was "proof of your telling me I am not alone in my struggle."[35] In 1969, she appeared in *International Women's Who's Who* and was appointed chairman of the State Advisory Board of Education for the Western State. In her letter of acceptance of the appointment she wrote, "May I never let womanhood down."[36] A year later, FRK was awarded the Lenin Peace Prize by the Supreme Soviet of the USSR. The USSR ambassador to Nigeria, A. Romanov, wrote to FRK that the award of the medal was in "recognition of your noble activities for many years in promoting friendship and mutual cooperation between Nigerian and Soviet peoples." He enclosed also a letter of congratulation signed by the chair of the Soviet Women's Committee, Valentina Nikolaeva-Tereshkova.[37] In 1973, the military governor Brigadier General C. O. Rotimi appointed FRK to serve on the management committee of the Egba Local Government Council. There were many less well known honors, as well.

▲▲▲

In an article in the September 8, 1974, issue of *Sunday Punch*, FRK commented at length on her relationship with her son Fela. She argued in support of his music and her own continuing intention to struggle to mobilize "women, youth and peasants of [Nigeria] . . . by educating them on how to choose their own leaders instead of allowing them to be bought and corrupted. . . . Our people have suffered too many instances of corruption by so-called leaders whose only intention in taking office is to amass wealth at the expense of the people." In May 1975, *New Breed* magazine carried a lengthy interview with her that the reporter called "the most exciting interview I have ever had with a woman in over a decade of full-time writing."[38] In the course of the interview, FRK commented on everything from the 1948 overthrow of the Alake to her belief in women's liberation.

In an April 9, 1976, profile of FRK, the *Daily Times* discussed specific people's lives whom FRK had influenced, including Hajiya Gambo, a Zaria (Northern Nigeria) woman political activist who fought for woman suffrage in the North (not granted until 1977) and who went on a pilgrimage to Abeokuta to meet and learn from FRK. The same article asked, "Who did not learn from Mrs. Kuti?" and also chronicled her influence on Kwame Nkrumah's organizing of Ghanaian women. The interviewer wrote, "In an unpainted building she often sits gingerly in an old chair making dresses for her grandchildren on an electric sewing machine. Above her, in a framed glass, is inscribed this didactic poem which seems to be her philosophy of life":

The best thing to give your enemy—
forgiveness
to your opponent, tolerance
to a friend, your heart
to your mother, conduct that
will make her proud of you,
to your child, a good example
to yourself, respect,
and to all men, charity.

In a June 14, 1989, issue, the popular newspaper *Guardian* profiled Titilayo Ajanaku, the female chairperson of the Abeokuta Local Government Area, under the banner "Another Mrs. Ransome-Kuti for Abeokuta." Ajanaku was quoted in the article as saying, "I remember vividly when I was campaigning, what people were saying was that another Mrs. Ransome-Kuti has come. It brought back memories of the past, and they rallied round me." Other politically active women, such as Margaret Ekpo, a longtime activist particularly in the Eastern Region, attributed their political acumen and inspiration to FRK.[39]

Within Nigeria, Funmilayo Ransome-Kuti's name will forever be associated with the rights of women and social, political, and economic justice for the exploited and oppressed. She was a woman who, though she could easily have converted her class privileges into personal gain and comfort, practiced what she preached by integrating her personal life with the political causes she espoused and for which she worked. Yet she was very much a human being, often direct and sometimes abrasive in her desire to make her point and achieve her goals. Perhaps these qualities account for the fact that she had very few close personal friends. Modupe Moore and Susan F. Adeyinka (regarded by many as her two closest friends) seem to have been her only intimate friends. Undeniably, FRK had a very assertive personality. Once she decided what she wanted, or what was right (two things she often conflated), whether in her personal or public life, she possessed a singular determination to have her way.

This book illustrates public examples of this, whether political or legal in nature, family anecdotes highlight it on the personal level. FRK was notorious for driving to Lagos late at night with several AWU women colleagues in tow. She would often arrive, for instance, at her son and daughter-in-law's home (Olikoye and Sonia) and gruffly ask, "Where shall we sleep? What shall we eat?" One of her former attorneys reported that if she wished to speak with him on one of her late night sojourns she would throw stones at his bedroom window to awaken him.

After her 1961 car accident, her children insisted she hire a driver, a rather common employee in Nigeria at that time, for roads were often rough and hazardous. She refused at first but finally consented. She could never get along with her drivers, however, and fired them one after another. Her daughter Dolupo remarked that even when someone else was driving, if her mother was in the car, "the two of you would be driving together."

Though considered fair-minded, FRK rarely changed her mind once it was made up. While she upheld the best interests of the women she felt she represented, she was not a "team player" with unconditional loyalty to any organized body. Her only lasting loyalty lay with her principles, and she was always willing to buck the tide, even to lose, rather than compromise a stand to which she was wedded.

Each of her children has been profoundly affected by her sense of social justice, patriotism, and Pan-Africanism. The eldest Ransome-Kuti child and only daughter, Dolupo, is a retired head nurse who currently resides in the almost legendary Ransome-Kuti home in Abeokuta. She runs a small restaurant on the ground floor. Dolu, as she is affectionately known, lived with and helped care for her mother in the last few years of her life. In 1971, when Dolu first returned to Abeokuta at her brothers' urging (she was the only sibling not married at the time) to care for her mother, FRK told her, "I don't want any looking after," remaining an aging but fiercely independent and competent woman.

The second child, Professor Olikoye Ransome-Kuti, was Minister of

Health for Nigeria from 1985–92. He is a medical doctor specializing in pediatrics, a former professor at Lagos University Teaching Hospital, and a recipient of several prestigious awards. Among them are the Leon Bernard Foundation Award from the World Health Organization in 1986 and the Morris Paetry (UNICEF founder) Award for contributions to child health in 1989. To date, he is the only person to have won both awards. He instituted many innovative health programs in Nigeria, particularly those aimed at decreasing infant mortality and developing community health programs in rural areas. He dedicated years to developing his Primary Health Care Scheme aimed at "guaranteeing basic health services to the greatest number of Nigerians" (*Daily Times,* July 17, 1989, and Aug. 29, 1981; *Guardian,* July 13, 1989). In 1996, he was working in Washington, D.C., for the World Bank on Africa-related projects.

The third child, Fela Anikulapo-Kuti, is the well-known musician of Pan-African philosophy. In 1977, during the Pan-African Arts Festival (FESTAC) hosted by Nigeria, the internationally known African American superstar musician and songwriter Stevie Wonder visited Fela at his Shrine nightclub in Lagos. One musical critic once wrote of Fela in the *New York Times:* "Musically, Fela is James Brown, Bob Dylan and Mick Jagger all rolled into one. Politically he is Stokely Carmichael, H. Rap Brown and Huey P. Newton all rolled into one."[40] Fela continues to play his music, which is critical of both the government and the bourgeois lifestyle. Fela is the subject of two documentary films, one by the British director Dennis Marks and one by the French director Stephane Tchalgadjieff. One Chicago newspaper, the *Reader,* in a lengthy profile of Fela on December 20, 1985, wrote that both films "explore the matrix of political, intellectual and musical forces that helped shape Fela into a folk hero and political scapegoat." The same article adds that "Fela . . . modeled himself on his mother, a freedom fighter in the struggle for independence and later a leader of the women's suffrage movement." In a November 29, 1982, *West Africa* magazine review of *fela, fela: this bitch of a life* by Carlos Moore, the Nigerian writer Ben Okri (winner of the Booker Prize for Literature in 1990) comments on the tremendous influence FRK had on Fela, though Okri is highly critical of the book and feels that Nobel laureate Wole Soyinka's book, *Ake: The Years of Childhood,* is far better and, in his words, "immortalizes" Funmilayo Ransome-Kuti. A number of other articles testify to Fela's close relationship with his mother (e.g., *Nigerian Sunday Times,* Apr. 27, 1986). Fela's son Femi and Dolu's daughter, Frances, are both musical stars in Nigeria and continue the musical tradition begun by their great-grandfather J.J., the singing reverend.

The youngest child, Dr. Bekolari Ransome-Kuti, is a medical doctor who until recently had a private practice in Lagos. He is also a former national vice president of the Nigerian Medical Association. In 1988 he was appointed by the Commonwealth Medical Association to serve in the Eminent Persons Advisory Group on Human Rights and was chairman of the Committee for the Defense of Human Rights in Nigeria. On August 26, 1989, the Nigerian newspaper *Guardian* published his lengthy letter entitled "Open Letter to President Babangida," which decried what he saw as the lengthening shadow of government oppression of the free expression of ideas, among other things. Several months later, on April 10, 1990, an article appeared in the *Daily Times* reporting that Wole Soyinka held a press conference calling for an open inquiry into an alleged attempt by government security forces to abduct Beko Ransome-Kuti and another human rights activist. During the May 1992 disturbances in Nigeria, Beko chaired a coalition of pro-democracy groups concerned about whether the military government headed by General Ibrahim Babangida was making serious attempts to abide by their promise to hold civilian elections (*New York Times*, May 23 and 31, 1992). The authorities detained him shortly thereafter.

Between 1992 and 1995 Beko was in and out of jail, due to his activities as chairman of the Campaign for Democracy headquartered in Lagos (*National Concord*, June 18, 1993; *Nigerian Tribune*, July 19, 1993). The Campaign for Democracy was organized at Jos in May 1992 and is a human rights organization that also campaigned actively for free elections in Nigeria (*Guardian*, Feb. 13, 1994). Though Nigerian elections were finally held in 1993, the results were annulled by the military (chap. 1; *New York Times*, May 23 and 31, and June 17, 1993). In July 1994, Beko was charged with treason. In August 1994, a bomb was thrown at his home which at that time was serving as headquarters for the Campaign for Democracy. In September 1994, Beko filed a suit against the military government for unlawful arrest and detention and, though his trial for treason has been suspended, he was recently sentenced to fifteen years imprisonment by a military tribunal (*P.M. News*, Aug. 31, 1994; *Daily Times*, Oct. 20, 1995). Beko's daughter Nike, a lawyer and civil rights activist, is campaigning for her father's release with the courage and conviction of her grandmother. The political situation in Nigeria is in such a state of flux at this time that it is impossible to predict the outcome of these affairs.

The Ransome-Kuti children inherited from both parents a keen sense of social justice, a generosity of the spirit that accepts others' problems as their own, and frequently a dedication to involvement in public life even at the expense of their comfort and personal lives. The Nigerian newspaper *Vanguard* carried an editorial on July 12, 1985, that, addressing the Ransome-Kuti children, stated in part, "It is as though your illustrious parents decided that not only were they going to be absolutely patriotic citizens, ready for the big fight to save Nigeria from all manner of scourges, they also decided to raise a brood of their own kind." Olikoye Ransome-Kuti commented in a 1981 interview, "We were brought up along with the schoolchildren [at his parents' school in Abeokuta] and we learnt to live amongst people. My parents were always involved with the community and my mother always fought for the rights and development of women as persons in their own right" (*Daily Times,* Aug. 29, 1981).

Clearly, the Ransome-Kutis gave their children an example of both personal and public politics that respected the rights of both women and men, a legacy of respect for the individual, and a dedication to public service. Almost twenty years after her death, FRK conjures in the public mind powerful images of a crusader for women's equality and justice for all. She steadfastly refused to accept any title, yet she is recognized nationally and internationally as the "mother" of Nigeria's women and an important nationalist figure. We must also see in her life some of the thinking of the collective womanhood who supported her. The list of important women political activists of the twentieth century is incomplete without her name.

Notes

1. Dolupo Ransome-Kuti, interview, Abeokuta, June 1, 1989.

2. Bekolari Ransome-Kuti, interview, Lagos, June 15, 1989; Olikoye Ransome-Kuti, interview, Lagos, June 17, 1989.

3. Letters of May and June 1952, IORK Papers.

4. Odugbesan, "Béére," 2; Bekolari Ransome-Kuti, interview; Olikoye Ransome-Kuti, interview.

5. IORK Papers.

6. Her sons reported that she discussed her decisions with them and with the reverend and that all counseled her to continue her work. Bekolari Ransome-Kuti, interview; Olikoye Ransome-Kuti, interview.

7. Christina Groves was principal of St. Anne's School, Ibadan, in 1959–73.

8. Moore, *fela, fela: this bitch of a life,* 52.

9. Copy of prayer, biography box, FRK Papers.

10. Davidson Nicoll, interview, London, July 1, 1987.

11. FRK, interview, *Woman's World.*

12. Letter dated Apr. 11, 1971, FRK Papers.

13. FRK to Oyewole, Nov. 12, 1968, FRK Papers.

14. FRK to Owa, memorandum, Feb. 7, 1968, FRK Papers.

15. FRK to Owa, June 15, 1968, FRK Papers.

16. FRK, memorandum, June 2, 1968, FRK Papers.

17. Report in FRK Papers.

18. *Daily Times,* Nov. 8, 1974.

19. Letter dated Sept. 12, 1974, FRK Papers.

20. Letter dated Sept. 20, 1974, FRK Papers.

21. "The Distribution of Late Mr. D. O. Thomas' Properties at Ifo and Abeokuta," undated typescript, biography box, FRK Papers. Information confirmed by an interview with Ebenezer Taiwo Thomas, Lagos, June 16, 1989, and by FRK's handwritten draft of a will found in the same box.

22. Litigation box, FRK Papers. Unless otherwise noted, all information on FRK's legal affairs came from this box.

23. The land is registered as no. 56 on p. 56 in vol. 750, Lagos Land Registry, Ikeja, Lagos.

24. Olikoye Ransome-Kuti, interview; Bekolari Ransome-Kuti, interview.

25. Dolupo Ransome-Kuti, interview.

26. In general, see Moore, *fela, fela: this bitch of a life.* See also, *Sunday Tribune,* Nov. 18, 1984.

27. Moore, *fela, fela: this bitch of a life,* 109–10.

28. The Shrine was originally known as the Afro Spot. See Idowu, *Fela,* 43.

29. Bekolari Ransome-Kuti, interview.

30. FRK's account is in *Punch,* May 5, 1978, and *Daily Star,* Feb. 25, 1978; Fela's account is in Idowu, *Fela,* 60–64; Bekolari Ransome-Kuti, interview.

31. Bekolari Ransome-Kuti; Idowu, *Fela,* 62.

32. Idowu, *Fela,* 60–63.

33. I. S. Oguntoyinbo to FRK, May 1948, FRK Papers.

34. Song, FRK Papers.

35. FRK to T. O. Lambo, Oct. 11, 1968, FRK Papers.

36. FRK to State Advisory Board of Education for the Western State, Mar. 25, 1969, FRK Papers.

37. Romanov to FRK, June 18, 1970, FRK Papers.

38. *New Breed,* May 1975, 23–31.

39. Margaret Ekpo on videotape of Nina Mba book launching, Lagos, July 6, 1984. Videotape in possession of Nina Mba, Lagos.

40. Idowu, *Fela,* 83.

Bibliography

Archives

Egba Council Archives, Abeokuta
   Minutes of meetings of the Egba Native Authority Council (subsequently
      the Abeokuta Urban District Council)
   Selected records of the Abeokuta Women's Union
Nigerian National Archives, Abeokuta
   Elliot Commission File
Nigerian National Archives, Ibadan
   Chief Secretary's Office
   Office of the Commissioner of the Colony of Lagos
   Abeokuta District Office
   Abeokuta Provincial Office

Official Publications

Annual Digests of Educational Statistics, 1957–61
Debates of the Federal House of Representatives, 1951–56
Minutes of Evidence of the Commission of Inquiry into the Egba Disturbances, 1918
Report of the Commission of Inquiry into the Egba Disturbances, 1918
Report of the Commission of Inquiry into Conditional Sales, 1948

Personal and Organizational Papers

Arthur Creech-Jones Papers, Rhodes House, Oxford
Herbert Macaulay Papers, Manuscripts Section, University of Ibadan
Chief Dr. M. A. Majekodunmi Papers, his home, Lagos
National Council of Women's Societies, records, Ibadan Office of NCWS

Nigerian Women's Party, records, in possession of Tinuola Dedeke in 1976 (deceased), Lagos
Funmilayo Ransome-Kuti (FRK) Papers, seen at both her home in Abeokuta and now housed at Manuscripts Section, University of Ibadan Library
Reverend I. O. Ransome-Kuti (IORK) Papers, Manuscripts Section, University of Ibadan
Ladipo Ṣolanke Papers, Gandhi Memorial Library, University of Lagos
Reginald Sorensen, autobiography, House of Lords Record Office, London

Newspapers and Magazines

Abeokuta Weekly Herald (Abeokuta)
Daily Service (Lagos)
Daily Star (Lagos)
Daily Times (Lagos)
Daily Worker (London)
Guardian (Lagos)
New Breed (Lagos)
Nigerian Pioneer (Lagos)
Nigerian Tribune (Lagos)
Punch (Lagos)
Reader (Chicago, Illinois, USA)
Service (Lagos)
Sunday Punch (Lagos)
Sunday Times (Lagos)
Times (London)
West Africa (London)
West African Pilot (Lagos)
West African Review (London)

Interviews

Members of Ransome-Kuti Nuclear and Extended Family
    Comfort Oluremi Adebayo (FRK's sister), Ibadan, June 7 and 10, 1989
    Chief R. Oluwole Coker (FRK's cousin), Lagos, Aug. 2, 1981; June 15 and 16, 1989
    Frances Kuboye (née Ransome-Kuti) (FRK's granddaughter), Lagos, June 15, 1989
    Dr. Bekolari Ransome-Kuti (FRK's son), Lagos, June 15, 1989
    Dolupo Ransome-Kuti (FRK's daughter), Abeokuta, June 18, 1989

Funmilayo Ransome-Kuti, Abeokuta, Jan. 26, Apr. 13–16, Oct. 29–30, 1974;
  Mar. 14 and 15, 1975; Apr. 3, 6, and 13, June 10, 15, and 23, July 7 and 12,
  Aug. 10 and 12, 1976
Dr. Olikoye Ransome-Kuti (FRK's son), Lagos, June 5, 17, and 22, 1989
Sonia Ransome-Kuti (FRK's daughter-in-law), Lagos, June 3, 8, and 12, 1989
Ebenezer Taiwo Thomas (FRK's half-brother), Lagos, June 15 and 16, July 10,
  1989
W. Olunbunmi Thomas (FRK's sister-in-law), Lagos, June 15, 1989
Associates of Funmilayo Ransome-Kuti
  Chief Margaret Ekpo, Lagos, Jan. 24, May 21, 1974; Oct. 6, 1976
  Wuraola Fagbemi (deceased), Abeokuta, June 27, 1974
  Amelia Osimosu (deceased), June 3, 1974; June 17, 1976
  Victoria Soleye, Abeokuta, Apr. 12, 1974
  Eniola Soyinka, Abeokuta, June 24, 1974
Contemporaries of Funmilayo Ransome-Kuti
  Lady Oyinkan Abayomi, Lagos, May 22, 1975; Apr. 28, May 15, June 12, 1976
    (deceased)
  Sir Adetokunbo Ademola, Lagos, Nov. 16, 1974 (deceased)
  Lady Kofoworola Ademola, Lagos, Jan. 31, 1976
  Remilekun Aiyedun, Lagos, Oct. 6, 1976 (deceased)
  Tinuola Dedeke, Lagos, Apr. 8, 10, and 19, 1976 (deceased)
  Archdeacon E. O. Alayande, Lagos, Feb. 12, 1991
  Chief Olisa Chukura, Lagos, June 12, 1989; Ibadan, Aug. 9, 1989
  Barrister Akin Delano, Lagos, June 4, 1976
  Chief Dr. M. A. Majekodunmi, Lagos, June 10, 1989
  Nora Majekodunmi, Lagos, June 10, 1989
  Professor Davidson Nicoll, interview, July 1, 1987
  Dr. O. Maja, Lagos, July 1, 1976
  Chief Ayo Rosiji, Lagos, June 20, 1989; June 14, 1990

Books and Articles

Abeokuta Women's Union (AWU). *The Constitution, Rules and Regulations for the
  Women's Union.* Abeokuta: Bosere Press, 1948.
Adebesin, F. *Egba History and Life Review.* Abeokuta: ENA Press, 1931.
Adeniyi, A. *A Philosophy for Nigerian Education.* Ibadan: Heinemann, 1972.
Adewoye, O. "Law and Social Change in Nigeria." *Journal of the Historical Society
  of Nigeria* 3, no. 1 (1973): 149–58.
Afigbo, A. E., E. A. Ayandele, R. J. Gavin, J. D. Omer-Cooper, and R. Palmer.

The Making of Modern Africa. Vol. 1: *The Nineteenth Century.* London: Longmans, 1986.

Ajayi, J. F. A. *Christian Missions in Nigeria, 1841–1891: The Making of a New Elite.*
London: Longmans, Green and Co., 1965.

———. "The Development of Secondary Grammar School Education in Nigeria." *Journal of the Historical Society of Nigeria* 2, no. 4 (1963): 517–35.

———. "Nineteenth-Century Origins of Nigerian Nationalism." *Journal of the
Historical Society of Nigeria* 2, no. 2 (1961): 196–210.

Ajayi, J. F. A., and M. Crowder, eds. *History of West Africa.* London: Longmans, 1971.

Ajayi, J. F. A., and R. Smith. *Yoruba Warfare in the Nineteenth Century.* Cambridge:
Cambridge University Press, 1964.

Ajayi, J. F. A., and T. N. Tamuno. *The University of Ibadan, 1948–1973.* Ibadan:
University of Ibadan Press, 1973.

Ajisafe, A. K. *Abeokuta Centenary and Its Celebrations.* Lagos: Ife-Olu Printing
Works, 1931.

———. *History of Abeokuta.* Lagos: Kash and Klare, 1964.

———. *The Laws and Customs of the Yoruba People.* London: George Rutledge
and Sons, 1924.

Akinjogbin, I. A., and E. A. Ayandele. "Yorubaland before 1800." In *Groundwork
of Nigerian History.* Ed. O. Ikime. Ibadan: Longmans, 1980. Pp. 121–43.

Akinsanya, J. A. *An African "Florence Nightingale" : A Biography of Kofoworola A.
Pratt.* Ibadan: Vantage, 1987.

Aloba, A., ed. *The Fall of a Ruler; or, The Freedom of Egbaland.* Abeokuta: Egba
Women's Union, 1948.

Anene, J. C. *Southern Nigeria in Transition, 1885–1906.* Cambridge: Cambridge
University Press, 1966.

Anyiam, F. *Men and Matters in Nigerian Politics, 1934–1958.* Lagos: Published by
the author, 1959.

Ariwoola, O. *The African Wife.* London: Kenton Press, 1965.

Asiwaju, A. I. "The Western Provinces under Colonial Rule." In *Groundwork of
Nigerian History.* Ed. O. Ikime. Ibadan: Longmans, 1980. Pp. 429–45.

———. *Western Yorubaland under European Rule, 1989–1945.* Atlantic Highlands,
N.J.: Humanities Press, 1976.

Atanda, J. A. "Indirect Rule in Yorubaland." *Tarikh* 3, no. 3 (1970): 16–28.

———. "The Yoruba Ogboni Cult: Did It Exist in Old Oyo?" *Journal of the Historical Society of Nigeria* 6, no. 4 (1973): 365–72.

Awe, B. "The Iyalode in the Traditional Yoruba Political System." In *Sexual
Stratification: A Cross-Cultural View.* Ed. A. Schlegel. New Haven, Conn.:
Yale University Press, 1977. Pp. 144–60.

Awolowo, O. *AWO: The Autobiography of Chief Obafemi Awolowo.* Cambridge: Cambridge University Press, 1960.

Ayandele, E. A. *The Missionary Impact on Modern Nigeria, 1842–1914: A Political and Social Analysis.* London: Longmans, 1966.

Azikiwe, N. *The Development of Political Parties in Nigeria.* London: Office of the Commissioner in the United Kingdom for the Eastern Region of Nigeria, 1957.

Babolola, E. A. *My Life Adventures.* Ibadan: Caxton Press, n.d.

Baker, P. *Urbanization and Political Change: The Politics of Lagos, 1917–1967.* Berkeley: University of California Press, 1974.

Bascom, W. "The Principle of Seniority in the Social Structure of the Yoruba." *American Anthropologist* 46 (Jan.–Mar. 1942): 37–46.

———. "Urbanization among the Yoruba." *American Journal of Sociology* 60, no. 5 (1955): 446–54.

———. *The Yoruba of Southwestern Nigeria.* New York: Holt, Rinehart and Winston, 1969.

Beir, H. U. "The Position of Yoruba Women." *Presence Africaine* 1 (1955): 39–46.

Biobaku, S. O. *The Egba and Their Neighbours.* Oxford: Clarendon Press, 1957.

———. "Madam Tinubu." In *Eminent Nigerians of the Nineteenth Century.* London: Cambridge University Press, 1960. Pp. 33–41.

———. "Historical Sketch of Egba Traditional Authorities." *Africa* 22 (1952): 35–49.

———. *The Origin of the Yoruba.* Lagos: University of Lagos Press, 1971.

———, ed. *Sources of Yoruba History.* Oxford: Clarendon Press, 1973.

Burton, R. F. *Abeokuta and the Cameroons Mountains.* London: Tinsley Brothers, 1863.

Childs, S. H. "Christian Marriage in Nigeria." *Africa* 16, no. 1 (1946): 238–46.

Coker, F. *A Lady: A Biography of Lady Oyinkan Abayomi.* Ibadan: Evans Brothers, 1987.

Coker, G. B. A., ed. *Family and Property among the Yoruba.* Lagos: African Universities Press, 1966.

Cole, P. *Modern and Traditional Elites in the Politics of Lagos.* Cambridge: Cambridge University Press, 1975.

Coleman, J. S. *Nigeria: Background to Nationalism.* Berkeley: University of California Press, 1958.

Connah, G. *African Civilizations: Precolonial Cities and States in Tropical Africa.* Cambridge: Cambridge University Press, 1987.

Cromwell, A. M. *An African Victorian Feminist: Adelaide Smith Casely-Hayford, 1868–1960.* London: Frank Cass, 1986.

Crowder, M. *Story of Nigeria.* London: Faber, 1973.

————. *West Africa under Colonial Rule.* London: Hutchinson, 1968.

Crowder, M., and O. Ikime, eds. *West African Chiefs: Their Changing Status under Colonial Rule and Independence.* Ile-Ife: University of Ife Press, 1970.

Delano, I. O. *Josiah Ransome-Kuti.* Ibadan: Oxford University Press, 1968.

————. *Oba Ademola II.* Ibadan: University of Ibadan Press, 1969.

Doi, A., and J. Parratt. "Polygamy in Yoruba Society: A Religious or Sociological Issue?" *Africa Quarterly* 8 (1968): 52–58.

Ekundare, R. *Economic History of Nigeria, 1860–1960.* London: Methuen, 1973.

————. *Marriage and Divorce under Yoruba Customs.* Ile-Ife: University of Ife Press, 1969.

Ekwensi, C. *When Love Whispers.* Intro. Funmilayo Ransome-Kuti. Onitsha, Nigeria: Tabansi Bookshop, 1948.

Fafunwa, A. B. *History of Education in Nigeria.* London: George Allen and Unwin, 1974.

Fadipe, N. A. *The Sociology of the Yoruba.* Ibadan: University of Ibadan Press, 1970.

Fajana, A. *Education in Nigeria, 1842–1939: An Historical Analysis.* Ikeja, Nigeria: Longmans, 1978.

Folarin, A. *The Demise of the Independence of Egbaland.* Lagos: Tika-Tore Printing Works, 1916.

————. *A Short Historical Review of the Life of the Egba, 1829–1930.* Abeokuta: Egba Native Administration Press, 1931.

Hinderer, A. *Seventeen Years in Yoruba Country.* London: Jackson and Halliday, 1872.

Hodgkin, T. *Nigerian Perspectives.* London: Oxford University Press, 1960.

Holy Trinity Church History Committee. *The History of the Holy Trinity Church of Gbagura, Abeokuta, 1889–1989.* [Gbagura]: Holy Trinity Church, n.d.

Huxley, J. *Memories.* London: George Allen and Unwin, 1970.

Idowu, M. K. *Fela: Why Blackman Carry Shit.* Lagos, Nigeria: Opinion Media, 1986.

Ikime, O. "Colonial Conquest and Resistance in Southern Nigeria." *Journal of the Historical Society of Nigeria* 6, no. 3 (1972): 251–70.

————. *The Fall of Nigeria.* London: Heinemann, 1977.

Johnson-Odim, C. "Class and Gender: A Consideration of Yoruba Women during the Colonial Period." In *Women and Class in Africa.* Ed. I. Berger and C. Robertson. New York: Holmes and Meier, 1985. Pp. 237–54.

————. "Female Leadership during the Colonial Period: Madam Alimotu Pelewura and the Lagos Market Women." *Tarikh* 7, no. 1 (1981): 1–10.

————. "Grassroots Organizing: Women in the Anti-Colonial Struggle in Southwestern Nigeria." *African Studies Review* 25, nos. 2/3 (1982): 137–57.

————. "Lady Oyinkan Abayomi: A Profile." In *Nigerian Women in Historical*

Perspective. Ed. Bolanle Awe. Lagos: Sankore Publisher; and Ibadan: Book-craft, 1992. Pp. 149–62.

Johnson, S. *History of the Yorubas from the Earliest Times to the Beginning of the British Protectorate.* 1921. London: Rutledge and Kegan Paul, 1966.

Kasunmu, A. B., and J. Salacuse. *Nigerian Family Law.* London: Butterworth, 1966.

Kirke-Greene, A. H. M., ed. *The Principles of Native Administration in Nigeria: Selected Documents, 1900–1947.* London: Oxford University Press, 1965.

Little, K. *African Women in Towns.* Cambridge: Cambridge University Press, 1973.

———. *West African Urbanization: A Study of Voluntary Associations in Social Change.* Cambridge: Cambridge University Press, 1970.

Lloyd, P. C. "Divorce among the Yoruba." *American Anthropologist* 70, no. 1 (1968): 67–81.

———. "The Traditional Political System of the Yoruba." *Southwestern Journal of Anthropology* 10 (1954): 366–84.

———. "Sacred Kingship and Government among the Yoruba." *Africa* 30, no. 3 (1960): 321–37.

———. *Yoruba Land Law.* London: Oxford University Press, 1962.

Mabogunje, A. L. "Some Comments on Land Tenure in Egba Division, West-ern Nigeria." *Africa* 31 (1961): 258–69.

———. *Urbanization in Nigeria.* London: University of London Press, 1968.

———. "Yoruba Market Women." *Ibadan,* no. 11 (1961): 14–17.

———. *Yoruba Towns.* Ibadan: University of Ibadan Press, 1962.

Mabogunje, A. L., and J. D. Omer-Cooper. *Owu in Yoruba History.* Ibadan: University of Ibadan Press, 1971.

Mackintosh, J. P. *Nigerian Government and Politics.* London: George Allen and Unwin, 1966.

Mann, K. *Marrying Well: Marriage, Status, and Social Change among the Educated Elite in Colonial Lagos.* London: Cambridge University Press, 1985.

Mba, N. E. *Nigerian Women Mobilized: Women's Political Activity in Southern Nigeria, 1900–1965.* Berkeley: University of California, Institute of International Studies, 1982.

Moore, C. *fela, fela: this bitch of a life.* London: Allison and Busby, 1982.

Muckenhirn, E. F. *Secondary Education of Girls in Western Nigeria.* Ann Arbor: University of Michigan Press, 1966.

O'Barr, J. F. "Making the Invisible Visible: African Women in Politics and Policy." *African Studies Review* 18, no. 3 (1975): 19–27.

Olusanya, G. O. "Constitutional Developments in Nigeria, 1861–1960." In *Groundwork of Nigerian History.* Ed. O. Ikime. Ibadan: Longmans, 1980. Pp. 518–44.

————. *The Second World War and Politics in Nigeria*. London: Evans Brothers, 1973.

————. *West African Students Union and the Politics of Decolonisation, 1925–1958*. Ibadan: University of Ibadan Press, 1982.

Oyemakinde, W. "The Pullen Marketing Scheme: A Trial in Food Pricing Control in Nigeria, 1941–1947." *Journal of the Historical Society of Nigeria* 6, no. 4 (1973): 413–24.

Post, K. *The Nigerian Federal Elections of 1959: Politics and Administration in a Developing Political System*. London: Oxford University Press, 1963.

Post, K., and G. Jenkins. *The Price of Liberty: Personality and Politics in Colonial Nigeria*. Cambridge: Cambridge University Press, 1973.

Ransome-Kuti, F. "Letter to the Editor." *West Africa* 1840 (May 1952): 490.

————. "The Status of Women in Nigeria." *Journal of Human Relations* (Autumn 1961): 67–72.

————. "Women Are Used as Tools at Elections." *Sunday Times*, June 2, 1957, 7.

————. "Women Should Play a Bigger Part in the Elections." *West Africa* 1810 (1951): 1015.

Sklar, R. *Nigerian Political Parties*. Princeton, N.J.: Princeton University Press, 1963.

Smith, R. S. *Kingdoms of the Yoruba*. London: Methuen, 1969.

Smyke, R., and D. Storer. *Nigerian Union of Teachers: An Official History*. Ibadan: Oxford University Press, 1974.

Soyinka, W. *Ake: The Years of Childhood*. 1981. New York: Vintage, 1989.

————. *Ibadan: The Penkelemes Years, A Memoir, 1946–1965*. Ibadan: Spectrum Books, 1994.

————. *Isara: A Voyage around Essay*. Ibadan: Fountain Publications, 1989.

Tamuno, T. N. *The Evolution of the Nigerian State: The Southern Phase, 1894–1914*. Ibadan: Longmans, 1972.

————. *Nigeria and Elective Representation, 1923–1947*. London: Heinemann, 1966.

Women's International Democratic Federation (WIDF). *That They May Live: African Women Arise*. Berlin: WIDF, 1954.

————. *The Women of Asia and Africa: Documents*. Budapest: WIDF, 1948.

————. *Women of the Whole World* (quarterly). Berlin: WIDF.

Unpublished Sources

All unpublished manuscripts are in authors' possession, unless otherwise noted.

Afigbo, E. A. "Women in Nigerian History." Ms., n.d.

Awe, B. "Iyalode Efunsetan Aniwura." Ms. 1977.

———. "Notes on the Institution of the Iyalode within the Traditional Yoruba Political System." Ms. 1974.

———. "The Rise of Ibadan as a Yoruba Power in the Nineteenth Century." Doctoral Dissertation. Oxford University, 1964.

Babatunde, S. O. "Change in Yoruba Marriage and Family." B.S. thesis. University of Ibadan, 1973.

Balogun, S. "Pressure Groups and Interest Articulation: A Study of Egba Women's Union, 1947–51." B.Sc. thesis. University of Ibadan, 1974.

Bird, M. "Social Change and Kinship Marriage among the Yoruba of Western Nigeria." Doctoral dissertation. University of Edinburgh, 1958.

Brown, S. H. "A History of the People of Lagos, 1852–1886." Doctoral dissertation. Northwestern University, 1964.

Byfield, J. "Women in Politics: A Profile of Funmilayo Ransome-Kuti." M.A. thesis. Columbia University, 1982.

Ejikeme, A. "Core-Periphery Relations in an International Women's Organization: The Case of WILPF in Nigeria, 1950–1970." Ms. 1992.

Fajana, A. "The Evolution of Educational Policy in Nigeria, 1842–1939." Doctoral dissertation. University of Ibadan, 1969.

Harunah, H. B. "The Evolution of Central Administration in Abeokuta, 1830–1898." M.A. thesis. University of Lagos, 1983.

Işola, K. S. "A History of Ifo, 1890–1986." Undergraduate thesis. Ogun State University, 1987.

Jenkins, S. "Government and Politics in Ibadan." Doctoral dissertation. Northwestern University, 1965.

Johnson-Odim, C. "Nigerian Women and British Colonialism." Doctoral dissertation. Northwestern University, 1978.

Laleye, C. O. "Political Consciousness among Egba Women, 1945–1948." B.A. thesis. University of Ife, 1972.

Lloyd, P. C. "Local Government in Yoruba Towns." Doctoral dissertation. Oxford University, 1958.

Marshall, G. "Women, Trade, and the Yoruba Family." Doctoral dissertation. Columbia University, 1964.

Muckenhirn, E. F. "Secondary Education of Girls in Western Nigeria." Doctoral dissertation. University of Michigan, 1966.

O'Connor, Sr. G. A. "The Development of Rural Administration in Egbaland, 1898–1918." Paper presented to a department of history seminar. University of Ibadan, November 13, 1975.

———. "The Status and Roles of West African Women." Doctoral dissertation. Columbia University, 1964.

Odugbesan, C. "Bééère: The Achievements and Contributions of a Brave Nigerian Woman Leader." Ms. May 11, 1968.

Pallinder-Law, A. "Government in Abeokuta, 1830–1914, with Special Reference to Egba United Government, 1898–1914." Doctoral dissertation. University of Gotsberg, 1973.

Saibu, K. "A History of Ifo, c. 1890–1980." B.A. thesis. Ogun State University, June 1987.

Ward, E. "The Yoruba Husband-Wife Code." Doctoral dissertation. Catholic University of America, 1938.

Index

▲ ▲ ▲

CHERYL JOHNSON-ODIM received a Ph.D. in history from Northwestern University and is presently chair of the history department at Loyola University Chicago. She is the coeditor of *Expanding the Boundaries of Women's History* (1992) and *Restoring Women to History: Women in Africa, Asia, Latin America and the Caribbean, and the Middle East* (1988) and has contributed to many edited collections and scholarly journals. Her areas of specialty include women's history in southwestern Nigeria and third-world feminist theory.

NINA EMMA MBA received a Ph.D. in history from the University of Ibadan and is presently with the history department at the University of Lagos. She specializes in the study of women in Nigeria and in promoting gender studies in that country. The author of *Nigerian Women Mobilized: Women in Southern Nigerian Political History, 1900–1965* (1982) and *Ayo Rosiji: Man with Vision* (1992), she is working on the biographies of other activists in twentieth-century Nigeria.